GUIDE TO JOINING THE MILITARY

ARMY ★ NAVY ★ MARINE CORPS ★ AIR FORCE ★ COAST GUARD

PETERSON'S

 **PETERSON'S**

About Peterson's

Peterson's provides the accurate, dependable, high-quality education content and guidance you need to succeed. No matter where you are on your academic or professional path, you can rely on Peterson's print and digital publications for the most up-to-date education exploration data, expert test-prep tools, and top-notch career success resources—everything you need to achieve your goals.

For more information, contact Peterson's, 3 Columbia Circle, Suite 205, Albany, NY 12203-5158; 800-338-3282 Ext. 54229; or find us online at www.petersonsbooks.com.

Photography Credits:
MEPS photos in Chapter 5 courtesy of U.S. MEPCOM.
Air Force photos in Chapters 1, 3, and 7 courtesy of U.S. Air Force.
Army photos in Chapters 1 and 3 courtesy of U.S. Army.
Coast Guard photos in Chapter 7 courtesy of U.S. Coast Guard.
Army photos in Chapter 7 courtesy of U.S. Army and the author.
Marine Corps photos in Chapters 3 and 7 courtesy of U.S. Marine Corps.
Navy photos in Chapters 1 and 7 courtesy of U.S. Navy.

ISBN 978-0-7689-3837-1

Printed in the United States of America

10 9 8 7 6 5 4 3 2 1   15 14 13

Third Edition

Dedication

In memory of my father, Artie Ostrow, who fought proudly in the European Theatre during World War II.

This third edition is also dedicated to those who have served, currently serve, and will serve this great nation.

Acknowledgments

To acknowledge all the people and organizations that assisted me in the research for this project would double the number of pages contained in the book! Many people throughout the Department of Defense and elsewhere provided guidance, information, inspiration, and encouragement to ensure that this project was a success.

Some of the organizations I'd like to thank include:

Air Force Recruiting   Marine Corps Recruiting

Army Recruiting   Navy Recruiting

Coast Guard Recruiting   Reserve Recruiting counterparts for each branch as well as
                                     the components of the National Guard.

I would also like to thank:
The Public Affairs (PA) officials of all the military services
PA officials of each of the services' Basic Training sites
USMEPCOM (especially its PA staff)

Most of all, I want to thank my family for their continual support during the writing of this book; my children (and their spouses), Scott II (Anne), Matthew (Kerri), Brittany, Corey, Jennifer, and Mary, and of course, my wife Susie.

I'd like to especially acknowledge Scott and Brittany who are currently serving our country; Scott as an Active Duty Air Force officer, and Brittany as an enlisted member of the Air Force Reserve (after serving time on Active Duty).

CONTENTS

PART ONE: PREPARE YOURSELF

In this chapter, you will learn about military recruiters, their training, their tactics, and their procedures. You'll also learn what a recruiter can—and cannot—promise you.

This chapter discusses the factors that you must consider to make an informed decision on whether to join the military. It includes an assessment to help you determine if the military can fulfill your needs.

This chapter tries to dispel some of the common misconceptions and stereotypes about women who serve in the armed forces and provides you with resources for finding detailed information about women in the military. There are several "testimonials" from women who are serving and have served in the military.

This chapter does not prepare you for the ASVAB. However, it provides a general overview of the examination and its parts, along with some helpful hints to prepare you for the ASVAB.

Perhaps the most traumatic and memorable experience in the entire enlistment process is the applicant's first trip to the MEPS. This chapter outlines the purpose of the MEPS and reassures you that the MEPS is not an indicator of what life is like in the military.

PART TWO: WHAT TO EXPECT AFTER ENLISTMENT

Most applicants wind up in a Delayed Enlistment Program (DEP). In this status, the applicant has already sworn in and is awaiting his or her "ship date" to Basic Training. As an enlistee, you can remain in DEP status for up to a year. A lot can happen between the day you swear in and the day you ship. In this chapter, I discuss avoiding certain things, keeping in shape, and keeping the recruiter informed.

This chapter outlines the Basic Training in each military branch. You will find sample training schedules as well as basic advice for getting through boot camp.

PART THREE: MILITARY BASICS

This chapter lists the occupational groups each branch of the armed forces offers. These are not specific jobs but rather "fields," such as electronics or mechanics.

Besides the "basic" military pay, there are lots of other benefits that add up to an attractive compensation package. This chapter outlines those, as well as the various forms of military pay, allowances, and educational opportunities.

Besides Active Duty, a great way to serve your country, get some excellent training, receive educational benefits, and get paid doing it is as a member of the Guard or Reserve. The purpose of this chapter is to familiarize you with the Reserve components and their many benefits.

To aid you in your research for more information on joining the military, this chapter provides you with contact points for information about each military branch, for Department of Defense websites, and commercial websites that deal with military careers. This chapter also contains other useful information that will help you get a head start on Basic Training.

A SPECIAL NOTE TO PARENTS

Although this book was written to be used by individuals who are trying to decide whether to join the military, it can also be used by parents to help their children make the right decision. If you are a concerned parent who is reading this book because your child is interested in joining the military, I urge you to read on.

It is not the intent of this book to persuade or dissuade your child from joining the military. Rather, its primary purpose is to give you and your child an honest look at the "enlistment process." In addition, there is an entire chapter dedicated to an inside look at Basic Training (or what you might know as Boot Camp).

Your child has probably seen recruiting commercials on television and received several colorful brochures, and viewed enticing ads and videos online that are designed to show the benefits of joining the military. Although this book covers the many benefits of military life, it also separates the hype from the reality of enlisting.

Although I made the military my career (a career I wouldn't trade for anything else in the world), I must admit that life in the military, while exciting and rewarding, isn't always quite the same "As Seen on TV." Even though those burgers you get at fast-food restaurants somehow don't look exactly like the photo up on the menu board, they still taste good.

I don't have to tell you that your job as a parent is to offer guidance to your children and help them to make the right decisions in planning their futures. However, if your child is old enough to be considering a military enlistment, the one thing you cannot do is mandate what decision your child makes.

If your child is under 18, he or she cannot enlist without your consent, so if you hold back your consent, your child will not be able to enlist—for now. However, my experience has been that in the rare occasions when parents have not given permission for their child to enlist, the individual will wait until he or she turns 18 and will enlist anyway. Holding back consent just causes resentment.

Instead of creating animosity, you should use this book and work with your child to determine whether the military is the right choice for him or her. Remember that you don't necessarily have to agree with your child's decision—you just have to support it.

If you wish, you might want to meet with the recruiter to discuss the options available to your son or daughter. However, I would not recommend that you attend the first meeting your child has with the recruiter. During the first meeting, the recruiter will ask your child some personal questions and will expect some honest answers. No matter how close a child is to his or her parents, there are things the child may not want his or her parents to know. Also, whatever information your child has given to the recruiter is protected from disclosure. Therefore, you shouldn't ask the recruiter for details of the information provided by your child; he or she is forbidden by law to discuss that with you.

The prospect of their child serving in the military initially scares most parents (especially mothers). It is a natural reaction for parents to be distrustful of military recruiters. For some parents, this distrust is based on a personal experience; for others, it comes from the "bad press" that military recruiters and the military itself have received over the years.

Instead of discouraging, or worse forbidding, your child from pursuing enlisting in the military, you should be proactive in gaining as much information as possible about the opportunities available to him or her in the military.

You will find a wealth of information on the Internet. Some useful links are listed in Chapter 11, "Contact Information." I would like to forewarn you, though, that most of these websites (either branch-specific or Department of Defense)—although offering valuable information—focus on encouraging their visitors to enlist in the military. Knowing that, you should use the information they provide and the information contained in this book to help your child make an informed decision. Remember that, ultimately, it is your son's or daughter's decision to make, not yours.

As a postscript, I would like to address those parents who are trying to encourage a child who has no interest in the military to enlist. You may believe that your child needs to "grow up" or "get her act together."

Although many young military members do a lot of "growing up" and maturing in Basic Training, that will never occur if your child was forced into the decision to join the military. The military is not a "scared-straight" program to help troubled youths solve their behavioral problems. However, if you believe that your child needs some direction in his or her life and think that the military could provide that direction, you may want to do some additional research and use this book to show your child the opportunities the military has to offer.

Good Luck!
Scott A. Ostrow, Ed.D.

INTRODUCTION

Recent world events have once again brought the military into the public eye. The first Gulf War brought the war into our living rooms and helped launch around-the-clock all-news networks.

The second Gulf War turned up the on-screen action tenfold. With embedded "journalists," the world is provided with blow-by-blow coverage in, sometimes, real time.

The U.S. military offers its members high-tech training and experience—with pay—and even helps finance a college education. Indeed, every year thousands of young people pursue a military career and enjoy the benefits it offers. Yet thousands more consider joining the military and decide against it. The reasons why vary, but many choose not to enlist because they lack knowledge of the benefits a military career can offer, whereas others simply mistrust recruiters based on the horror stories they've heard from acquaintances. Sadly, many make the decision against joining the military without ever setting foot in a recruiting office.

In the past, military recruiters have been compared to used-car salesmen—and we all know what kind of bad reputation used-car salesmen have. However, despite the stereotype, we still buy automobiles from salesmen. Yet the smart shopper arms himself or herself with knowledge before going to a used-car lot. He or she prepares himself or herself with information about the car that he or she wants to buy—what the car should cost, the available options, and its safety record. Most important, the shopper determines whether the car of his or her dreams will suit his or her needs.

The main thrust of this book is to transform you into an educated consumer. You will learn how to determine if the military is the right choice for you. After that, you will learn how to deal with that salesman they call a recruiter. Just as the car buyer does his or her homework to get the best deal from the salesman, you will learn how to do the homework necessary to get what you want from your recruiter.

For the most part, military recruiters are highly trained and skilled salespeople. Their job and sole purpose in life is to find, qualify, and, ultimately, enlist people for military service. Although the training and education benefits are excellent in the military, recruiters are not in the business of college counseling, nor are they employment agents. The bottom line is that we need a military to defend our country and Her allies. As an Airman, a Soldier, a Coast Guardsman, a Marine, or a Sailor, that is your primary reason for being. Military recruiters are employed to ensure that only the best (mentally, physically, and morally) individuals join our nation's military.

Despite what you may have heard, most military recruiters have a high degree of integrity. Why then all those horror stories of "how my recruiter lied to me"? In most cases, it's a matter of "selective listening" on the applicant's part. This book helps you to understand the enlistment process and keeps you from being a selective listener.

Another purpose of this book is to dispel some of the myths about recruiters and military life. Things have changed quite a bit from the time when your Uncle Joe served in Vietnam, yet many times we rely on stories from friends and relatives to get our information about the military. Just as you would probably turn to the Internet to research a school paper and not your Uncle Joe's outdated encyclopedias, you should turn to someone who has up-to-date information about military benefits—your recruiter.

This book walks you step-by-step through the enlistment process; you will know what to expect at every turn. From the initial interview, through testing and the physical examination, and, ultimately, to taking the oath of enlistment, you will be prepared. Can you get through the enlistment process without this book? Of course. Millions have. But just as you wouldn't think of planning a trip without a good road atlas (or GPS) to guide the way, why would you want to take this journey without some sort of guidance? Think of this book as your roadmap to joining the military. There may be some detours along the way, but ultimately you will arrive at your destination a lot better off than if you hadn't used this valuable tool.

Take the time to read this entire book, to study, and to prepare for the meetings with your recruiter and your trips to the Military Entrance Processing Station (MEPS), just as you would for any test or job interview. The key to the entire enlistment process is preparation. Given the proper preparation, you will succeed in getting what you want. Although you won't become an expert on the military enlistment process overnight, it is my sincere hope that this book will help you to become familiar with the process so that your decision to join the military will be an educated one in which you are knowledgeable enough to get what you want from it.

Since the first edition of this book, similar books have been published, as well as a multitude of websites offering "advice" to people interested in joining the military. It is important to note that *Guide to Joining the Military* was written by someone who has experience in military recruiting. Although much research went into its writing, a great deal of the information contained in this book is based on the experience and knowledge of the author. Additionally, this book was written to provide the reader with essential information about joining the military. This is not a book on military history, although you'll find some useful historical information contained in these pages.

While critics of this book have argued that much of the information contained in this book may be researched on the Internet, and, I agree there is a plethora of information about the military on the web...too much to sift through! The myriad of information available on the Internet is a bit like having a six-pack of soda without the plastic "thingy" that holds them all together--this book is that plastic "thingy" (and more)!

This book is separated into three sections. Each covers a specific aspect of the enlistment process. Therefore, without further introduction, let's get started on the adventure that is joining the military.

PART ONE

PREPARE YOURSELF

1 YOUR FIRST MEETING WITH A RECRUITER: FACING THE BEST-TRAINED SALESPERSON ON EARTH

In this chapter, you will learn about military recruiters, their training, their tactics, and their procedures. You'll also learn what a recruiter can—and cannot—promise you.

How can you tell if a military recruiter is lying to you? His lips are moving!

Is that what you think of military recruiters? If so, I hope you will feel differently by the time you've finished reading this chapter.

If you are reading this book, you probably either have been contacted by a recruiter or seen some sort of advertisement that interested you, or perhaps someone you know has suggested that you explore a military career. Notice I've used the term "military career" instead of "military job." The reason is simple. Although the military is a place to get a start and to learn a skill, it is also a way of life, not a job. In addition, the opportunities for those who pursue them are endless.

You are now at the crossroad of a journey that may change your life. Do or don't you make an appointment to see a recruiter? Many who have come before you have chosen not to talk to a military recruiter, while many others chose to give the recruiter a chance to make his pitch. Many of those who chose to take that chance joined the military. Those who chose not to take that chance will never know what might have been.

Enough with the melodrama! If you're having doubts about whether to meet with a recruiter, I'm sure you have your reasons. Some common reasons why people are reluctant to meet with a recruiter include:

- I'll be pressured into joining—I just can't say no to any salesman.
- I don't think I'll like the military; I don't like rules and regulations.
- My friend's dad was in the army (I think), and he hated it.
- I don't like getting up early in the morning.
- They wouldn't want me; I have nothing to offer them.
- He or she has nothing to offer me.

When I was younger, I used to get calls constantly from life insurance agents. They were relentless in their pursuit of getting me to make sure I had the peace of mind of knowing my family would be taken care of in the event of my untimely death.

After the millionth telephone call I'd received and after the millionth time I repeated, "I'm sorry, I'm not interested," I decided I'd take a different approach. I started inviting the agents to my house. However, before I did that, I did my homework. Yes, they were right: I needed supplemental life insurance, for my family's sake. But were they giving me the best deal I could get? After listening to sales pitch after sales pitch, I finally agreed to buy a life insurance policy. However, it was on my terms, and I believe I got the best deal I could. More important, every time I received a telephone call from a life insurance salesman after that, I was able to say, "I've checked all of my available options, and I am certain that I have made the right decision." Soon, most of the phone calls ceased.

Before I decided to explore the possibility of supplemental life insurance, I had reasons why I didn't need it. Just as the reasons why some people won't meet with a military recruiter, my reasons were unfounded—I lacked knowledge about life insurance and I distrusted insurance salesmen. My main reasons for not purchasing life insurance were:

- I'm never going to die.
- My wife has my military life insurance policy. When she's done with that, she can go out and get a job!
- I'll be dead, so who cares what happens after that.
- I can take the money I'd spend on insurance and invest it.

Sure, they weren't good reasons not to see the insurance agent, but they were my reasons and they were all I had.

So, what is the moral of this story? Do your homework, meet with a recruiter, and make an informed decision. You, too, will be able to say, "I've checked all of my options, and I am certain I have made the right decision."

How do you decide which recruiter you meet with first? That's an easy question to answer: meet with the one with whom you've already had some contact or the one who is listed first in your Google search. It doesn't really matter, because if you take my advice, you'll eventually speak with recruiters from all of the services.

Why the Military Needs Recruiters

Although the military, as a whole, has gone through massive draw-downs in the past twenty years, it still must recruit an approximated 353,000 new people each year to keep pace with the number of people leaving its ranks. People leave the military for several reasons: some retire after twenty years of service, some get out to pursue a civilian occupation (most times using the skills they learned in the military), and others leave to pursue higher education. Whatever their reasons for leaving, they leave and must be replaced.

The military must attract enough qualified individuals each year to maintain a high level of readiness and be able to perform its mission. This is where the recruiter enters. It is not enough to advertise an "800-number" on television and wait for the calls to come flooding in (that only works for Ginsu knives and the exercise DVDs). The military must depend on its recruiters to get out into the communities, schools, youth groups, and wherever else they can reach America's youth to keep its numbers strong.

Who Is "The Recruiter?"

All recruiters may look the same to you. You may not be able to distinguish an Army recruiter from an Air Force recruiter. In fact, unless you've done some research, you probably don't know much about the differences between the missions of the Army and the Air Force.

Although I will refer to all recruiters in a generic sense by calling them "military recruiters," or just "recruiters," make no mistake: each recruiter works for his or her branch of the service and does not represent any other branch.

Why do I tell you this? Occasionally, a recruiter will speak to an applicant about the opportunities that are not available from another branch. Don't let an Army recruiter tell you what an Air Force recruiter can't offer you. Instead, let the recruiter tell you what the Army can give you, and then let the Air Force recruiter tell you what the air force can and cannot offer you.

Each branch of the armed forces uses different criteria to select its recruiters. However, they all have one thing in common: they employ experienced enlisted personnel from within their ranks to "sell" their product. This sets military recruiters apart from the majority of "salespeople."

"Live from New York, it's . . . an Air Force recruiter."

Recruiters know what they are selling; they lived and breathed the military long before they started selling it. The military recruiter is both an expert on and an advocate of his or her product. Therefore, he or she can provide information, guidance, opinion, and an occasional story or two.

Recruiters do not start their military careers as salespeople—they come from all walks of military life. They are mechanics, cooks, administrators, electricians, and just about anything else you can name. They come to recruiting, most often, with no sales background at all. You may ask: how does a cook become so good at selling? The answer is a simple one: they attend recruiting school.

WHAT RECRUITERS ARE TRAINED TO DO

Each branch of the military runs its own unique recruiting school whose primary mission is to turn "cooks" into highly effective salespeople in a matter of weeks. In that short time, the recruiters must learn not only how to sell but also how to complete all the paperwork necessary for enlistment. It doesn't end there. They must also learn and become familiar with all of the enlistment criteria, such as what makes someone physically unfit to enlist. They must learn how to be public speakers, how to deal with school and community officials, how to be job counselors, and a myriad of other things. What they learn in weeks would take months, even years, of training elsewhere.

Although recruiters learn a multitude of things in recruiting school, the primary focus is sales: how to contact, or prospect for, potential applicants and then convince them to join the recruiters' particular military branch.

Prospecting for Applicants

Unless you took the first step and made the initial contact, your recruiter somehow obtained your name and contact information. In fact, if the recruiter made the initial contact by telephone, you may have asked him, "How did you get my phone number?" Military recruiters have many ways to get your name. Here are just a few:

- a list provided by your school
- referral from a friend, family member, classmate, or coworker
- in response to your request for information
- your high school yearbook and a little investigative work
- the Armed Services Vocational Aptitude Battery (ASVAB) examination you took at school

Selling the Interview

Once the recruiter has made contact, it is his or her job to get you to come in for an interview. As with any job, you can't be hired without a formal interview. Depending on your interest level, you may or may not agree to the interview. If you don't agree, it is up to the recruiter to sell the interview.

Sure, you may use excuses for not meeting with the recruiter. You may say, "Can you e-mail me some information?" Or, maybe you'll say, "I'd like to think about it some more." Or, maybe you'll use my favorite, "I don't have time for an interview." Believe me; if you have a reason, or an excuse, for not meeting with the recruiter, he or she has at least one response to overcome that reason. Take my advice; if you're reading this book, you already have some level of interest in at least checking out what the military has to offer. Make the appointment, and show up for it! Don't agree to an appointment that you have no intention to keep. Not keeping appointments speaks volumes about your character.

Selling "The Military"

Later in this chapter, I'll discuss your first meeting with the recruiter and how to handle yourself during the initial interview. I'll cover the sales pitch and how to respond to it. At this point, I have provided a simplified outline of the sales process in the following figure. As you review it, remember that you will probably spend an hour or more with the recruiter during your first interview.

It is the recruiter's job to find your primary motivator for joining the military—it may be to obtain money for education, to obtain technical training, or to secure employment. This is where the comparison of a recruiter's methods to a car salesman's methods begins. When you walk into a car dealership, the conversation would probably sound something like this:

Salesman: "What are you looking for in a car?"

Customer: "I need a seven-passenger minivan to transport my family."

If the salesperson doesn't sell minivans and only has five-passenger sedans, it is unlikely that he or she will get you to buy a sedan. It is difficult to sell a product that just can't fit a customer's needs. The recruiter must not only sell you a product that meets your needs, but also first determine your needs. This can be extremely difficult, especially if you don't express those needs to him or her or if you just are unsure of those needs. The following conversation rarely, if ever, occurs in a recruiting office:

Recruiter: "What are you looking for from an enlistment in the military?"

Applicant: "I want to complete a degree in biology at XYZ University, have enough leisure time to go bowling with the guys, and can you throw in good pay, too?"

WHAT THE RECRUITER CAN AND CANNOT PROMISE YOU

As a recruiter, one of the lines I heard more often than most when trying to get a prospective applicant in for an interview was, "I'll come in tomorrow for an interview, but I won't sign anything." My response to that was always along the lines of "I wish it were that simple to enlist someone." Just as you wouldn't expect to be hired on the spot after your first job interview with a civilian company, the same is true for the military. You must jump over many hurdles before you can qualify to wear a military uniform.

When you spoke to the recruiter to make an appointment for an interview, he or she probably asked you some preliminary questions concerning your health, your education, and any involvement with law officials. If you passed this initial inquiry, you made it over the first hurdle. When you meet the recruiter for the first time, he or she will probe even deeper into these areas to determine whether you initially qualify for enlistment. Assuming that you agree to enlist after listening to the recruiter's sales presentation, here is a list of the hurdles that you must get over to enlist eventually:

- questions regarding your medical history to ensure that you do not have, or have not had, a medical disqualifying condition
- questions regarding any involvement with law officials, including traffic tickets and arrests as an adult or a juvenile

- questions regarding illegal drug usage
- passing the Armed Services Vocational Aptitude Battery (ASVAB)
- a complete (and I do mean *complete*) physical examination
- a background check

I present a more detailed explanation of these hurdles later in this chapter. However, as you can see from this list, you are in no danger of a recruiter enlisting you for basic training after your initial interview.

So what can the recruiter promise you? The answer is simply this: not much! What the recruiter can promise is that he or she will treat you fairly throughout the enlistment process. He or she can ensure that you fully understand the steps to enlistment; that he or she will not lie, or misrepresent, anything to you; and that you are fully prepared for enlistment. The recruiter should be your advocate, not your babysitter. Do not expect the recruiter to hold your hand during the process. You are responsible for your own actions, just as you will be expected to be when you are on active duty.

COMMON MISCONCEPTIONS ABOUT RECRUITERS

There are some common misconceptions that people have about recruiters and recruiting. Here are a few:

- **Recruiters are on quotas and receive a "bonus" for every new recruit they enlist.**
  Recruiters receive their regular military pay plus a standard "professional pay" every month. They receive the same pay whether they enlist one, two, or twenty people every month. Of course, if they want to keep their jobs, they'll try to enlist as many people as possible.
- **Recruiters will lie, cheat, and steal to get you to enlist.**
  As I mentioned, some recruiters would do whatever it takes to get someone to enlist; so be careful, but not cynical. The majority of recruiters will not misrepresent themselves or their service. Most successful recruiters rely on referrals from satisfied applicants—if you are unhappy with your experience with your recruiter, you won't refer others to him or her, and he or she knows that.
- **They'll trick me into signing a contract, and then it will be too late.**
  Remember that enlisting in the military is a long and involved systematic process that consists of many steps. It is the recruiter's job to prepare you for each step.

Now that you have a better understanding of who the recruiter is, it is almost time to meet with him or her, but not before you read the rest of this chapter. It will better prepare you for this first meeting. Although the recruiter is your advocate and not your opponent, you should do your homework to make sure you are ready for the "battle." Just as you would prepare for a visit to the local car dealership to buy a new car, you should prepare for your first meeting with your recruiter.

Your Responsibilities During the Recruiting Process

During the recruiting process, you have several responsibilities. They include:

- keeping all your appointments and arriving on time for them
- studying for the ASVAB
- getting enough sleep before the ASVAB and physical examination
- being open and honest with your recruiter and the MEPS staff
- being an active, not a selective, listener

PRIORITY ONE: BE HONEST

Of all your responsibilities, being honest with your recruiter is paramount. Telling white lies and half-truths will eventually catch up to you—maybe not at first, maybe not while you are at Basic Training, but some day. Not telling the truth about past physical problems or past involvement with law enforcement officials are the fastest ways to get yourself in a heap of trouble. Remember these simple rules:

- Divulge all involvement with law enforcement, even if you weren't convicted or even if the court told you your records would be closed and eventually expunged.
- Tell about all diagnosed medical conditions. Do not conceal anything. Conversely, do not make anything up. If you never were diagnosed with asthma, even though your mother told you that you had it, you never had it! I cannot tell you how many people who never had asthma disqualify themselves.
- Do not, under any circumstances, lie because someone has told you to do so. This includes your recruiter, your brother, and your mother.

PRIORITY TWO: BE AN ACTIVE, NOT A SELECTIVE, LISTENER

Do recruiters lie? There are good and bad people in all professions, and military recruiters are not excluded. Aside from those few bad apples that give recruiters a bad name, most misunderstandings attributed to "my recruiter lied to me" come down to a phenomenon called selective listening.

Selective listening occurs when an applicant (or, using the car dealership example, the customer) hears only the parts of the recruiter's (salesperson's) presentation that interests him or her. For example, a customer leases a car for three years and at the end of the lease he or she is ready to trade in the car for a new one. He or she works out the deal for his or her new vehicle and notices an additional charge of $1,000. Of course, he or she questions the charge and receives the following response: "Your three-year lease allowed for a maximum of 30,000 miles (an average of 10,000 miles per year), and your vehicle's odometer reads 40,000 miles. Your contract states that you will be charged $.10 per mile for every mile exceeding 30,000. At $.10 per mile, 10,000 miles equals $1,000." The customer leaves the car dealership $1,000 poorer, totally disgusted, and in search of a car salesperson that won't "lie" to him or her. Isn't it ironic that when he or she first leased the vehicle, he or she didn't "hear" the part of the sales presentation that talked about exceeding the mileage, yet when he or she found out it was going to cost him or her $1,000, he or she heard loud and clear?

Sometimes salespeople do their best to gloss over these "minor details," helping the customer to be a selective listener. "The maximum mileage allowed is 30,000. I've never seen anyone exceed that mileage after only three years." Is the salesperson lying in this example? Maybe not, but it's a matter of semantics.

Be an active listener, not a selective one. Make sure you understand everything that someone presents to you. Do not be afraid that you will look stupid if you ask for clarification. Remember that the recruiter is the expert; you are not. If you think you don't understand something, you're probably correct in that assumption. Ask your questions, and listen to the answers.

Establishing the Interview

Most appointments to meet with a recruiter occur over the telephone, although you may have met the recruiter somewhere in person, such as at your school or at a job fair. No matter how the first contact was made, it all comes down to your committing to an appointment.

NEGOTIATING THE APPOINTMENT DATE AND TIME

If you have decided to meet with a recruiter (and I'll assume you have based on the fact that you are reading this book), all that remains is deciding on a good time to meet with him or her. Because you are the customer, the recruiter should accommodate your schedule and meet with you when it is convenient for you. Most recruiters will use some variation to the following tried-and-true method of giving a prospective applicant an "option" of when to meet for an interview. It goes something like this:

Recruiter: "I am glad you decided to investigate the opportunities the [insert service name here] has to offer. The next step is a face-to-face interview so we can determine if we'll be able to meet your needs."

Applicant: "Sounds good to me. When can we meet?"

Recruiter: "I have openings on Monday and Wednesday. Which is better for you?"

Applicant: "Wednesday would be better."

Recruiter: "Great! What's better for you, mornings or afternoons?"

Applicant: "Afternoons are generally better."

Recruiter: "Okay, I have an opening at three and another at five. Which is better for you?"

Applicant: "Five would be better."

Recruiter: "Good. I'll see you on Wednesday afternoon at five, then."

Who was in control of the conversation? Although it seemed like the recruiter was being very accommodating, she or he was in total control of the situation. When you take a closer look at the conversation, you can see that the recruiter gave the applicant only a few choices of interview times. What if the applicant had been available only on Thursdays between 2 and 4 p.m.?

Although recruiters do spend some time in face-to-face contact with applicants, they spend most of their time doing other things, such as making appointments over the telephone. This gives recruiters some flexibility in their daily schedule and allows them to switch activities to accommodate applicants.

In this example, there is no problem if it is convenient for the applicant to meet with the recruiter when the recruiter states that he or she is available. But if the applicant isn't available, then what?

The answer is simple. The applicant should just say, "I'm sorry, but I have a full schedule during the week. I am available on Thursday afternoons between 2 and 4 p.m., and also any time on Saturday."

At this point, the recruiter will either agree to an appointment that is in line with the applicant's schedule or offer an alternative. It is important to note that recruiters do have lives outside of their jobs, so don't be unreasonable. Don't insist on meeting on Sunday at 2 p.m., although some recruiters may take you up on it if that is truly the only free time you have. However, if your free time is indeed that limited, how will you get the time off to do the processing for enlistment, such as testing and taking the physical examination?

If you make a reasonable request for a time to meet with the recruiter and he or she tells you he or she can't make it, ask about the following week, or perhaps the week after that. Most recruiters (the good ones anyway) will want to get you into the office as soon as possible and will rearrange their schedules, if possible, to accommodate you.

The following true story is an example of an inflexible recruiter who focused more on his needs than on those of his applicants.

After determining that an applicant could not meet at a time convenient for the recruiter, the following conversation ensued:

Applicant: "I'm in school all week, but I can meet you any weekday after 5 p.m. or any time on Saturday."

Recruiter: "Sorry, but my last appointments are at 3:30, and I don't work on Saturdays."

Applicant: "Well, okay, maybe we'll be able to meet in a few months when I'm on summer vacation."

Two things resulted from this conversation. First, the prospective applicant never contacted the recruiter again and never enlisted. Second, this particular recruiter was not happy when his supervisor found out what had happened. One thing is certain: this recruiter would never survive in a commission-based sales environment where the customer always comes first.

If you find yourself in a similar situation with a recruiter who is unwilling to be flexible after you make reasonable demands concerning when to meet for your interview, find another recruiter. If he or she doesn't have the time for you now when you represent new business, how will he or she treat you once you've already made the purchase, that is, enlisted?

Unfortunately, finding another recruiter may not be that easy. Depending on the service, recruiters work a wide geographic area. Also, most branches have rules against their recruiters "poaching" applicants from other recruiters' zones—that is, enlisting applicants who live in an area covered by another recruiter. However, most recruiter supervisors would probably make an exception if an applicant were having a problem with a particular recruiter.

If it isn't feasible for you to seek another recruiter, you have three choices. First, you can go to another branch of the military. Second, you can change your schedule to accommodate the recruiter. Third, you can forget the whole thing.

Of the three choices, the first one is probably your best. However, I would not recommend that you forget about enlisting because of a bad experience with one recruiter.

THE WALK-IN APPLICANT

Often when people take the initiative to see a recruiter, they will simply walk in to a recruiter's office without an appointment. Although this may seem like a good idea, it isn't.

Would you ever consider walking in to the corporate office of a large company and demand an interview or ask for information about the company? Probably not. The same holds true for your recruiter's office. Most successful recruiters rely on a schedule to get all of their planned daily activities accomplished. By walking in without an appointment, you may throw a wrench into the recruiter's entire work schedule for that day. In addition, he or she may be in the middle of an interview with a prospective applicant. How would you feel if you were being interviewed and the interviewer ignored you while he or she dealt with someone else?

Perhaps a recruiter told you to "stop by anytime." If he or she did, he or she more than likely told you that because you couldn't take time out of your schedule to set up an appointment, and he or she thought an open invitation may result in your wandering into the office someday. Or perhaps you've been thinking about enlisting for a while when you just happen to walk by a recruiting office and decide to stop in for some information, like I did.

If being a walk-in applicant is the only way you can find the time to see a recruiter, then I would recommend it. However, if you can make an appointment with a recruiter, I suggest you do that instead. By dealing with walk-in applicants, the recruiter must meet with someone he or she knows nothing about, so he or she is 'flying blind' until he or she can ask you some questions and establish a rapport with you.

As a high school JROTC teacher, quite a number of my students over the years have enlisted in the military either active duty, guard, or reserve. Many have come to me out of desperation because they have tried to meet with a particular recruiter who was never in his or her office. In a few cases, students have enlisted in another branch because that recruiter happened to be in his or her office when the other recruiter wasn't: What a way to start a career! If you really want to investigate becoming a Marine, for example, make an appointment to see the Marine Corps recruiter!

INTERVIEW SETTINGS

Although most initial interviews with recruiters occur in the recruiter's office, there may be an occasion when the recruiter might suggest another setting for the meeting. The two most popular alternatives are the applicant's residence and the applicant's school.

Although an alternative settings may be more convenient for the applicant, I suggest that the recruiter's office is the best setting for the initial interview. Just as it is possible to be treated for an injury out on the street by an ambulance crew, I would much rather be treated by a doctor in a hospital. An ambulance crew has limited resources "out in the field," and so does the recruiter. If given the choice, meet the recruiter in his or her office. This will also give you the advantage of seeing your recruiter in his or her environment. During your interview, your recruiter undoubtedly will be interrupted several times, usually by telephone calls from other applicants—how he or she handles those interruptions will tell you a lot about your recruiter. Does your recruiter take the time to speak to the person on the other end of the telephone? Does he or she politely dismiss the caller with a sincere promise to call back? Or, is he or she short and impolite with the caller and doesn't even write a note so he or she can remember to call back? Remember that someday you may be the person on the other end of the telephone. Is he or she the kind of salesperson who will treat you well while you're thinking about buying and then forget about you once the sale has been made?

Preparing for the Interview

Once you have an appointment date set, if you think that all you have to do now is sit back and wait for your alarm clock to buzz that morning, think again. You need to prepare for your interview.

OBTAIN THE NECESSARY PAPERWORK

The recruiter may have asked you to bring along some documents to your appointment. Although some, if not most, people are put off by this, it will save you from having to make multiple trips to the recruiter's office, if you decide to proceed in the enlistment process.

The documents requested will probably include:

- your Social Security card;
- your birth certificate (usually the one issued by the state or county, not by the hospital);
- your driver's license; and
- your high school diploma (if applicable).

Although you will eventually need a copy of your birth certificate to enlist, you may begin the process as long as you have your Social Security card. You can furnish the other documents later, although doing so will slow the enlistment process.

If you cannot locate your birth certificate, your recruiter may be able to assist you either in getting a new one or by verifying your birth certificate information by telephone.

STUDY FOR YOUR INTERVIEW

Besides dressing appropriately, the one thing that the experts will tell you about preparing for an interview is to do your homework and find out as much as you can about the company with which you are interviewing. Meeting with a military recruiter is no exception.

In addition to reading this book to prepare you to deal with a recruiter, you should review any literature you may have received from that service, and visit recruiting and other websites. After you've reviewed all the material, get out a pencil and paper and write down any questions you may have. You should also talk to any friends who have either recently enlisted in that particular military branch or whom that particular recruiter interviewed.

The smart recruiter will try to learn as much about you as possible before the initial interview; this gives him or her a competitive edge when dealing with you. I can assure you that he or she is doing his or her homework before the interview, just as you should do.

When I dealt with new applicants, they were amazed at how much I knew about them. It was as if I should have been working for one of those psychic networks. In reality, I would do a little investigative work before the interview. This was particularly easy when dealing with high school seniors. Because I had several seniors from each of the local high schools in my Delayed Entry Program (DEP) waiting to leave for Basic Training, I was able to get information from them. Also, I would have them bring in their yearbook so I could get information about a potential applicant's school activities.

As you'll see in a later section, the first thing a recruiter will do when meeting a new applicant is gain rapport. That is, he or she will try to "connect" with the applicant by putting him or her at ease, and at the same time, by showing interest in the applicant's accomplishments, hobbies, and other interests.

What I have just described will occur if you are dealing with a professional, successful recruiter. If the recruiter has not done his or her investigative work or has tried and was unable to gather any information about you, he or she will spend more time establishing rapport.

GUIDELINES FOR PROPER DRESS: APPEARANCE AND INTERVIEWING PROTOCOL

The following rules apply to the meeting with your recruiter, as well as most job interviews you may have.

Dress Appropriately

Although it is not necessary, or even advisable, to wear a suit or equivalent attire for women applicants, you should dress neatly.

Be Timely

Ensure that you have accurate directions to the recruiter's office, and then allow yourself plenty of time to get there. Take into account the usual traffic conditions at the time of your interview. If you are going to be late for any reason, make sure you call to let the recruiter know.

Be Mentally Alert

Make sure you get plenty of rest before an early appointment; if you are meeting in the afternoon or evening, don't schedule an appointment after a big track meet or a final examination. It is important that you have the ability to give the recruiter your undivided attention.

Be Polite

Even if you've determined that you are not interested in what the recruiter has to say, remain polite and give him or her the respect you would expect in return. Most important, don't use foul language.

Don't Smoke, Chew Gum, or Eat Anything During the Interview

Do I need to say more about this?

Remember to Bring the Required Documents

Bring all the documents described, if the recruiter requested you to do so. Also, don't forget to bring your notepad with the questions you've written.

Leave Your Phone in the Car or Turn it Off

You wouldn't answer a call or a text during a job interview, would you? The same goes for your meeting with the recruiter. If there is no way you can make it through an hour-long meeting to discuss your future without your phone, there is no way you're going to make it through Basic Training!

Discussing test results.

The Interview Session—An Overview

You will probably spend an hour or more with the recruiter during your first interview. Every interview follows the same basic plan. Your recruiter will, in the following order:

- establish rapport with you;
- determine your eligibility for enlistment;
- ask you questions to find your primary motivator(s) for enlisting;
- determine whether the military can meet your needs/wants; and
- make his or her closing sales pitch.

I describe each of these phases in detail in the following sections.

Establishing Rapport

As I mentioned, the first step the recruiter will take when meeting you face-to-face is establish a rapport with you. Hopefully, he or she will have done his or her homework and will be ready for you.

Most recruiters will use the first few minutes of the interview to put you at ease and, at the same time, learn a little more about you. More than likely, the recruiter will also spend some time talking about his or her favorite subject: himself or herself!

The first reaction most applicants have when meeting their recruiters for the first time is intimidation. Most of us equate someone in uniform as an authority figure, especially if that person is wearing a chest full of medals. Do not let this make you feel uneasy; although you do need to treat your recruiter with respect, do not allow him or her to dominate you because of his or her appearance and demeanor.

Allow the recruiter to get to know you better. At the same time, you will get to know the recruiter somewhat better. You will also know by this point whether the recruiter has been doing his or her homework.

The recruiter may start rattling off some names of your classmates or friends. He or she will do this in order to prove to you that he or she has dealt with people you know and that they are satisfied with the way he or she has treated them.

At some point in the conversation, your recruiter will ease out of the rapport step and start asking some specific questions about your medical and criminal history. He or she will also ask some questions about any use of illegal drugs. These questions will allow the recruiter to make some preliminary decisions regarding your eligibility for enlistment.

Determining Your Enlistment Eligibility

Unlike most employers, the military can, and does, impose stringent eligibility requirements on its applicants. These requirements include mental, physical, and moral standards. Your recruiter's job at this point is to ensure that you, at least tentatively, meet these standards.

Depending on your answers, your recruiter will either proceed with the interview process or inform you of your ineligibility for enlistment and tactfully dismiss you.

MORAL REQUIREMENTS

Your recruiter may have asked you some questions about law violations when he or she called to set up the interview. Even if he or she did, he or she will ask you again during the interview. Despite what you might have heard, enlisting in the military is not an option for criminals facing jail time, although I've heard stories that many years ago it was common for a judge to allow offenders to enlist in the military instead of going to jail.

Meeting the moral requirements for enlisting is not difficult for the average law-abiding citizen. Even minor indiscretions may not disqualify you for enlistment. As you'll see later in this section, certain law violations may even be waived to let some individuals who have made mistakes in the past get a fresh start in the military.

Your obligation is to tell your recruiter the truth, not the truth as you see it. Although your recruiter is taking you at your word to determine your eligibility at this point, someone eventually will verify what you tell him or her before you enlist.

Your recruiter more than likely will check with local and state law-enforcement agencies to search for any involvement you may have had with the law. Later in your processing, the investigation will be more in-depth. The section in Chapter 5 entitled "Background Screening" further explains this process.

One important fact to remember at this time is that you must divulge information about all law violations no matter when they happened—this includes crimes or offenses committed as a juvenile, no matter what your attorney or a judge told you. Your recruiter will probably stress this point and impress on you the importance of revealing all past law violations. Sometimes, for one reason or another, a recruiter may not stress the significance of telling the entire truth. He or she may not want to go through the "hassle" of submitting a morals waiver, or your offense may not be eligible for waiver, and he or she doesn't want to lose you as an applicant. Whatever the reason, this behavior is unacceptable. It is unlikely that your recruiter will come straight out and tell you to lie, but it may take the form of, "That's really not important to mention" or something similar. If this happens, find yourself another recruiter; if he or she can ask you to lie, what lies is he or she capable of telling you? Remember that you alone are responsible for any false statements that you make.

Each military branch has its own set of standards concerning disqualifying law violations. In some cases, even small offenses, such as traffic violations, can be disqualifying if there are enough of them in a short period.

MORALS WAIVERS

It is possible that you may be eligible to enlist in the military, even if you commited a law violation that has made you ineligible. Depending on the circumstances, you may receive a morals waiver.

Recruiters do not automatically grant waivers; in most cases, a recruiter will not even offer a disqualified applicant the possibility of a waiver. It is up to the applicant to initiate the conversation concerning a waiver. The conversation may go something like this:

Recruiter: "I'm sorry, but based on what you have just told me about your law violations, I am afraid that you are ineligible for enlistment."

Applicant: "Isn't there anything I could do to enlist? I made a stupid mistake two years ago. Can't you do anything for me?"

Recruiter: "Since you asked, and you sound so sincere, there is a possibility that we can get you a waiver for enlistment."

Because the applicant in this example initiated the conversation, the recruiter was free to offer him or her the option of a morals waiver. However, usually the recruiter also has the option of not offering the applicant that option. If a particular recruiter refuses to run a waiver, find another recruiter who will. In addition, what may require a waiver with one branch of the military may not require one with another; so, if necessary, try another branch.

Who Can Grant a Morals Waiver?

A recruiter cannot grant morals waivers. The level at which the waiver is granted depends on the severity of the legal violation that the interviewer committed, and how long it takes for a decision about a morals waiver depends on the level of the approval authority.

Increasing Your Chance of Getting Your Waiver Approved

There are several ways to increase your chances of getting your waiver approved; there are also mistakes you can make that will more than likely result in a disapproved waiver. First, though, here is the number one rule regarding morals waivers: in most cases, you must divulge the information about the law violation yourself before an approval authority will consider a waiver. In other words, if you told the recruiter that you had no law violations and then something came up on a police check, you would be disqualified automatically. Had you disclosed the same offense to your recruiter, you may have received a waiver. The bottom line is this: tell the truth.

You will be required to write a statement concerning the law violation that led to your disqualification. It is important that your letter is clear and sincere; in most cases, it is the only way you can tell the waiver-granting authority about yourself. Here are some tips for writing your statement:

- Take responsibility for your own actions; do not blame others for what you've done. If you were convicted of assault, don't say, "I was an innocent bystander. He walked into my fist." If you were in a fight, even if you didn't start it, take responsibility for your part in it.
- Tell the waiver authority how much out of character this behavior was for you. If you had never been in a fight before and have never been in trouble with the law, write that in your statement.
- Take your time, write neatly, and, if allowable, type the statement, proofreading for spelling and grammar. The waiver authority will be looking at the whole person when determining whether to grant a waiver.
- Be polite in your writing; use "sir" or "ma'am" in addressing the waiver authority. Use words like please and thank you.
- Do not make derogatory comments about the police, the courts, the judge, etc. This shows how well, or badly, you deal with authority figures.
- Stress what you can offer the military, such as skills or work ethic, and not what you want from the military.
- Request a face-to-face interview to discuss your waiver request.

The statement does not have to be long; it just has to be accurate and cover the details about the law violation. A good example of a well-written letter requesting a waiver appears on the next page.

Notice how the applicant takes full responsibility for his actions and doesn't place blame on others, although he could have. Although a letter like this does not guarantee that this applicant will receive the waiver, the chances are good that he or she will.

Law Violations

This section lists examples of law violations. I would warn you not to use these examples to disqualify yourself before you even talk to a recruiter. Although no list can be complete, this one comes very close.

If, by chance, you were convicted of a violation not listed in your recruiter's recruiting regulation, he or she probably will make a determination as to what violation on his or her list most closely matches yours. If he or she is smart, he or she will not make the determination him- or herself, but will ask for guidance up his or her chain-of-command.

I have divided this list into different levels of violations; all military branches use a similar method to determine the level of waiver approval. The level of the law violation depends on the individual branch.

July 29, 2013

Dear Sir:

I am requesting a waiver to enlist in the United States Army. I believe that it would be in the best interest of the Army to grant this request.

On August 1, 2010, a group of my friends and I decided to go to the beach for the day. We were there for about an hour when we decided to go for a swim. When we returned about 15 minutes later we found another group of teenagers on our blankets.

When we asked them to get off our blankets, they started cursing at us and one of them started pushing one of my friends. Before I knew what was going on, everybody was fighting, and some-one pushed me to the ground.

The fight lasted about 5 minutes, until the police arrived. We were all taken to the Main Street police station and later released to our parents.

I went to court on October 1, 2010, and was found guilty of disturbing the peace and unlawful assembly. I paid a $50 fine, and because of my age (16), I received 30 hours of community service, which I completed on January 15, 2011.

I have never been in trouble before this incident and feel ashamed because of it. I should have contacted the police or the lifeguard when we found the other teenagers on our blankets. That would have solved the whole problem without fighting.

I hope that this one isolated incident does not keep me from enlisting in the Army. I am a good student and a trustworthy person. I believe the Army could use someone like me.

Thank you for the opportunity to apply for enlistment in the Army. If you wish, I am available to meet with you in person to discuss this matter.

Very Respectfully,

Joe Applicant

Level-One Offenses

These offenses are serious and require the highest level of waiver approval.

- Aggravated assault with a dangerous weapon, intentionally inflicting great bodily harm with intent to commit a felony
- Bribery
- Burglary
- Carnal knowledge of a child under sixteen years of age

- Draft evasion
- Extortion
- Indecent acts or liberties with a child under sixteen years of age, molestation
- Kidnapping, abduction
- Manslaughter
- Murder
- Perjury
- Rape
- Robbery

Level-Two Offenses

These offenses, although serious, are less serious than level-one offenses and usually require approval at a level above the local waiver approval authority. Level two contains some of the same offenses found in level one, but are considered at the lesser level if adjudicated when the applicant was a juvenile.

- Arson
- Aggravated assault with a dangerous weapon, intentionally inflicting great bodily harm with intent to commit a felony
- Attempting to commit a felony
- Breaking and entering a building with intent to commit a felony
- Breaking and entering a house
- Bribery
- Burglary
- Carrying a concealed firearm or unlawful carrying of a firearm
- Carrying a concealed weapon (other than a firearm), possession of brass knuckles
- Child pornography offenses
- Conspiring to commit a felony
- Criminal libel
- DUI/DWI (driving under the influence of, while intoxicated, or impaired by, alcohol or drugs)
- Embezzlement
- Extortion
- Forgery: knowingly uttering or passing a forged instrument (except for altered identification for purchase of alcoholic beverages)
- Grand larceny
- Grand theft
- Indecent assault
- Involuntary manslaughter
- Leaving the scene of an accident (hit-and-run) involving personal injury
- Lewd, licentious, or lascivious behavior
- Looting
- Mail or electronic emission matters: abstracting, destroying, obstructing, opening, secreting, stealing, or taking

- Mail: depositing obscene or indecent matter (includes electronic or computerized e-mail/bulletin board systems, and files)
- Maiming or disfiguring
- Marijuana: simple possession or use
- Negligent homicide
- Pandering
- Perjury
- Prostitution or soliciting to commit prostitution
- Public record: altering, concealing, destroying, mutilating, obliterating, or removing
- Riot
- Robbery
- Sedition or soliciting to commit sedition
- Selling, leasing, or transferring a weapon to a minor or an unauthorized individual
- Sexual harassment
- Willfully discharging firearms endangering life, or shooting in a public place

Level-Three Offenses

Less serious than levels one and two, yet more serious than a traffic ticket, level-three offenses usually can be waived at the local level.

- Adultery
- Assault (simple)
- Breaking and entering a vehicle
- Check—insufficient funds (amount more than $50, worthless, or uttering with intent to defraud or deceive)
- Conspiring to commit a misdemeanor
- Contempt of court (includes nonpayment of child support or alimony required by court order)
- Contributing to the delinquency of a minor (includes purchase of alcoholic beverages)
- Desecration of a grave
- Discharging a firearm through carelessness or within municipal limits
- Drunk in public, drunk and disorderly, public intoxication
- Failure to stop and render aid after an accident
- Indecent exposure
- Indecent, insulting, or obscene language communicated directly or by telephone
- Killing a domestic animal
- Leaving the scene of an accident (hit-and-run) with no personal injury involved
- Liquor or alcoholic beverages: unlawful manufacture or sale
- Malicious mischief
- Resisting, fleeing, or eluding arrest
- Removing property under lien or from public grounds
- Slander
- Shooting from highway or on public road

- Shoplifting, larceny, petty larceny, theft, or petty theft (age fourteen or older or stolen goods valued over $50)
- Stolen property: possession of, or knowingly receiving stolen property
- Unlawful or illegal entry
- Unlawful use of long-distance telephone lines or any electronic transmission method
- Use of telephone or any electronic transmission method to abuse, annoy, harass, threaten, or torment another
- Wrongful appropriation of motor vehicle, joyriding, or driving without owner's consent

Level-Four Offenses

Approved at the local level, these offenses are not usually disqualifying unless you've committed more than one of them.

- Abusive language under circumstances to provoke breach of peace
- Altered identification when intent is to purchase alcoholic beverages
- Careless or reckless driving
- Check—($50 or less, insufficient funds, or worthless)
- Curfew violation
- Committing or creating nuisance
- Damaging road signs
- Disorderly conduct, creating disturbance, or boisterous conduct, disturbing the peace
- Failure to appear, comply with judgment, answer or disobey summons
- Failure to comply with officer's direction
- Fare evasion
- Fighting, participating in a brawl
- Illegal betting or gambling: operating illegal handbook, raffle, lottery, punch board, or watching a cockfight
- Juvenile noncriminal misconduct: beyond parental control, incorrigible, runaway, truant, or wayward
- Liquor or alcoholic beverages: unlawful possession or consumption in a public place
- Littering or dumping refuse near highway or other prohibited place
- Loitering
- Possession of indecent publications or pictures (other than child pornography)
- Purchase, possession, or consumption of alcoholic beverages by a minor
- Racing, drag racing
- Shoplifting, larceny, petty larceny, theft, or petty theft (committed under age 14 and stolen goods valued at $50 or less)
- Trespassing on property
- Unlawful assembly
- Vagrancy
- Vandalism, defacing or injuring property
- Violation of fireworks law
- Violation of fish and game laws

Level-Five Offenses

Consideration for waivers is at the local level for multiple convictions of level-five violations.

- Blocking or retarding traffic
- Crossing yellow line, drifting left of center
- Disobeying traffic lights, signs, or signals
- Driving on shoulder
- Driving uninsured vehicle
- Driving with blocked or impaired vision
- Driving with expired plates or without plates
- Driving without license in possession
- Driving without registration or with improper registration
- Driving wrong way on a one-way street
- Failure to display inspection sticker
- Failure to have vehicle under control
- Failure to keep right or in proper lane
- Failure to signal
- Failure to stop or yield to a pedestrian
- Failure to yield right of way
- Faulty equipment
- Following too close
- Improper backing
- Improper blowing of horn
- Improper passing
- Improper parking
- Improper turn
- Invalid or unofficial inspection sticker
- Leaving key in ignition
- License plates improperly or not displayed
- Operating overloaded vehicle
- Playing vehicle radio/stereo too loud
- Speeding (does not include racing)
- Spinning wheels, improper start
- Seatbelt violation
- Zigzagging or weaving in traffic

Morals Waiver Summary

Each branch of the military grants morals waivers on a case-by-case basis to applicants who are ineligible for enlistment. Being granted a waiver depends on the circumstances surrounding the law violation(s), your age at the time of the incident(s), your current level of maturity, and your level of sincerity.

Although you may be granted a morals waiver, you are, essentially, still not technically "qualified" for enlistment. Because of this, you must be flexible when it comes time to choose a military career field (job). You will read more about this in Chapter 5.

PHYSICAL REQUIREMENTS

Although some branches of the military will require you to meet some physical fitness requirements before enlistment (most people of enlistment age are in good enough physical condition to meet those standards), they rely on Basic Training to get you in the proper physical conditioning for military service.

The physical requirements that will concern your recruiter during your initial interview are your overall health and medical history. As you'll see in Chapter 5, you will be subjected to a thorough physical examination.

In addition to the physical examination, you will be "grilled" for information concerning your medical history at the MEPS.

As with law violations, your recruiter may not press you to reveal details concerning your medical history. As with the law violations, your recruiter may tell you it may be best if you do not disclose certain things. I will give you the same advice as I have previously given: if your recruiter asks you to conceal or withhold information, find yourself another recruiter.

Your recruiter should have asked some preliminary medical history questions over the telephone before he or she made the initial appointment. The recruiter made a determination of your eligibility based on your answers to those questions.

Unless there is something visibly wrong with you, your recruiter will have to take your word on your present health and your medical history. The one exception to this is your weight. You will be required to get on the scale so your recruiter can determine if you are within weight standards.

On a lighter note (no pun intended), there is an urban legend involving recruiters who convince female applicants that they must get undressed to get an accurate reading on the scale. At no time should any applicant, male or female, remove any clothing as part of the interview process with the recruiter. Of course, you will be required to get undressed at the MEPS for your physical examination.

Divulging Medical History Information

The rule is simple: when it comes to divulging information about your medical history, divulge everything!

Although you should disclose all information about your medical history, make sure that you divulge information about problems that a physician has diagnosed. All too often applicants will disqualify themselves by telling their recruiter that they had an illness with which they were never diagnosed. A popular example of this is asthma.

Many times, applicants are intimidated by the strong wording about what can happen to you if you lie on the application forms. If you are unsure about a particular question, inform the recruiter that you must confirm the information before answering it. That might mean you could resolve it right away by making a telephone call or you may need to get back to your recruiter. However, in no case should you feel compelled to answer a question about which you are uncertain.

Chapter 5, which deals with MEPS processing, contains more information on this subject.

Just as it is possible to be granted a morals waiver for disqualifying law violations, you may be granted a medical waiver for certain disqualifying medical conditions. However, unlike morals waivers, the recruiting chain of command has no control of waiver approval.

Medical Waivers

A Marine Corps Recruiter discusses options with an applicant.

As with a morals waiver, it is up to the applicant to request a medical waiver. You may be told, however, that no waivers may be granted for your disqualifying condition. Although this might be true, ask to see it in writing, if possible. Some recruiters don't want the hassle of bothering with medical waivers because, in most cases, they are too time-consuming and many times are not granted, leaving the recruiter with nothing to show for his or her efforts.

If your condition truly cannot be waived, try another branch of the military; although similar, the standards are not 100 percent the same for all services.

Initiating a Medical Waiver

Usually a recruiter can initiate a medical waiver by getting all the documentation concerning an applicant's disqualifying condition and forwarding it to the MEPS for determination. The MEPS Chief Medical Officer (CMO) may then take one of several steps. He or she may:

- request that the applicant come to the MEPS to process and then make a final determination (sometimes a waiver may not even be required);
- ask for further tests to be accomplished; or
- disapprove a waiver (at his or her level).

If the CMO wants you to process at the MEPS, he or she will evaluate you at that time and make a determination. If you pass your physical at that time, you are on your way to enlisting. If he or she requires further tests, the CMO will evaluate the results of those tests. Then he or she either may ask you to come to the MEPS for further evaluation or deny you a waiver based on the information you provided. If the CMO disapproves your waiver request either initially, after reviewing the additional tests, or after evaluating you at the MEPS, you may request through your recruiter that your waiver request be up-channeled—that is, sent to a higher authority for review.

The level at which a waiver must be approved depends on the service. However, one thing is true of all military branches: the further a medical waiver has to be up-channeled, the more likely it will be disapproved and the longer it will take for a final decision.

Disqualifying Medical Conditions

Remember, at this stage, the recruiter is evaluating you solely by the information you have provided to the recruiter. For instance, if you have epilepsy, the recruiter would have no idea of that, unless you had a seizure in his or her office. Therefore, the recruiter can only find you tentatively physically qualified for enlistment. Final determination on your fitness for enlistment will occur at the MEPS. The waiver process may also begin at that time if a CMO finds a disqualifying condition at the MEPS.

The following disqualifying conditions are typical for all branches of the military. Do not use this list to disqualify yourself for enlistment but rather as a guide to make you aware of the physical standards criteria. If you are completely healthy and never were hospitalized, I would advise you not to review the following disqualifying conditions. I found myself getting sick just writing them!

Waiver approval procedures differ among services and change from time to time, so it is important to get up-to-date information from your recruiter.

MEDICAL CONDITIONS THAT MAY RESULT IN DISQUALIFICATION

Category	Condition
Abdomen and Digestive System	Abdominal surgery within sixty days
	Cirrhosis
	Colon, megacolon, diverticulitis, regional enteritis, or ulcerative colitis—spastic colon if more than moderate
	Fistula in anus

MEDICAL CONDITIONS THAT MAY RESULT IN DISQUALIFICATION

Category	Condition
	Gallbladder removed and symptoms continue—special diet required
	Gallstones—current
	Hemorrhoids—symptomatic
	Hepatitis—within six months
	Hernia—if present
	Intestinal obstruction—within five years
	Pancreas—any acute or chronic disease
	Rectum—stricture or prolapse
	Resection of any portion of the digestive tract
	Scars that show bulging or herniation, prevent full activity, or cause pain
	Splenectomy (except for trauma)
	Tumors
	Ulcer
Allergies	Allergic manifestations—a reliable history of life-threatening generalized reaction with anaphylaxis to stinging insects or reliable history of moderate to severe reaction to common foods, spices, or food additives
	Asthma, including reactive airway disease, exercise-induced bronchospasm, or asthmatic bronchitis—at any age
	Hay fever and skin allergies
Blood and Blood-Forming Tissue Disease	Anemia (unless permanently corrected by therapy)
	Bleeding and clotting disease
	Enlarged spleen
	Immunodeficiency diseases
	Leukemia
	Low white count
	Myeloproliferative disease or myelodysplactic disease
Dental	Diseases not easily corrected
	Inability to eat an ordinary diet
	Orthodontic appliances (acceptable to enter Delayed Entry Program [DEP] but must be removed before going on Active Duty)
Ears and Hearing	Acute or chronic otitis media of any type
	Infection of canal—if acute or chronic
	Loss of ear

MEDICAL CONDITIONS THAT MAY RESULT IN DISQUALIFICATION

Category	Condition
	Mastoidectomy
	Mastoiditis—if acute
	Meniere's syndrome
	Middle ear infections—if acute or chronic
	Perforated eardrums
	Severe scarring of eardrums—with associated hearing loss of more than 20 dB
	Smallness or closing of ear canal
	Tumors of canal
Endocrine and Metabolic Disorders	Most disorders, except simple low thyroid that is being controlled medically
	Hypothyroidism, symptomatic, or uncontrolled by medication
Extremities (Orthopedic)	Amputation of:
	Big toe
	Hand, foot, arm, or leg
	More than one-third of distal portion of thumb
	One joint on two or more fingers (except little finger)
	One or more small toes if it interferes with function
	Two joints of index, middle, or ring finger
	Fractures:
	Bones (major) within six months
	Healed improperly
	Injury (bone)—without fracture disqualified for six weeks
	Metal retained for repair of fracture
	Joints:
	Arthritis—other than mild
	Cartilage (knee)—torn, unless surgically repaired, more than six months since surgery and rehabilitation completed
	Deranged joint (unstable)
	History of anterior cruciate ligament knee or posterior cruciate ligament injury
	Ligament (knee) surgery
	Significantly impaired joint function
	Muscles—weakness, paralysis, or contracture
	Neuroma—refractory to medical treatment
	Osteomyelitis—in past two years or if extensive or recurrent

MEDICAL CONDITIONS THAT MAY RESULT IN DISQUALIFICATION

Category	Condition
	Plantar fasciitis—refractory to medical treatment
	Retropatellar knee pain syndrome (chronic)
	Scars—if extensive, deep, adherent, or painful
	Silastic or other devices implanted to correct orthopedic abnormalities
	Soft bones (such as osteoporosis)
	Ununited fractures—except ulnar styloid process
Back, Spine, and Sacroiliac Joints	Congenital deformities
	Curvature of the spine—if more than moderate
	Infections
	Recurrent back pain
	Ruptured disc
	Spondylolisthesis
	Symptomatic healed fractures
Eyes	Absence of lens or lens implant
	Blind in one eye
	Corneal scars or ulcers
	Double vision
	Glaucoma
	History of surgery to modify the refractive power of the cornea
	Night blindness
	Nystagmus
	Opacities of cornea or lens
	Refractive error of 8.00 diopters or more
	Torn or diseased retina
	Vision requiring contact lens for correction
Genitourinary System (Males)	Absence of both testicles
	Hydrocele or left varicocele—if painful or any right varicocele unless urologic evaluation reveals no disease
	Undescended testicle
	Urethritis—acute or chronic
Genitourinary System (Females)	Congenital absence of uterus
	Infections—if acute or recurrent
	Irregular periods or no periods
	Menopausal symptoms if caused by surgery—thirteen-month waiting period

MEDICAL CONDITIONS THAT MAY RESULT IN DISQUALIFICATION

Category	Condition
	Painful periods
	Pelvic inflammatory disease—acute or chronic
	Vagina—congenital abnormalities that interfere with physical activities
	Vulva—condyloma accuminatum and dystrophic conditions
Kidneys	Albuminuria (protein in the urine)
	Bed-wetting
	Kidney disease (absence of one kidney)
	Kidney stones—if in past year, or more than twice, or on both sides at any time, or present now
Head and Neck	Concussions—more than mild within three months
	Depressed fractures of the skull
	Loss of portion of the skull—larger than the size of a quarter
	Severe contusions or lacerations within three months
	Unsightly deformities, scars, etc.
Heart and Vascular System	High blood pressure, especially if it requires medication or dietary restriction
	Heart disease
Lungs and Chest	Acute disease of the lungs, pneumonia, bronchitis, etc.—chronic lung disease if more than mild
	Asthma—at any age
	New growth of breast
	Removal of any part of the lungs
	Removal of breast (females)
	Tuberculosis—within two years, or active two or more times
Mouth	Harelip—unless repaired
	Mutilations
	Perforation of hard palate
Nose	Chronic rhinitis (allergy)
	Hay fever—if not controllable
	Perforated nasal septum
	Sinusitis—acute or chronic (if more than mild)
Neurologic Disorders	Arteriosclerosis
	Brain hemorrhage
	Congenital malformations
	Degenerative and hereditodegenerative disorders

MEDICAL CONDITIONS THAT MAY RESULT IN DISQUALIFICATION

Category	Condition
	Disturbances on consciousness—head injury resulting in unconsciousness or amnesia
	Early posttraumatic seizures—occurring within one week of injury (five-year waiting period)
	Embolism
	Incoordination
	Intellectual deficit
	Late posttraumatic epilepsy—occurring more than one week after injury
	Multiple sclerosis
	Muscular atrophies and dystrophies
	Organic personality disturbances
	Paralysis
	Paroxysmal convulsive disorders—epilepsy, seizures, fits, etc. (except fever fits before age 5)
	Recurrent headaches—when interferes with normal function or history of such headaches within three years
	Sensory disturbance
	Severe head injury with associated abscess or meningitis (within five years)
	Sleep disorders
	Tremors
Psychiatric	Alcohol or drug dependence (or history of)
	Anabolic steroids requiring professional care within one-year period before examination or if it is determined that the applicant has accepted their use as a pattern behavior
	Character and behavior disorders, manifested by:
	Dependency
	Homosexual conduct
	Immaturity
	Instability
	Personal inadequacy
	Repeated inability to maintain reasonable adjustment at school, work, or with family

MEDICAL CONDITIONS THAT MAY RESULT IN DISQUALIFICATION

Category	Condition
	Chronic history of academic skills or perceptual defects secondary to organic or functional mental disorders that interfere with work or school after age 12; current use of medication to improve or maintain academic skills
	Personality disorders, manifested by:
	Chronic alcoholism
	Drug addiction
	Repeated and frequent encounters with law enforcement
	Sleepwalking or eating disorders that are habitual and persistent—since age 12
	Stammering or stuttering—unless mild
	Psychoneurosis—if hospitalization required
	Psychosis at any time
	Suicide attempts—history of suicidal behavior
Skin	Acne—severe
	Any skin condition aggravated by sunlight, high humidity, or extreme heat or cold
	Contact dermatitis involving rubber or other materials used in protective equipment
	Cysts, pilonidal, if evidenced by the presence of a tumor mass or a discharging sinus—history of pilonidal cystectomy within one year before examination
	Eczema—if chronic and resistant to treatment
	Fungus infections—if extensive and resistant to treatment
	Lupus erythematosus
	Psoriasis
	Scars—if extensive, deep, or adherent and may interfere with wearing military clothing or equipment
	Urticaria (hives)—if chronic
Tumors	Any tumor or history of benign tumors of:
	Anywhere—if large
	Auditory canal
	Bone, if subject to trauma
	Brain, spinal chord, or central nervous system
	Eye
	Kidney, bladder, testicle, or penis—uterus, ovary, or breast
	Tongue, if interferes with function

MEDICAL CONDITIONS THAT MAY RESULT IN DISQUALIFICATION

Category	Condition
Miscellaneous Conditions	Any tumor if malignant (even if removed and cured), with exception of small, early, basal cell carcinoma of skin
	Benign tumors of the peripheral nerves that interfere with function, have malignant potential, or interfere with military duty or the wearing of the uniform or military equipment
	Cold urticaria and angioedema, hereditary angioedema
	HIV/AIDS—tested positive for HIV/AIDS-related complex
	Malignant hypothermia
	Motion sickness—frequent, incapacitating after 12th birthday
	Organ transplant recipient
	Residual of tropical fevers and various parasitic or protozoal infections that prevent the satisfactory performance of military duty
	Rheumatic fever within two years—history of recurrent attacks
	Sydenham's chorea at any age

I realize that the temptation is just too much for most people, so you probably read the entire table of disqualifying conditions. Hopefully, you didn't pick up any new diseases as you read it.

USE OF ILLEGAL DRUGS

The military has a zero-tolerance policy for drug use among its members. Therefore, all applicants are required to be drug-free. Besides illegal drugs, the abuse of prescription drugs is also disqualifying.

Each branch has its own policy on granting waivers for past drug use, and because policy changes often, the specifics are not listed here. Like the other waivers, the applicant must initiate the request for a drug waiver. In determining whether to grant a waiver, the military will consider the following :

- the type of drug
- the number of times used
- age at the time of use
- length of time since you used the drug
- any law violations connected to your drug use (this, of course, would require a double waiver—one for the law violation and one for the drug use)
- your sincerity about any future drug use

As with the initial morals and physical qualifications, your recruiter must take your word concerning your past and present involvement with drugs. One thing is for certain, though, if you get to MEPS and have drugs in your bloodstream, there will be no waivers granted.

OTHER ELIGIBILITY REQUIREMENTS

The recruiter will cover a few more qualification areas, such as citizenship and whether you have any dependents.

Citizenship

Certain military occupations require U.S. citizenship. Your recruiter will determine your status by reviewing your birth certificate, naturalization documents, and the like.

Dependency

Dependency does not refer to your dependency on someone else; it refers instead to others' dependency on you. This includes single parents, spouses of military members with minor children, and married applicants with multiple dependents.

If you have dependents, the recruiter will more than likely tell you that you are ineligible for enlistment. However, as with other criteria, you may be able to obtain a waiver. As with other types of waivers, the recruiter can only make a dependency determination if the applicant asks for one; it will not be offered. The recruiter reviews each dependency waiver on a case-by-case basis.

Isn't it discriminatory to make an applicant with dependents ineligible for enlistment? The answer is no. Consider the following:

- Because military members sometimes are deployed away from home for extended periods of time, single parents may be required to make semi-permanent arrangements for the care of their children.
- If both parents are military members, a military deployment may turn one of the spouses into a temporary single parent. What happens if that remaining parent then is deployed?
- Considering the salary of a person just starting out in the military, it would be irresponsible for the military to allow someone with many dependents to enlist and try to support a family.

MENTAL REQUIREMENTS

Mental requirements perhaps are the only part of the qualifications for enlistment that cannot be waived; the mental requirements begin with the ASVAB examination.

If you've already taken the ASVAB (at school or for another recruiter), your recruiter will have you complete a form called the 680-3A. Signing this form does not obligate you to anything, but it does allow your recruiter to gain access to your ASVAB scores.

If you haven't taken the ASVAB, your recruiter may ask you to take the Enlistment Screening Test (EST). This short exam, administered by your recruiter, will give him or her an idea of how you'll do on the ASVAB.

Based on the results of the EST, your recruiter will either proceed with the interview or inform you that you will need additional study to pass the ASVAB.

Chapter 4 covers the ASVAB examination, includes a few sample questions, and provides some common-sense test-taking techniques. If you are serious about getting yourself more prepared for the ASVAB, I suggest that you purchase a study guide.

If you've passed all the preliminary qualifications hurdles, it will be time for the recruiter to get down to the real nitty-gritty of the interview.

Probing to Find Your Primary Motivator(s)

I enjoy cop shows on television, especially detective shows. I'm usually pretty good at solving the crime before the end of the show. There is always a common thread between all the detective shows I've ever watched—usually the first thing all the detectives look for before anything else is motive!

The reason is simple: nearly all crimes are committed for a reason. Maybe the motive is money, maybe it's revenge, or perhaps it's hatred. Whatever the reason, it all comes down to motive.

The same is true of sales or recruiting: every buyer or applicant has at least one motive for buying, or in this case, enlisting. In the case of military recruiting, it is up to the recruiter to uncover your motives for enlisting. It helps, of course, if you know your own motives.

STATE YOUR MOTIVES

For one reason or another, some applicants feel that they need to conceal their motives for enlisting from their recruiter. Often, applicants will force a situation where the recruiter must coerce the applicant to reveal his or her true motive(s) for enlisting.

Consider the example of the police detective trying to establish a motive for a crime. The conversation might go something like this:

Detective: Why did you kill him?

Suspect: I didn't!

Detective: Didn't you discover that the victim was stealing from your company bank account?

Suspect: Yes, but why would I kill him for that?

Detective: Maybe it's because you were listed as the beneficiary on his life insurance policy and you wanted to get back the money he stole from you.

Suspect: Okay, okay, you got me; that was my motive.

(I'm sure it's clear why I'm not writing detective novels—but even this illustration will serve my purpose.)

In the case of a detective questioning a suspect, the suspect has everything to gain by not revealing his or her motive. In fact, he or she will do everything in his or her power to prevent the police from finding it. In sales, the exact opposite is true. Take a car buyer, for example. Suppose you want to buy a car that will serve your needs. You stroll down to the dealership looking for a small, fuel-efficient car with a large trunk, so you can easily load the gear you use on your frequent camping trips. In most cases, you would probably tell the salesman, up front, what you are looking for so that he or she can show you the right vehicle to meet your needs. Rarely would you play the detective-suspect game with a salesperson. The same holds true for dealing with your recruiter. You need to let him or her know, up front, what it is you expect from an enlistment in the military. Don't worry that your motives may appear totally selfish, or maybe even weird, because seasoned recruiters have heard them all. Some common motives include:

- money for college
- technical training
- security of steady employment
- travel
- patriotism
- discipline
- pride

Your motives may be many or just one; it may be one of those listed or one completely different. Be sure you know what your motive or motives are before you meet with your recruiter so you can be straightforward with him or her.

Have you ever purchased something and then later said to yourself, "Why on earth did I ever buy this?" The reason this happened is because you had no clear motives in mind when you purchased the item. Or, you had clear motives in mind and then purchased something that did not meet what motivated you to go to the store in the first place.

Motives can also translate to "needs" and "wants." Showing you how the specific branch of the military can meet these needs and wants is the job of the recruiter. Once your motivators are on the table, your recruiter will move on to the next step, which is showing you how his or her service is the one that can best meet those needs and wants.

Meeting Your Needs and Wants

This is where the sales or recruiting process starts to get tricky. What if after finding your primary motivation for enlisting the recruiter realizes that the service he or she represents is not the best to meet your needs or wants? In most cases, the answer is easy: he or she will force a "fit," and someday in the future you'll find yourself saying, "Why on earth did I ever buy into this?"

Just as you wouldn't expect a car salesman to say, "You know, it doesn't appear that a Chevy will meet your needs, so why don't you try a Ford?" rarely will you hear a recruiter say, "The Army doesn't seem to be the best solution to your needs, but I'm sure the Navy can meet them." The recruiter who can admit that you might be better off shopping elsewhere is saying a lot about himself or herself and the service he or she represents.

THE BENEFITS DUMP

The approach your recruiter takes in demonstrating how his or her service can meet your needs will vary from recruiter to recruiter. Generally, though, recruiters will engage in what is known as a "benefits dump" —that is, they will throw all the benefits their service has to offer at you and hope some of them interest to you. Here's a little secret that I'll share with you that they probably won't: the basic benefits of military service are the same for all branches of the military:

- the same pay scales
- medical care
- dental care
- GI Bill for higher education
- housing allowance
- thirty vacation days with pay, per year
- privileges at base stores
- availability of recreational activities, such as golf courses and swimming pools
- retirement plan

After you've been subjected to the deluge of benefits, your recruiter will more than likely try to sell you on the "exclusive" benefits of his or her particular service.

(I will cover these and other basic benefits in more detail in Chapters 9 and 11.)

THE PRESSURE IS ON

Although the actual "sale" has already begun, it is now that the real pressure begins. It is at this point that you must be on the offensive.

During the benefits dump, most recruiters will make it sound as if they have an exclusive on the basic benefits, but now you know better! If the recruiter can satisfy your needs (motivator) with the basic benefits, he or she will more than likely try at this time to make the sale. If, however, he or she doesn't believe that your needs have been satisfied, he or she will employ his or her skills to convince you that his or her service is the one to get what you want.

Recently one of my students, who was about to graduate, was extremely excited to tell me that she had missed school the day before in order to join the military. When I asked her why she had selected the specific branch, she said that the recruiter told her that it had the best pay... if only she had read this book!

THE ART OF PERSUASION

Recruiters, just like any well-trained salespeople, are trained in the art of persuasion. That is, they are taught to get people to agree with them and ultimately to buy their product.

They will use all sorts of tactics and techniques to convince you to agree to enlist. At this stage of the game, most recruiters will try to match your wants with the benefits of their particular service. The recruiter will make everything make sense and lead you down a path that comes to only one conclusion: enlist in their particular branch!

The typical recruiter will give what amounts to a sales pitch and will ask feedback questions along the way to ensure that you are on track and following down the path he or she is creating for you. Here's how part of the conversation may go:

Recruiter: "Okay, Sue, from what you have told me, your primary interest is to get some training in the area of computers. Is that correct?"

Applicant: "Yes, that's correct."

Recruiter: "Well, Sue, the Navy has many jobs that are directly related to computers. We have computer programming jobs, computer repair jobs, and data processing jobs. In addition, Sue, many Navy jobs require sailors to work directly with computers. Does that sound interesting to you?"

Applicant: "So far, yes. But how much training will I get to prepare me for my job?"

Recruiter: "I'm glad you asked that, Sue, because I want to tell you that the Navy has some of the best computer training you'll find anywhere. In addition, we do it all at an accelerated pace because, for the time you'll be in school, that's your only job. You'll be focusing on your studies and won't have any other duties to worry about. You'll also receive your full pay the entire time. This is starting to sound better and better, isn't it?"

Applicant: "Yes, it is!"

Recruiter: "Great, Sue. I'm sure we'll be able to find you a Navy job that meets your needs of providing computer training. Let me ask you this: if I could guarantee you computer training, would you be ready to take the next step?"

Applicant: "I think so. What is the next step?"

Recruiter: "The next step is to take the ASVAB and then the physical."

Applicant: "When can I take the ASVAB and physical?"

Recruiter: "Sue, I know you're busy, so I'd suggest that you do one-stop processing. You'll take the ASVAB on Tuesday evening at the MEPS, stay at a hotel overnight at our expense, and then take your physical the next day. How does that sound?"

Applicant: "Sounds great."

Recruiter: "Good, before we arrange the ASVAB and physical, we need to complete some paperwork. Are you ready to get started?"

Applicant: "Sure, let's get started."

Notice how the recruiter laid a path for the applicant to follow. The recruiter asked several feedback questions to ensure that the applicant was still on the path and not getting lost. Also, like many salespeople, recruiters use the applicant's name a lot (a trait that I never liked). Good recruiters will also look for nonverbal cues to make sure their applicants are following them down the path. Positive body language and an applicant nodding in agreement are signs that he or she is on the way to enlistment.

My advice at this stage of the game is to keep 'em guessing; it's not time to buy quite yet. Don't get overly enthusiastic about anything your recruiter has presented. Answer feedback questions matter-of-factly, not emotionally.

When my wife and I were looking for a house to buy, I gave her the following instructions when we pulled up to each house: "Show no emotion; don't say anything positive about the house while we're inside; and, definitely don't start telling them where you would put your furniture or what color you'd paint each of the rooms."

Why did I give such explicit instructions? The answer is simple: I didn't want the seller to know I was eager to buy. I wasn't rude to the seller, but I also wasn't giving her or him signals that I had already made up my mind.

Unfortunately for recruiters, conversations with applicants rarely go as smoothly as the example given here. Usually, applicants will respond negatively to feedback questions:

Recruiter: "Great, Sue, I'm sure we'll be able to find you a Navy job that meets your needs of providing computer training. Let me ask you this: if I could guarantee you computer training, would you be ready to take the next step?"

Applicant: "No, I don't think so."

In this situation, the recruiter is met with an objection. It is up to the recruiter to identify and overcome it.

OVERCOMING OBJECTIONS

Part of a recruiter's training deals with overcoming applicant objections. However, before he or she can overcome them, he or she must identify them.

The true objection in the example is not, "No, I don't think so." Rather, it is whatever motivated the applicant to say "no." What the applicant may have been trying to say was:

- "No, I don't think so. You haven't told me enough about the training I'll receive."
- "No, I want to know more about the jobs I might be doing after the training."

Or, there may be other concerns holding back the applicant. It is the recruiter's job to identify them. Once the recruiter has identified the objections by asking probing questions, he or she can begin to overcome them. In the given scenarios, he or she would probably give Sue more information to answer her concerns and continue to ask feedback questions such as, "How does that sound?" or "Does that answer your question?" in order to get Sue to agree to continue processing for enlistment.

Sometimes, the objection may not be that the applicant needs more information; rather, it may be that the applicant doesn't think that proceeding is the right choice. For example, "No, I don't think so. I'm not ready for a commitment to the Navy."

There are as many objections as there are applicants, and it is up to the recruiter to probe deeper to overcome every objection.

There are several methods a recruiter can use to try to overcome an objection such as fear of commitment. One of the most popular methods is the "feel, felt, found" approach. For example:

Applicant: "No, I don't think the Army is right for me because I don't think I'd make it through Basic Training."

Recruiter: "I understand how you **feel**; many people have **felt** the same way. This is what other people have **found:** Basic Training was not as hard as they believed it would be. They found that Basic Training actually helped them realize just how much they could accomplish if they put their mind to it."

Recruiters may use variations of "feel, felt, found" and may also just come out and ask you, "Why do you feel that way?" or "What makes you say that?" or something else along those lines. The bottom line is that the recruiter will ensure all your objections are uncovered and put to rest so that he or she can close the sale and get you to commit.

What If I Have Objections?

If you have any objections, let the recruiter know about them. By hiding objections, you may be sending a signal to the recruiter that you are ready to buy, when in fact you are not. Give the recruiter every opportunity to answer your concerns, and then let him or her know if he or she has answered your questions to your satisfaction.

Sometimes the objection may be that you have heard what the recruiter has to offer and you are just not interested. If this is the case, let the recruiter know that, and tell him or her matter-of-factly that you are just not interested in proceeding. Of course, at this time any good recruiter will say something to the effect of "I understand why you would say that. Many people have felt the same way, this is what they have found . . ." If this is the case, end the conversation right there. Do not feel pressured or obligated to continue. The most important thing is not to continue in the enlistment process if you don't intend to enlist. There is nothing worse for a recruiter than having an applicant complete all the paperwork, take the ASVAB and physical, and then not enlist. Believe me, despite how he or she feels at the time, a recruiter would much rather you be up front in the beginning than go through all the steps of enlistment and lose you in the end. If you just need more time to think things through, let the recruiter know that. If, however, you've already made up your mind not to enlist, don't tell him or her you'll think about it. Assuming that your recruiter has satisfied all your questions and you are still interested in enlisting, the recruiter will no doubt move to the next step of closing the sale.

Closing the Sale

A recruiter will usually wait until he or she is sure that he or she has overcome all your objections and has sold you on all the benefits of enlisting in his or her particular service before trying to close the sale. However, sometimes recruiters may notice certain buying signals from an applicant during the interview and may try closing during an earlier step of the process; this is called a trial close.

Consider the car dealership example again for a moment. Most salespeople will tell you all about the features of a car, will answer all your questions, will allow you to test drive a car, and may even talk about financing options before asking you, "Would you like to buy this car?"

On the other hand, if you walk into the dealership, tell the salesperson how much you love the car, how you've always wanted one, and rave about the car's features, chances are he will say at the first opportunity, "So when will you be ready to take delivery of the car?" In this case, you've sold yourself; the salesperson has no need to sell you any further. How easy would it be for you to negotiate a better price in such a situation? The same is true for applicants; that's why it is so important for you to maintain a "poker face" when dealing with your recruiter. Let him or her know you are interested, but don't make it too easy for him or her, and don't get emotional about the sale (remember my example of looking for houses).

THE CLOSING PITCH

Recruiters have learned many techniques for closing a sale. They range from impending doom ("You've got to make up your mind right now or the offer will expire") to making a list of the pros and cons (remarkably, the pros always seem to win). Some recruiters may close by painting a mental picture of life in the military and then paint you into the picture. Some are more subtle: They may just say, "Okay, if you don't have any other questions, let's get started," or "Is there any reason we shouldn't get started with the paperwork?"

If you are ready to proceed at that point, then, by all means, do so. If you have doubts or there are still unanswered questions, stop the process right there. It's okay to go home and think about it. Do not agree to proceed with the enlistment processing if you are not ready to do so. Believe me, the recruiter and the service that he or she represents, will be there in a week, a month, or whenever you make up your mind.

Although recruiters have learned to sell their particular service branch, they also are taught to sell the "enlistment process" piece by piece. In other words, they sell the initial interview, and then they sell the ASVAB examination and the physical. The reason for this is they believe that the further you get into the process, the more committed you will become to enlisting—and they are right. Almost no one wants to go home after they've told all their friends and family members that they are processing for enlistment in the military and have to say, "I didn't enlist."

What makes matters even worse is that some recruiters will encourage applicants that aren't 100 percent sold on enlisting to continue processing. The conversation may go something like this:

Applicant: "I'm not sure if the Air Force will be right for me. I may want to attend college in the fall."

Recruiter: "No problem, I understand that, but let's get you tested and get your physical so that if you decide later that you want to join, they'll be out of the way."

This type of behavior is one of a weak recruiter—one who throws as many applicants as he or she can against the wall to see which ones stick. Again, my advice is that if you aren't sure that enlisting is what you want to do, don't do it! You can take the ASVAB and physical examination when you decide to enlist.

Along similar lines, sometimes a recruiter will tell you to enlist just in case college doesn't come through. Then, you'll at least have the military to fall back on, and if you do go to college, he or she eventually will get you out of the DEP. If your recruiter does this, get yourself another recruiter, if possible. This behavior is not only the sign of a weak recruiter but also a desperate one!

What am I trying to say with all of this? Proceed only when you, not the recruiter, are ready.

Gathering Your Thoughts

At this point, you've decided on one of the following courses of action:

- You have a strong desire to enlist and will proceed with enlistment processing.
- You have an interest in enlisting, but you are not fully committed and you want to think about it some more before continuing with the enlistment process.
- You have no desire to enlist and will not proceed with the enlistment process.

IF YOU HAVE A STRONG DESIRE TO ENLIST

After your initial interview, if you have a strong desire to enlist and want to proceed with the enlistment process, I caution you to proceed with care. Gather as much information and literature as you can from the recruiter, and make sure you've asked all the questions that you want answered.

After you've gathered all the data, go home and read through Chapter 2 of this book. Once you've done that, if you still fit in the "strong desire" category, I suggest that you go for it!

IF YOU HAVE SOME INTEREST IN ENLISTING

If you are unsure how to proceed, don't commit to further processing. Again, although your recruiter may push you into further processing, you need to insist on putting off continuing until you've made up your mind.

Do not agree to further processing just to pacify a pushy recruiter. This happens quite often, unfortunately, when an applicant is not committed to enlisting, but will continue in the enlistment process because it is easier than saying no to the recruiter. Some recruiters may even tell you that you can take the ASVAB and physical for their particular service, and if you decide to join another branch, you'll already have them done and won't have to go through it again. Although that may be true, it's complete nonsense. Wait to take the ASVAB and physical until you are sure that you want to enlist and you are certain of the branch you want to join.

Before you leave the recruiting office, let the recruiter know that you would like some time to think things over. Set a time for the recruiter to contact you (usually one to three weeks) for a decision. You should do this because the recruiter will probably start calling you (sometimes the day after the interview), and you need to let him or her know that you want some time to think about it seriously without being hounded by him or her. Don't give the recruiter the old, "Don't call us, we'll call you" line. That just shows the recruiter you are probably not interested and, once again, you will start receiving persuasive telephone calls from him or her.

If your recruiter hasn't offered any names and telephone numbers of people he or she has enlisted to whom you can talk, ask for some. Recruiters will often encourage members of the DEP to talk with applicants. This enables the applicant to talk with people who have recently gone through the enlistment process.

If you do get some names and telephone numbers, make the calls! Here are some of the things you may want to ask:

- For what job did you enlist?
- Was it the job you originally wanted?
- Why did you join?
- Why did you choose this particular branch over the others?
- Did you have any problems with the recruiter?
- Was the recruiter honest with you?
- How was MEPS? Are there any surprises for which I should look out?
- How was the ASVAB? Any tips on taking it?
- If you had to do it all over again, would you?

Of course, you should ask questions about anything else that may concern you.

Finally, you should obtain as much literature as you can. Go home, review all the material, search the Internet for more information, and read through Chapter 2 of this book to ensure that you have answers to all of your questions.

IF YOU HAVE NO DESIRE TO ENLIST

After your initial interview, if you find you have no desire to enlist, be up front with the recruiter and tell him or her so. Do not make another appointment, do not tell him or her to call you, do not tell him or her that you will call him or her, and definitely do not agree to further enlistment processing!

Recruiters can be persuasive, and people sometimes will agree to things to appease them. If after looking at a car in a dealer's showroom you find you do not intend to buy the car, would you have the salesperson work out the financing for you just because he or she was pushy? Although it sounds ridiculous, people do it every day with recruiters; unable to say no, they continue with the enlistment process with no intention of ever enlisting.

Ask the recruiter not to call you (this may or may not do any good), but thank him or her for his or her time. Do take some literature with you; review it when you get home, and, even though you've decided not to enlist, read Chapter 2 of this book anyway.

REPEAT AS NECESSARY

Because you should talk with recruiters of most, if not all of the military branches, you should fit into one of the three categories for each of the services.

Also, the "some desire" category will need to be turned into either "strong desire" or "no desire." Once you've narrowed down the branches to those for which you have a strong desire, it will be time to choose the right branch for you. Of course, you may find that none of the branches meet your needs. In that case, the military is not the right option for you and you have some options of what to do with this book:

- Pass it along to someone else.
- Try to sell it at a garage sale or on ebay.
- Put it on a shelf and leave it there.
- Use it to level out an uneven table.

What's Next?

If you agree to proceed with the enlistment process, your recruiter will schedule you to take the ASVAB, if you haven't already taken it, and the physical examination. The paperwork will begin at this point, but don't worry; you aren't committed to anything until you raise your right hand and take the oath of enlistment (see Chapter 5).

FILLING OUT THE PAPERWORK

You will have to complete forms about your health, law violations, and involvement with drugs. Your recruiter will also complete the application for enlistment, the DD Form 1966. You will have to sign this form and attest to its accuracy, so make sure that it is accurate before signing. You can find an example of the DD Form 1966 in the Appendix. More than likely, the form will also contain additional comments that you must initial. Each service has special requirements concerning Basic Training, certain policies, and so on, of which it wants you to be aware, so they are listed on the DD Form 1966. One such policy is the requirement for applicants to view certain videos dealing with Basic Training. Review the sample form so that you can become familiar with it before you see the actual one. Pay particular attention to the statements on page 3 and the certification on page 4. To use the car dealership example: Imagine being able to take the time to read an application for a loan or lease before being asked to sign on the dotted line. Well, here's your chance!

SCHEDULING THE ASVAB AND PHYSICAL EXAMINATION

Chapter 4 covers specific details about the ASVAB and where to take it. Chapter 5 contains information concerning the physical examination.

Your recruiter will encourage, and some will almost insist, you to take the ASVAB and physical as soon as possible. Although this is not necessary, by taking the two as soon as possible, you are showing a commitment to enlisting. However, if you are being pushed to get them done by some deadline, I can assure you that the deadline is an arbitrary one created by your recruiter.

Chapter Summary

The purpose of this chapter was to get you better prepared to meet with your recruiter for the first time and to give you some insight into what to expect from your initial interview. If you take nothing else away from this chapter, take these key points:

- Do your homework before the initial interview.
- Be honest with your recruiter.
- Be polite but firm.
- Do not allow anyone, including your recruiter, to get you to lie.

- Do not feel pressured or obligated to continue with the enlistment process.
- Continue at your own pace, but remember that the enlistment process has a logical flow that should not be prolonged unnecessarily.
- Remember that there are rarely any "special, limited-time offers" that won't be available next week (after you've had some time to think about it).
- If the recruiters tells you that you are ineligible for enlistment, ask for a waiver.
- If the recruiter tells you that a waiver cannot be granted, ask to see it in writing.

You should now be well on your way to making a decision that may change your life. Chapter 2 helps you with that difficult task.

2 GETTING THE FACTS TOGETHER: SHOULD I OR SHOULDN'T I ENLIST?

This chapter discusses the factors that you must consider to make an informed decision on whether to join the military. It includes an assessment to help you determine if the military can fulfill your needs.

Facts or Emotion?

Once you have met with your recruiter(s), and received some basic information, as well as conducted some research on the Internet, you will need to decide whether to proceed with the enlistment process. Your decision must be based on facts and whether your needs can be met by enlisting in the military.

People rarely buy anything based on their needs; instead, they buy based on their emotions. We see it on a daily basis in advertising, from automobiles to soft drinks. We rarely see an automobile commercial that gives statistics about how the car is engineered, how long it will last, the gas mileage, and other technical specifications. Instead, we see people driving around having a good time without a care in the world. We see snowboarding, skydiving, and mountain climbing in ads to sell soft drinks, not details about the product's nutritional value.

The reason for this is that advertising agencies know that you will buy based on how you feel rather than what you think. Because of this tendency to buy based on emotion rather than reason, it is important to separate the feelings from the facts so that you can base your decision primarily on the facts.

The reason I said primarily on the facts and not solely on the facts is quite simple: we are all human and cannot be totally without emotion. For instance, you may decide that joining the military is the right choice, so you narrow your decision to two services. After comparing the two, you may not be able to choose based on the facts, so the decision may come down to which service has the better looking uniform.

The First Decision Point

There are two big questions here. First, is the military right for me, and second, if the first answer was yes, which branch is right for me?

Consider the car analogy again for a minute. Suppose that you have to decide whether to buy a new car or repair your current car. The first choice you make will determine your next course of action. You will have to weigh the facts to determine if you will purchase a new car. Once you've decided to buy a car rather than repair your old one, you must then decide exactly what make and model will best meet your needs.

The next section, "Choosing the Military (Needs Assessment)," will help you decide whether the military is the right choice for you. If you decide it is, the following section, "Choosing the Branch to Join," will help you in determining which branch of the military will best meet your particular needs.

In the previous chapter, you learned about your "primary motivators" for contacting a military recruiter or agreeing to an interview. You'll use these primary motivators to determine whether enlisting in the military is the right thing for you to do.

Choosing the Military (Needs Assessment)

You should have made a list of your primary motivators before you set foot in the recruiter's office. Whether your list was long—containing such items as money for college, job security, opportunity to travel, technical training, and good pay—or contained only one item, such as having full-time employment, the number of items on your list is not what's important. What is important is that you are able to satisfy those motivators.

Whatever your list contains, the first course of action is to collect your list of primary motivators and put them in order of importance to you. This process, known as rank ordering, will help you determine if you should proceed with the enlistment process.

However, it should be noted that at this time you may not have all the information necessary to determine whether you should enlist. For instance, if your most important primary motivator is receiving technical training, you will not know if the military can meet this motivator unless you have taken the Armed Services Vocational Battery (ASVAB) and physical examination. If this is the case, you must assume that you will qualify for technical training and base your decision on the information provided to you by your recruiter. It will then be necessary for you to return to this chapter and reevaluate your situation if needed.

RANK ORDERING YOUR LIST

Rank ordering your list is a simple process of deciding which motivators are most important to you and then listing them in order of importance. List your most important motivator as number one, your next most important as number two, and so on.

If we apply the car-buying scenario here, your primary motivators may be finding a car that costs under $20,000, has a four-cylinder engine, gets at least 30 miles to the gallon, has leather interior, is available in blue, and has a sunroof. If you put those motivators in rank order, your list might look something like this:

1. costs less than $20,000
2. gets at least 30 mpg
3. has a sunroof
4. has leather interior
5. available in blue

You'll notice that the number one, or most important, motivator is cost, whereas the last, or least important, motivator is color. The more important the motivator, the less likely you'll be willing to settle for something different or to live without it altogether.

MEETING YOUR NEEDS (MOTIVATORS)

After you've rank ordered your motivators, proceed to the process of going down your list and determining whether those motivators can be met by enlisting in the military. Simply write "yes" next to those that enlisting can fulfill and "no" next to those that enlisting cannot fulfill.

If you find that enlisting can meet all your motivators, that's great; but even if only some of your motivators can be met, you may still want to consider it. Seldom does a product meet all our needs and wants, and you may be able to make satisfactory compromises and still be happy with the outcome.

For instance, in the car-buying scenario, you may find that a particular car meets all of your needs but is not available in blue. Although the color of the car is important, it is the least important of all your motivators. For this reason, you may decide to purchase the car, despite that it isn't available in blue. Or, suppose you could get all your motivators met, even the color, but instead of $20,000 you would have to pay $21,000. You might decide that you're willing to compromise on the cost to get the car of your dreams.

However, if you were buying a car, you probably would compare several makes of cars to see if any of them could meet all your motivators before buying one that met just some of them. The same applies when determining whether to enlist. You should compare all the alternatives to enlisting—gather all the facts—before making a final decision.

COMPARING THE ALTERNATIVES

Several alternatives to enlisting may be available to you, such as going to work at a local company, attending college, or attending a local vocational school. You should perform the "yes/no" test on each of your motivators as they pertain to each of the available alternatives.

For example, let's assume that one of your alternatives is a job at the local factory and your primary motivators are in rank order:

1. money for college
2. technical training
3. job security
4. opportunity for travel

Let's further assume that the local factory offers its employees a college tuition assistance program similar to that offered by the military. It also has an on-the-job technical training program and a great trackrecord of keeping employees. However, because this is a local company, your opportunity for travel will be nonexistent.

You may need to modify your approach to your motivator list depending on the alternative. For instance, job security really does not apply when you are talking about attending college as an alternative. However, you might consider things like the job security of people in occupations related to your intended major or even the graduation rate of the college you are thinking about attending.

Although you are well on your way to making a decision, there is still one important piece of the puzzle that you must consider—the negative aspects of each alternative.

NEGATIVE ASPECTS

Returning to the car-buying scenario, let's assume that you have found a car that matches all of your motivators. However, the closest dealership is one hundred miles away, the particular make of car has a terrible maintenance record, and, after looking at the car, you just don't like the style. These are the "negative aspects" that you must consider.

When you go out to purchase your car armed with your motivator or needs list, you should have a list of negative aspects, at least in your mind, with which you just can't live when considering a new vehicle.

The same applies to enlisting in the military: there may be certain things about military service that would conflict with your desires. For instance, if you wanted to stay in the local area, you would probably not want to enlist for active duty, although you might want to consider enlisting in the Reserve or Guard.

PUTTING IT ALL TOGETHER

Once you have gathered all of your lists, it is time to make a decision. At this point, the decision can be whether to continue processing (i.e., take the ASVAB), or it could mean making the decision to enlist. Whatever your decision, it should be made based primarily on the facts, with little emotion as part of the equation. That said, I must also say that although I am "preaching" about keeping emotion out of the decision process, there may be times when emotion may be the one thing that will sway your decision. In fact, emotion may be your primary motivator.

EMOTION AS A PRIMARY MOTIVATOR

When I enlisted, I met several people who joined the military primarily for emotional reasons. For instance, someone had immigrated to the United States with his family. He lived well here (better than he could ever have hoped for in his home country), received a good education, and genuinely loved the United States. In his words, he wanted to pay something back to the country that had given him so much. His way of doing that was to enlist in the military. He didn't base his decision on facts; he was motivated solely by emotion.

In other cases, individuals enlisted because they wanted to keep a family tradition alive. They joined because their fathers and grandfathers had joined, and they wanted to follow in the footsteps of their forefathers.

The emotional reasons people have for enlisting in the military are many and aren't necessarily bad. However, as a word of caution, be careful of making any "buying" decision based on emotion alone.

THE NEXT STEP

If you've gotten this far, the next step may be easy or it may be extremely difficult. It all depends on the amount of homework you've done on each military branch you are considering.

Choosing the Branch to Join

If you are seriously considering joining the military, you probably have checked out at least two of the branches. I advise you to check them all out, even if it means just visiting their recruiting website. Although I was not interested in joining the Army, I did look at its brochures first to find out a little about its programs before I made my final decision (there was no Internet then).

A word of caution though: sometimes (in reality, most times) recruiting brochures and websites do not tell the complete story, and it is difficult to base your decision either for or against on the contents of a brochure or website. When I was a recruiter, people were always telling me that they weren't interested because of what they had read about it in a brochure. I'd usually say something like, "I understand why you wouldn't be interested in joining, but how could you be interested in something you know little about? That's why I'd like to take a few minutes to meet with you in person and tell you a little more about your opportunities."

Smooth sales talk? Perhaps, but it was the truth. Would you buy a car based solely on the information contained in a brochure or website? Probably not! And unless you totally hated the car based on the information in the brochure, you would probably not completely dismiss it as an option.

MAKING A CHOICE

After checking into the military branches that interest you, if there is clearly only one choice, then your decision has already been made (although I would have to question what you have based your decision on). But, if you are like most people (most people, that is, who have read this book and are taking my advice), you will have at least two branches in mind, so read on!

The process of choosing the right branch of the military for you is basically the same process that you used to determine if joining the military was right for you. You should start with your list of primary motivators and use the "yes/no" method to determine whether each branch can meet all or some of those motivators. Once you've determined which branch or branches can best meet your motivators, it's time to compare those branches. What the first branch meets, the second may not; but what the first branch doesn't, the second one might meet. Remember to look for the negative aspects as well as the motivators of each of the branches as you compare.

After making your comparisons, you may still find yourself with more than one choice. What do you do then? You could flip a coin, but I wouldn't advise it. Instead, you may want to look at some of these factors:

- Length of enlistment—Some branches may require a longer term for offering the same benefits that you could receive from another branch.
- Advanced pay grade—You may be entitled to an advanced rank in some branches based on certain enlistment options.
- Length and type of training—How long will the training you'll receive take? Usually the longer the training, the more in-depth and useful it is. You'll also want to consider how useful the training will be once you've left the military.
- Enlistment bonuses—I caution you about using an enlistment bonus as the only factor in deciding which branch to choose. But if it comes down to a tie between two branches and only one offers a bonus, it's not a bad reason to choose that branch.
- Additional pay and allowances—There may be additional pay you'd be entitled to that can only be offered by a particular branch. For instance, if you join the navy, you may be entitled to Sea Pay and Submarine Pay, something obviously not available if you join the Air Force.
- Ability to pursue higher education—Although all the military branches offer educational benefits, you must consider when you will be able to take advantage of these benefits. If you are in a job requiring twelve-hour shifts and being out in the "field" a great deal, when will you attend classes? Even online classes may be difficult to accomplish in the field.

Once you have considered these factors, and perhaps some of your own, you should be able to decide which branch is right for you. If you still haven't selected one branch over another, though, consider the following:

- Ask your recruiter if you can speak to someone who has joined recently.
- If there is a base nearby, you may be able to get a tour to get a look at its facilities.
- You may want to look for online blogs that cater to military members, and then ask a lot of questions.
- Talk to friends and family members who are serving in the military. However, be careful not to talk to individuals who have been out of the military for a while, because they probably do not have an understanding of "today's" military. Also, avoid individuals who left the military under less-than-desirable conditions (for example, someone who was discharged from Basic Training for non-compatibility).

If you still are having problems deciding, maybe you should choose the service with the best-looking uniform!

Guard and Reserve Opportunities

Other alternatives that may be available to you are the Air National Guard, the Army National Guard, and the Reserve components of the Air Force, Army, Coast Guard, Marine Corps, and the Navy. I provide more information about the Guard and Reserve in Chapter 10. However, at this point it is important to mention that depending on your primary motivators, the Guard and Reserve may be a more viable option for you than Active Duty.

You should seriously consider the Guard and Reserve if:

- you have "deep roots" in your local community and do not desire to leave home;
- you are attending college full time and wish to continue at your current school; and
- you currently have a full-time career and are only looking for additional income or some additional skills that you can apply to your full-time job.

The Guard and Reserve would probably not be an option for you if:

- you are looking for full-time employment; and
- you desire to leave your current surroundings.

When choosing between Active Duty and the Reserve, apply the primary motivator principles to help you decide your course of action.

Job Selection

You'll learn about the job selection process later, in Chapter 5, when I cover the Military Entrance Processing Station (MEPS).

I bring this up now because you may wish to use the primary motivator—needs assessment principles—when selecting the right military job. Keep in mind, though, that depending on your motivators, the job you wind up with might not play such a major role in your decision-making process.

For instance, if your primary and perhaps only motivating factor is getting money for college, your choice of jobs may be secondary to getting into the branch that can offer you the most money to pay for college. On the other hand, if your primary motivator is getting high-tech training, the job you choose would probably take precedence over which branch you select.

THE BUDDY SYSTEM

No, I'm not talking about swimming here. Many services offer a way for you and a friend or two to attend Basic Training and technical training together. This is a comfort to some people, and it may make you a little less homesick while you're away. However, things can happen that can separate you and your buddy. You, or your buddy, may not progress through training as planned because of an injury, not meeting physical fitness standards, etc.

Therefore, if you are considering going to training on the buddy system and you and your buddy's schedules are in sync, then go for it. On the other hand, if your buddy can't leave for six months and you can leave immediately, my advice to you is say "adios" to your buddy and leave for Basic Training.

Chapter Summary

In deciding whether to join the military and then choosing a specific branch to join, you must analyze and apply facts, not simply respond to emotions. Because most people buy based on feelings and not facts, it is important for you to determine your primary motivators, which are the needs you are looking to fulfill by joining the military.

Following the "rank-order-chart" procedure first will help you determine which of the military branches, if any, can meet your motivators. Once you have determined those branches, you must compare the military to your other alternatives, remembering to consider the negative aspects along with your motivators to get the "whole picture." You should also add the Guard and Reserve alternatives to the mix for consideration.

Joining the military is a big step, whether you go Active Duty or Reserve, regardless of which branch you choose. By following the advice offered in this chapter, you will be able to make a more informed and rational decision based on the facts.

If you choose to continue with processing for enlistment, your next step probably will be to take the ASVAB, if you haven't already done so. Chapter 4 familiarizes you with the ASVAB and offers some advice so that you can maximize your chances of doing well on this important test.

3 WOMEN IN THE MILITARY

This chapter tries to dispel some of the common misconceptions and stereotypes about women who serve in the armed forces and provides you with resources for finding detailed information about women in the military. There are several "testimonials" from women who are serving and have served in the military.

Most people reading this book would probably agree that in today's society the "gender gap" is becoming smaller. Throughout American society, women, for the most part, have the same opportunities as their male counterparts. That has not always been the case, and, in fact, the U.S. military has been a leader in promoting equality between the sexes.

In the Beginning

Since the beginning of our nation's military, women have found ways to serve. As far back as the American Revolution, women, masquerading as men, served alongside men, often going undetected.

It wasn't until the Spanish-American War in 1898 that women obtained a quasi-official role in the U.S. military. It was then that women nurses could serve in the Army, although not as regular members of the Army. In the social climate at the time, however, women were decades away from being able to vote in elections.

By the mid-1940s, the tide was about to turn for women serving in the armed forces. Although not fully integrated with their male counterparts, women were finally given military status. Although most women served as nurses and in administrative and support roles, some women learned to fly. They did not fly in combat, but they transported airplanes.

The 1970s saw a revolution for military women. Many more non-traditional jobs opened up for them, and the barriers that had previously existed began to crumble. By the time of the first Gulf War, women were an integral part of the country's Armed Forces.

FROM AN ARMY RETIREE:

"I entered the U.S. Army in June 1971, just two days after I graduated from high school. At that time, the only career ahead for girls was to find a man, marry, and have babies or work in a sewing factory. I couldn't picture myself doing these. I retired from the Army in 1991 as a Sergeant Major. I consider entering the Army as the first best decision of my life. It's a great place for a career-minded person to start out whether you become a 'lifer' or not."

By the Numbers

The percentage of women serving in the U.S. Armed Forces since 1973 (when the draft ended) has increased tremendously. In 1973, women comprised only 1.6 percent of the active duty force. By 2011, that number increased to 14.5 percent (204,700). Additionally, 5,800 women serve on active duty with the U.S. Coast Guard, which is part of the Department of Homeland Security.

Here is how the numbers break down by active-duty service Active Duty:

Enlisted	Total Number of Women	Percentage of Total Personnel
Total Department of Defense	166,815	14.2
Army	60,255	13.0
Navy	43,896	16.4
Marine Corps	12,363	6.9
Air Force	50,301	19.1
Coast Guard	4,454	13.3

Officer	Total Number of Women	Percentage of Total Personnel
Total Department of Defense	37,899	15.9
Army	15,760	16.1
Navy	8,520	16.0
Marine Corps	1,328	6.1
Air Force	12,291	18.8
Coast Guard	1,345	15.9

For most services, women comprise an even larger percentage of total personnel of the Reserve and Guard components:

Enlisted	Total Number of Women	Percentage of Total Personnel
Army Reserve	38,737	22.9
Navy Reserve	10,670	21.0
Marine Corps Reserve	1,562	4.3
Air Force Reserve	14,354	25.3
Coast Guard Reserve	1,001	15.1
Army National Guard	47,276	14.9
Air National Guard	16,986	18.6

Officer	Total Number of Women	Percentage of Total Personnel
Army Reserve	8,659	24.4
Navy Reserve	2,433	17.1
Marine Corps Reserve	264	6.9
Air Force Reserve	3,761	25.9
Coast Guard Reserve	267	20.4
Army National Guard	5,431	12.4
Air National Guard	2,514	17.4

Along with the increase in numbers of women serving in the military, the number of women serving in the senior enlisted ranks also increased dramatically. Until the late 1980s, women comprised less than 4 percent of the top three enlisted ranks. In 2011, women made up 10.8 percent of the top Army enlisted members, 16 percent of the Air Force, 8.3 percent of the Navy, 5.4 percent of the Marine Corps, and 7.8 percent of the Coast Guard top three enlisted grades.

FROM A NAVY WOMAN:

"I have been in the Navy for fourteen years. One of the best things I have ever done is join the Navy. When I joined, I had no goals and no real idea of what I would do with my life. Now I have six years to retirement, a wonderful job, and a chance to see more of the world than would have been possible had I not joined. I am now on my first ship and enjoying it. The Navy has enhanced my life more than I can say."

Misconceptions and Stereotypes

Throughout history, there has been quite a bit of stereotyping and gender bias about women joining the military. Some people still believe that women should be restricted to filling specific roles. During those years, people could not understand why a woman would want to do a "man's job."

Today, women are filling many "non-traditional" jobs in the civilian world, as well as in the military. Women are joining the military for many of the same reasons men are, such as patriotism, education, and training.

Even a gas mask doesn't take away a woman's femininity.

During my military career, I have worked with and for many women. They were able to maintain their femininity while serving in the military; it was never a choice between the two.

FROM A MARINE:

"My thoughts on service in the Corps are filled with many conflicting emotions that range from chest-burning pride to teeth-grinding frustration. There are some sentiments, such as graduation from boot camp or even in battalion formation, when standing shoulder-to-shoulder with my fellow marines and contemplating all that we have accomplished and will yet accomplish together fills me with an overwhelming sense of pride and esprit de corps. I really feel as if I belong here and that my individual contribution, although small, is by no means insignificant. I feel that I helped to bring us to where we are today and will shape where we will be in the future. Then there are times, like walking a post in the middle of the night on a cold, lonely windswept hillside in a foreign country or struggling to put one blistered foot in front of the other on a hump through the rock-strewn hills of Camp Pendleton, when I ask myself repeatedly, "Why am I here?" Through it all, the answer is simply the shining fact that I feel that I belong. Some intrinsic part of being a Marine fills a void within me better than any other way of life would. Though at times I may vehemently wish I were some place, any place, other than where I am at that given moment, I would not trade the experience for anything else in the world. I am what I was always meant to be. I am a Marine."

Military as a Leader

The military outpaces the civilian sector in equality and opening career "doors" for women. You will find military pay charts in chapter 9. Note that there is only one pay chart because there is no difference in military pay for men and women. This is not always the case for civilian jobs in today's society, because many women are paid less than men for doing the same jobs.

Military promotions are based on job performance and not on gender. Although we'd like to believe that is true throughout "corporate America," it is not true for all companies.

Although civilian women fight for healthcare for their children, military women and their families receive healthcare and support, such as low-cost child care and paid maternity leave.

FROM AN ACTIVE DUTY AIRMAN:

"I have almost twenty-one years in the Air Force and I'm a Chief Master Sergeant. I stayed in the Air Force for differing reasons throughout my career. As a young airman, I stayed in because I knew I had a pretty good deal. I was given room and board, excellent formal technical training, a job, and mentors galore! What other company will take individuals and invest in them what the military does? I stay in the Air Force now because I'm at the top. Respect at this pay grade is equal to that of our senior officers and civilian executives. I had the opportunity to make a difference in many young lives. You'll never find a more motivated person than one who has learned and grown in the Air Force. However, you are responsible for your growth. And if you don't take advantage of it while on active duty, you have missed a very rare opportunity in life."

Job Restrictions for Women

In the last edition of this book (2004) I reported that, "although women have come a long way in gaining the similar treatment as men in the military, there are still several military jobs from which women are restricted. For example, the Special Forces units, such as the Navy SEALs and the Army's Green Berets, are composed entirely of men, as are the crews of all Navy submarines and Army tanks.

However, women have increased in a number of positions once believed to be "male only." They are no longer restricted to the "rear" of the battlefield and have proved that they can perform jobs once viewed as too hard or too dangerous for women. Women are flying combat aircraft, and they are serving in combat units in direct contact with the enemy." Things have changed significantly since then!

By January 2016, most, if not all military jobs including positions in special forces units and navy submarines, will be open to women.

In 2013, Secretary of Defense Leon Panetta announced that the DOD would notify Congress of its intent to open all military units and occupations to women. This put an end to the ground combat exclusion and eliminating the last barrier to full integration of women in the U.S. military. The phase in of the new policy will take place over three years with the expectation of full implementation by January of 2016.

Each service will develop its own integration plan. However, there is also a provision that will allow an individual service to apply for a special exemption if it is determined that certain occupations or units should be closed to women. (WREI, Women in the Military, Eighth Edition, 2013)

Female Marines practicing drill at Parris Island.

FROM A COAST GUARDSMAN

"I've been in the Coast Guard close to fourteen years and, like any other job, some days are better than others. I can proudly say that the positive has outweighed the negative. I am fortunate to be a part of a team that specializes in lifesaving. I've had the opportunity to travel to my favorite locations and work search and rescue. I'm currently on board a ship and traveling to distant locations, enforcing fishery laws, marine safety, illegal immigrant control, and search and rescue. I miss my husband and family, but like we all know, sacrifices are part of the job. I believe the military is what you make it. It's only as good as you want it to be, and I am proud to be a part of it."

Recent Scandals

The military has always been under a microscope whenever there are allegations of sexual harassment or abuse. Most recently, in 2012, the Air Force investigated sexual assault charges against at least twenty-eight instructors at Air Force Basic Military Training (boot camp) in San Antonio, Texas. As of December 2012, five of the twenty-eight instructors were convicted by court martials. Instructors abused more than fifty-four female trainees. In addition to the instructors' convictions, the basic training Commander was relieved of command.

This recent scandal has one thing in common with other scandals that came before it: there was a complete investigation, and several high-ranking officials lost their jobs. These types of incidents happen every day in corporate America, with one exception: they rarely are publicized ,and are often settled through lawsuits with no one losing their jobs.

The military and its members are held to higher standards than their civilian counter parts. There is zero tolerance in the military for sexual abuse or harassment. What would result in "a slap on the wrist" to a civilian could end a military member's career.

Single Parents

It is possible to be a single mother and a soldier, sailor, marine, etc.; there are thousands of them. They manage to juggle the long hours of military life and life as a mother. Of course, they can't do it alone, and they must have a plan in place in case they are deployed away from home, have to work extra shifts, etc. Many single parents rely on help from family and friends to care for their children when they cannot.

Many women become single parents while already serving in the military (by divorce, etc). In the past, that would have qualified them for an immediate discharge from the military, but this does not apply in today's military. Joining the military as a single parent, however, usually requires a waiver for enlistment. Because there is no way a single parent could take care of a child while in training, the parent must also agree to give up custody of her child. Custody normally is given to an immediate family member, who then turns over custody to the parent when the parent has completed training.

Being a single parent in the military is not easy. However, if your goal is a career in the military, it is possible.

A Few Words About DACOWITS

Started in 1951, the Defense Advisory Committee on Women in the Services (DACOWITS) is composed of civilian and retired military women. Their job is to travel to military installations searching for women's military issues to report to the Department of Defense to bring about change.

In 2002, DACOWITS went through some major changes. Besides having the committee size cut by half, its duties changed to include issues dealing with military families. When DACOWITS started, women did not have much of a voice in the U.S. military. Much has changed since its creation. For more about this committee, check out its website at www.dacowits.defense.gov.

Air Force security forces member writing a traffic citation.

FROM A RETIRED AIR FORCE OFFICER (AND WEBMASTER OF MILITARYWOMAN.ORG):

"The military provides a wonderful opportunity to learn the traits to become outstanding and to be rewarded for dedication and willingness to work. It helps to develop confidence and strength of character. While there seems to be a sense of mystique that embodies the "military woman," and though we are not fully understood by our civilian counterparts, we are quite simply the average female who has been given extraordinary circumstances to develop into highly capable women.

My tenure in the military allowed me to travel to many locations, serve two European tours, and earn my baccalaureate and master's degrees. While these experiences and achievements can be finitely measured, the lifelong rewards of the military go into infinity, because the values and principles you learn become a part of who you are, a part of your essence. The Air Force really did allow me to 'Aim High.'"

Resources for More Information

This chapter could easily be expanded into an entire book. In fact, there are many books dedicated to women in the military. I tried to provide you with basic information about women in the military, and have given you a starting point. I do not claim to be an expert on women in the military; that would be unfair to the women who have served and are currently serving in the military. Fortunately, many experts can provide insight on what it is like to be a woman serving in the U.S. Armed Forces.

BOOKS

Women in the Military, An Unfinished Revolution by Major General Jeanne Holm, USAF, Retired.
This book covers women's role in the military through the first Gulf War. It is a fantastic resource.

Letters Home by Katherine Chance.
Although about a fictitious person, the account of Basic Training gives you a good idea of what to expect.

Women in the Military, Where They Stand
This thirty-six-page booklet is available for a nominal fee (approximately $3.00) from Women's Research and Education Institute (WREI). It provides statistics and numbers pertaining to women serving in the military. In addition, this booklet contains a chronology of milestones dealing with women in the military, as well as other useful information. The Web address is www.wrei.org.

WEBSITES

www.militarywoman.org
This website is an incredible source of information on just about every subject possible relating to women serving in the military. It also provides a forum for women who have served, are now serving, or are thinking of serving, to ask questions, to offer opinions, and to connect with others. Two retired women veterans (an Air Force officer and an Army senior enlisted member) run the site. They run the site in their "spare time," and the only reward they receive is the satisfaction of knowing that they are helping others. You will want to keep this site in your browser's favorites even after you join the military.

http://userpages.aug.com/captbarb/
This is an interesting website full of information, history, and opinion. The site is Captain Critical (or Capt. Barb).

www.4militarywomen.org
Alliance for National Defense is a nonprofit, educational organization that offers a monthly newsletter about issues relating to military women, a resource for speakers for educational events, and a library of publications by and about military women. It also provides information on scholarships, and monitors legislation and alerts members to issues.

www.va.gov/womenvet

The Center for Women Veterans, Department of Veterans Affairs, assures that women veterans receive benefits that are on par with male veterans. The site offers women veterans information about their VA entitlements, healthcare programs, and sexual abuse counseling. It also has links to other sites that may be of interest to women veterans.

www.deomi.org

The Defense Equal Opportunity Management Institute provides education and training programs in human relations and equal opportunity. It offers seminars and workshops, as well as its Core Equal Opportunity Advisor course. There is an online magazine, video catalog, and other resources available on its site.

www.defense.gov/fraternization

The Fraternization Policies of the Armed Forces site provides information about personal and business relationships that are prohibited between officers and enlisted members. There is a description of each branch's policies, including each service's definition of fraternization and examples of prohibited relationships.

There are many other resources available online, in your local library, and at bookstores.

HONORING THE WOMEN WHO SERVED

The Women in Military Service for America Memorial is the only major national memorial to honor the approximately two million uniformed women who have served in the nation's defense. Located at the gateway to Arlington National Cemetery, the memorial and its 33,000-square-feet education facility chronicles the history, and showcases individual stories, of servicewomen. To learn more about the memorial, its programs and activities, membership eligibility, and how to join, visit the website: www.womensmemorial.org or call 1-800-222-2294.

The Women in Military Service for America Memorial. Courtesy of Women's Memorial © Carol M. Highsmith

Chapter Summary

For decades, the military has been a leader in providing equal opportunities for women. The stereotypes of military women are just that, stereotypes, and are not realistic. Now, more than ever, the military is a place where women can and do succeed.

4 PREPARING FOR THE ARMED SERVICES VOCATIONAL APTITUDE BATTERY (ASVAB) EXAMINATION

This chapter does not prepare you for the ASVAB. However, it provides a general overview of the examination and its parts, along with some helpful hints to prepare you for the ASVAB.

Having an understanding of the Armed Forces Vocational Aptitude Battery (ASVAB) examination will increase your chances of scoring higher and consequently will qualify you for more military occupations. If you've already taken the SAT, you know how important it is to prepare for an examination that will, in all likelihood, shape your future. I am not comparing the ASVAB to the SAT; however, as with the SAT, you do not want to go into the ASVAB examination without preparation.

Unlike the SAT, the the military gives the ASVAB free of charge through the Military Entrance Processing Station (MEPS). There are two ways that you can take this examination. First, many high schools sponsor the ASVAB and offer it to all interested students. This is called the "institutional" ASVAB. If you choose to take the institutional ASVAB, you will take the examination with other students at your school. More than likely, there will be one or more military recruiters present to proctor the examination. This is their sole purpose for being there on test day; in fact, they cannot by regulations actively recruit during the ASVAB. However, when you complete the ASVAB answer sheet, you will be asked about your plans after high school—such as attending a two- or four-year college or vocational (or trade) school or enlisting in the military. If you do well on the ASVAB, military recruiters will contact you regardless of your intended plans. Of course, if you list your intention to join the military, you will be a prime candidate for enlistment and pursued by recruiters of all services. If you choose to enlist in the military, your high school or other institutional ASVAB scores can be used for purposes of enlistment. Your ASVAB scores will remain valid for two years.

The second way that you can take the ASVAB is referred to as the "production" ASVAB. Individuals who take this version of the ASVAB to pursue enlistment either did not take the institutional version or want to retake the examination in the hope that they will improve on their previous scores. There are specific rules on how often you may take the ASVAB; I discuss these rules later in the chapter.

You can take the production ASVAB in one of two places: at either one of the sixty-five MEPS or one of the 470 Mobile Examining Team (MET) sites. In either place, you will be taking the examination with others who have also decided to pursue enlistment in the military. There is one main advantage of taking the ASVAB at a MET site versus one of the MEPS—how the test is administered.

All MEPS administer the Computerized Adaptive Test (CAT) ASVAB. A computer administers this version of the examination. If you take this version of the ASVAB, you'd better be certain of your answers because you can only move forward through the questions; you cannot return to previous questions. Because of this, many of the tried-and-true test-taking techniques 'go out the window.' For instance, anyone who has ever taken a paper-based test knows that you should skip questions you are unsure of and return to them later. Also, most people will go back and review their answers if there is time remaining at the end of the test section. That is not possible with the CAT ASVAB. Also, the "Adaptive" part of the CAT refers to the test adapting to how well the test-taker is doing and adjusts the next question accordingly. In other words, if you are doing well on the examination, the questions get harder; if you are not doing particularly well, the questions get somewhat simpler. Therefore, I recommend avoiding the ASVAB administered at the MEPS in favor of a MET-site administered examination. Please note that some MET sites administer the I-CAT ASVAB, which is an online version administered exactly like the CAT ASVAB.

Also note that the institutional ASVAB does not include two of the subject areas, Assembling Objects and Coding Speed, while the paper-and-pencil version administered at the MET sites lacks the Coding Speed section. Only Navy applicants take the Coding Speed test.

WHAT IS THE ASVAB?

Now that you know about the different versions of the ASVAB, your next question is probably "What is the ASVAB?"

All military branches give the ASVAB examination to determine your basic skills, such as verbal and math, as well as your aptitude for other skills, such as electronics and mechanics. Your overall score, known as the Armed Forces Qualification Test (AFQT), will determine whether you meet the basic qualifications for enlistment, whereas the specific scores in other areas will determine if you have the aptitude for certain military career fields.

The ASVAB is divided into subject tests, which are presented in the following tables. Presently, the navy is the only service that uses the coding speed test in evaluating aptitude for a few career fields.

SUBJECT TESTS FOR THE CAT ASVAB

Subject	Total Questions	Minutes to Complete
General Science (GS) Tests knowledge of biological and physical sciences	16	8
Arithmetic Reasoning (AR) Tests ability to solve arithmetic word problems	16	39
Word Knowledge (WK) Tests ability to select correct word definitions and synonyms	16	8
Paragraph Comprehension (PC) Tests ability to extract information from passages	11	22

Subject	Total Questions	Minutes to Complete
Mathematics Knowledge (MK) Tests knowledge of general mathematics, including algebra and geometry	16	20
Electronics Information (EI) Tests knowledge of electronics principles	16	8
Auto Information (AI) Tests knowledge of automobiles technology	11	7
Shop Information (SI) Tests knowledge of tools and shop terminology and practices	11	6
Mechanical Comprehension (MC) Tests knowledge of mechanical and physical principles	16	20
Assembling Objects (AO) Tests spatial aptitude—the ability to perceive spatial relations	16	16
Coding Speed (CS) **For Navy applicants only** – Tests your ability to swiftly use a key to assign code numbers to words	84	7

SUBJECT TESTS FOR THE PAPER-AND-PENCIL ASVAB

Subject	Total Questions	Minutes to Complete
General Science (GS) Tests knowledge of biological and physical sciences	25	11
Arithmetic Reasoning (AR) Tests ability to solve arithmetic word problems	30	36
Word Knowledge (WK) Tests ability to select correct word definitions and synonyms	35	11

Subject	Total Questions	Minutes to Complete
Paragraph Comprehension (PC) Tests ability to extract information from passages	15	13
Mathematics Knowledge (MK) Tests knowledge of general mathematics, including algebra and geometry	25	24
Electronics Information (EI) Tests knowledge of electronics principles	20	9
Auto and Shop Information (AS) Tests knowledge of automobiles and related tools and terminology	25	11
Mechanical Comprehension (MC) Tests knowledge of mechanical and physical principles	25	19
Assembling Objects (AO) Test spatial aptitude—the ability to perceive spatial relations	25	15

Example test questions in each of these subject tests follow. Please note that the example provided for AI and SI sections are combined under the AS section. You can find more examples and practice tests in *Peterson's Master the ASVAB*. This guide provides excellent study tips, as well as many practice problems to hone your skills and to make you more comfortable with the ASVAB.

For more information on the ASVAB, I urge you to visit www.officialasvab.com.

ARMED FORCES QUALIFICATION TEST (AFQT)

As I mentioned in this chapter, the AFQT is a composite score used to determine your eligibility for enlistment. You will be placed in a "mental category" based on your AFQT score. This mental category has no real relevance and is only mentioned here so you can understand the terminology that may be used by your recruiter. For example, "mental category one" (CAT I) is a good thing to hear; conversely, "mental category four" (CAT IV) is not. Your only concern is whether you have a high enough AFQT (or QT) score to qualify. The formula for calculating your AFQT is based on the following ASVAB subject tests:

Arithmetic Reasoning + Mathematics Knowledge + 2 × Word Knowledge + 2 × Paragraph Comprehension

Preparing for the ASVAB

As discussed, to increase your chances for success, you must prepare for the ASVAB. If you've taken the SAT and done well on it, there is a good chance that you will score high enough on the AFQT to qualify for enlistment. However, the SAT will not prepare you for some of the other ASVAB subject areas, which will determine your aptitude for specific jobs in the military.

Sample ASVAB Test Questions

General Science (GS)

1. The chief nutrient in lean meat is

  1-A fat
  1-B starch
  1-C protein
  1-D carbohydrates

2. Which of the following is an invertebrate?

  2-A starfish
  2-B pigeon
  2-C gorilla
  2-D alligator

Arithmetic Reasoning (AR)

1. If three hoses of equal length connected together reach 24 feet, how long is each hose?

  1-A 6 feet
  1-B 7 feet
  1-C 8 feet
  1-D 9 feet

2. A salesperson earns 30% commission on each sale made. How large a commission would the salesperson earn for selling $160.00 of merchandise?

  2-A $36.00
  2-B $40.00
  2-C $48.00
  2-D $50.00

Word Knowledge (WK)

1. Small most nearly means

  1-A cheap
  1-B round
  1-C sturdy
  1-D little

2. The wind is variable today.

  2-A mild
  2-B steady
  2-C shifting
  2-D chilling

Paragraph Comprehension (PC)

1. In the relations of man to nature, the procuring of food and shelter is fundamental. With the migration of man to various climates, ever new adjustments to the food supply and to the climate became necessary.

According to this passage, the means by which man supplies his material needs are

  1-A accidental
  1-B inadequate
  1-C limited
  1-D varied

2. Twenty-five percent of all household burglaries can be attributed to unlocked windows or doors. Crime is the result of opportunity plus desire. To prevent crime, it is each individual's responsibility to

  2-A provide the desire
  2-B provide the opportunity
  2-C prevent the desire
  2-D prevent the opportunity

This test measures your ability to determine how an object will look when its parts are assembled mentally. Each item consists of five drawings. The problem is in the first drawing. Four answers, only one of which is correct, follow each problem.

Assembling Objects (AO)

Which figure best shows how the objects in the left box will touch if the letters for each object are matched?

1.

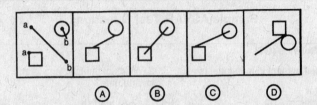

ⓐ   ⓑ   ©   Ⓓ

2.

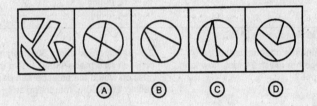

ⓐ   ⓑ   ©   Ⓓ

Auto and Shop Information (AS)

1. A fuel injection system on an automobile engine eliminates the necessity for

    1-A a manifold
    1-B a carburetor
    1-C spark plugs
    1-D a distributor

2. What happens if cylinder head torquing is not done in proper sequence?

    2-A It warps the piston rings.
    2-B It cracks the intake manifold.
    2-C It distorts the head.
    2-D It reduces valve clearance.

Mathematics Knowledge (MK)

1. If 50% of x = 66, then x is

    1-A 33
    1-B 66
    1-C 99
    1-D 132

2. What is the area of this square?

    2-A 1 square foot
    2-B 5 square feet
    2-C 10 square feet
    2-D 25 square feet

5 ft.

Mechanical Comprehension (MC)

1. Which post holds up the greater part of the load?

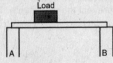

    1-A post A
    1-B post B
    1-C both equal
    1-D not clear

2. If all of the following objects are at room temperature, which will feel coldest?

    2-A book
    2-B metal spoon
    2-C wooden chest
    2-D blanket

Electronics Information (EI)

1. The safest way to run an extension cord to a lamp is

    1-A under a rug
    1-B along a baseboard
    1-C under a sofa
    1-D behind a sofa

2. In the schematic vacuum tube illustrated, the cathode is element

    2-A A
    2-B B
    2-C C
    2-D D

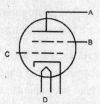

ANSWER KEY:

General Science (GS): 1. C 2. A
Arithmetic Reasoning (AR): 1. C 2. C
Word Knowledge (WK): 1. D 2. C
Paragraph Comprehension (PC): 1. D 2. D
Numerical Operations (NO): 1. C 2. A
Coding Speed (CS): 1. C 2. A 3. E 4. A 5. E
Assembling Objects (AO): 1. C 2. D
Auto and Shop Information (AS): 1. B 2. C
Mathematics Knowledge (MK): 1. D 2. D
Mechanical Comprehension (MC): 1. A 2. B
Electronics Information (EI): 1. B 2. D

For those who did not do well on the SAT, or did not take it at all, and for the other subject areas of the ASVAB, the only way to ensure success is by studying! A great place to start is by using *Peterson's Master the ASVAB*. When I say use, I don't just mean reading or browsing through the pages; I mean taking all the practice tests and going over them again and again. Remember, the ASVAB is a timed examination, and in certain areas it's not the difficulty of the questions that will get you in trouble; it's the amount of time you have to complete these problems.

Here are some other tips for doing well on the ASVAB:

- Read every day. Use a dictionary to look up definitions of words you don't understand.
- Read magazines dealing with mechanics, electronics, and automobiles.
- Practice math problems from your ASVAB study guide, SAT preparation books, or math textbooks.
- Attend SAT preparation classes.
- Ensure that you get enough sleep before the examination.
- Show up early enough for the examination so you don't feel rushed.
- Don't schedule the examination if you cannot devote enough time to prepare for it.
- When all else fails, guess! You will not get penalized for guessing. Answer all the questions.

Of course, if you have no mechanical or automotive background, you will not become an expert in time for the ASVAB. Just remember that the ASVAB measures your *aptitude* for a certain area, not necessarily your mastery of it.

Can you do well on the ASVAB without any preparation? The answer is a *definite maybe*! If you are a solid student who has also taken some shop classes or likes to work on cars, you will probably do okay on the ASVAB without any outside help. Remember, though, that the job and the training you receive in the military are based largely on your ASVAB results.

RETAKING THE ASVAB

If you've taken the ASVAB and believe you didn't do as well as you could have, request to take it again. Just as taking the SAT more than once sometimes results in higher scores, the same can be true for the ASVAB. Here are the rules for repeating the examination:

- You may retake the ASVAB after one month from the date of your first examination.
- You must wait another calendar month to retest a second time.
- You can take subsequent examinations every six months.
- Your last ASVAB results are good for two years from the test date.

If you are being pressured into using scores with which you are uncomfortable, it may be because the recruiter is trying to meet his or her own monthly recruiting goal and is more interested in enlisting you into any career field than enlisting you into a career field for which you are more suited. However, if you've taken the ASVAB more than once, with the same results, the recruiter is not obligated to wait for some "miracle" transformation to occur. It may be that even though you want a job in electronics, you are more suited for a position in a mechanical field.

WHO CAN USE MY ASVAB SCORES?

No matter which version of the ASVAB you take, any military branch can use it. You will be asked to sign a form called the 680-3-AE (an example is provided at the end of this chapter) to convert your scores for use by that particular service. Even if you take the production ASVAB for the Navy, for example, and then decide you'd rather join the Marines, you do not have to take the ASVAB again.

If you have taken the institutional ASVAB, your scores can also be used by your high school guidance counselor to determine what path you may choose after leaving high school.

Some high schools that offer the ASVAB to their students do not share the results or even the names of those who took the examination with the military. In these cases, the high school only uses the results for its own purposes in student counseling. Therefore, you should ask your school whether it plans to release the results to the military. If it does not, it will be up to you to contact the recruiter(s) of your choice to discuss the results, because he or she has no way of contacting you.

WHEN TO TAKE THE ASVAB

You have no control of the scheduling of the institutional ASVAB, but you do have some control over when you take the production ASVAB.

Your recruiter will try to get you to take the ASVAB as soon as possible. That is understandable, because there is a logical order in the enlistment process and the ASVAB is a major part of that process. Unlike a sale at your favorite store that happens only once a year, the ASVAB is given several times a week, depending on the location, and it probably will still be given next week if you decide to wait until then rather than taking it this week.

Usually, you can take the ASVAB on certain days at the MEPS and other days at a MET site. Ask your recruiter when the examination is given. Also, most MEPS schedule one Saturday a month to accommodate those who cannot lose a day of school or work. Do not miss an important final examination or midterm to take the ASVAB, because you can always schedule it for another day.

Another option you may have is "one-stop" processing. This is where you spend the night at a hotel (at the government's expense) and arrive at the MEPS early in the morning to take the ASVAB and physical examination on the same day. This works well for those who cannot miss time away from school or work.

Again, I'd like to emphasize that you should not be pressured into taking the ASVAB "as soon as possible." Take it only when you feel comfortable in doing so. Remember, however, that the recruiter has a job to do, and one of his or her duties is to get you tested. Therefore, be honest with him or her: if you have no intention of taking the ASVAB, say so. Or, if you need more time to study before you take it, tell him or her when you think you'll be ready.

UNDERSTANDING ASVAB RESULTS

Your recruiter should be able to thoroughly explain your ASVAB results to you, even if you took the ASVAB in high school. Rarely, high school guidance counselors are well-versed in interpreting ASVAB results. In any case, if your intentions are to enlist in the military, your results will be explained to you so you fully understand for which military occupations you qualify. I provide an example of the institutional ASVAB results summary following the Chapter Summary.

CHAPTER SUMMARY

Although this chapter has not prepared you for the ASVAB, it has served as an introduction to the test-taking process. If you take no other advice from what I've written in this chapter, please do all you can to prepare to do your best on this important examination, because the job and the training you receive in the military are based largely on your ASVAB results. Once again, I advise you to visit www.officialasvab. com for more information about the ASVAB.

Once you are mentally prepared for military enlistment, you must also prepare yourself for the next hurdle—the physical examination. The next chapter helps you to get through this sometimes seemingly impossible task.

ASVAB SUMMARY RESULTS

Student
12th Gr Female (Form 23G)
SSN: XXX-XX-9999
Test Date: Jul 11, 2006
Old Dominion H.S.
Hometown DC
Print No. XXXXX

ASVAB Results

	Percentile Scores			12th Grade Standard Score
	12th Grade Females	12th Grade Males	12th Grade Students	
Career Exploration Scores				
Verbal Skills	97	95	96	65
Math Skills	22	17	19	42
Science and Technical Skills	81	48	64	53
ASVAB Tests				
General Science	91	81	86	61
Arithmetic Reasoning	43	30	37	47
Word Knowledge	98	95	96	66
Paragraph Comprehension	92	91	91	62
Mathematics Knowledge	14	12	13	37
Electronics Information	13	10	11	38
Auto and Shop Information	53	21	37	45
Mechanical Comprehension	95	76	85	59

Military Entrance Score (AFQT) 57

12th Grade Standard Score Bands (graph with score scale 20 30 40 50 60 70 80; each test score marked with an "X")

EXPLANATION OF YOUR ASVAB PERCENTILE SCORES

Your ASVAB results are reported as percentile scores in the three highlighted columns to the left of the graph. Percentile scores show how you compare to other students - males and females, and for all students - in your grade. For example, a percentile score of 65 for an 11th grade female would mean she scored the same or better than 65 out of every 100 females in the 11th grade.

For purposes of career planning, knowing your relative standing in these comparison groups is important. Being male or female does not limit your career or educational choices. There are noticeable differences in how men and women score in some areas. Viewing your scores in light of your relative standing both for men and women may encourage you to explore areas that you might otherwise overlook.

You can use the Career Exploration Scores to evaluate your knowledge and skills in three general areas (Verbal, Math, Science and Technical Skills). You can use the ASVAB Test Scores to gather information on specific skill areas. Together, these scores (the snapshot of your current knowledge and skills). This information will help you develop and review your career goals and plans.

EXPLANATION OF YOUR ASVAB STANDARD SCORES

Your ASVAB results are reported as standard scores in the above graph. Your score on each test is identified by the "X" in the corresponding bar graph. You should view these scores as estimates of your true skill level in that area. If you took the test again, you probably would receive a somewhat different score. Many things, such as how you were feeling during testing, contribute to this difference. This difference is shown with gray score bands in the graph if you retest. Your standard scores are based on the ASVAB tests and composites based on your grade level.

The score bands provide a way to identify some of your strengths. Overlapping score bands mean your true skill level is similar in both areas, so the real difference between specific scores might not be meaningful. If the score bands do not overlap, you probably are stronger in the area that has the higher score band.

The ASVAB is an aptitude test. It is neither an absolute measure of your skills and abilities nor a perfect predictor of your success or failure. A high score does not guarantee success, and a low score does not guarantee failure, in a future educational program or occupation. For example, if you have never worked with shop equipment or cars, you may not be familiar with the terms and concepts assessed by the Auto and Shop Information test. Taking a course or obtaining a part-time job in this area would increase your knowledge and improve your score if you were to take it again.

USING ASVAB RESULTS IN CAREER EXPLORATION

Your career and educational plans may change over time as you gain more experience and learn more about your interests. *Exploring Careers: The ASVAB Career Exploration Guide* can help you learn more about yourself and the world of work, to identify and explore potential goals, and develop an effective strategy to realize your goals. The *Guide* will help you identify occupations in line with your interests and skills. As you explore potentially satisfying careers, you will develop your career exploration and planning skills.

Meanwhile, your ASVAB results can help you in making well-informed choices about future high school courses.

We encourage you to discuss your ASVAB results with a teacher, counselor, parent, family member or other interested adult. These individuals can help you to view your ASVAB results in light of other important information, such as your interests, school grades, motivation, and personal goals.

USE OF INFORMATION

Personal identity information (name, social security number, street address, and telephone number) and test scores will not be released to any agency outside of the Department of Defense (DoD), the Armed Forces, the Coast Guard, and your school. Your school or local school system can determine any further release of information. The DoD will use your scores for recruiting and research purposes for up to two years. After that the information will be used by the DoD for research purposes only.

MILITARY ENTRANCE SCORES

The **Military Entrance Score** (also called AFQT, which stands for the Armed Forces Qualification Test) is the score used to determine your qualifications for entry into any branch of the United States Armed Forces or the Coast Guard. The **Military Entrance Score** predicts in a general way how well you might do in training and on the job in military occupations. Your score reflects your standing compared to America's men and women 18 to 23 years of age.

Use Access Code: 123456789X

(for online Occu-Find and FYI)

Access code expires: Jul 15, 2007

Explore career possibilities by using your Access Code at

www.asvabprogram.com

SEE YOUR COUNSELOR FOR FURTHER INFORMATION

DD FORM 1304-5, JUL 05 - PREVIOUS EDITIONS OF THIS FORM ARE OBSOLETE

FOR USE OF THIS FORM, SEE USMEPCOM REG 680-3

REQUEST FOR EXAMINATION
THE INFORMATION PROVIDED CONSTITUTES AN OFFICIAL STATEMENT

FOR OFFICIAL USE ONLY

PRIVACY ACT STATEMENT AUTHORITY: Sections 505, 508, 510, and 3012 of Title 10 U.S. Code and Executive Order 9397. PRINCIPAL PURPOSE: The requested information on this form will be used to properly process and identify the individual requesting an examination at a military entrance processing station (MEPS). ROUTINE USE: Record is maintained with other enlistment processing records. DISCLOSURE: Voluntary; refusal to provide required data could result in denial of enlistment.

A. SERVICE PROCESSING FOR

B. PRIOR SERVICE [ ] YES [ ] NO

NUMBER OF DAYS :

C. SELECTIVE SERVICE CLASSIFICATION

D. SELECTIVE SERVICE REGISTRATION NUMBER

1. SOCIAL SECURITY NUMBER — —

2. NAME (Last, First, Middle Name (and Maiden, if any), Jr., Sr., etc.)

3. CURRENT ADDRESS (Street, City, County, State, Country, ZIP Code)

4. HOME OF RECORD ADDRESS (Street, City, County, State, Country, ZIP Code)

5. CITIZENSHIP (X One)
- a. U.S. AT BIRTH (If this box is marked, also X (1) or (2))
  - (1) NATIVE BORN
  - (2) BORN ABROAD OF U.S. PARENT(S)
- b. U.S. NATURALIZED
- c. U.S. NON-CITIZEN NATIONAL
- d. IMMIGRANT ALIEN (Specify)
- e. NON-IMMIGRANT FOREIGN NATIONAL (Specify)
- f. ALIEN REGISTRATION NUMBER (As applicable)

6. SEX (X One)
- a. MALE
- b. FEMALE

8. MARITAL STATUS (Specify)

9. NUMBER OF DEPENDENTS

7.a. RACIAL CATEGORY (X one or more)
- (1) AMERICAN INDIAN/ ALASKA NATIVE
- (2) ASIAN
- (3) BLACK OR AFRICAN AMERICAN
- (4) NATIVE HAWAIIAN OR OTHER PACIFIC ISLANDER
- (5) WHITE

7.b. ETHNIC CATEGORY (X One)
- (1) HISPANIC OR LATINO
- (2) NOT HISPANIC OR LATINO

10. DATE OF BIRTH (YYYYMMDD)

11. RELIGIOUS PREFERENCE (Optional)

12. EDUCATION (Yrs/Highest Ed Gr Completed)

13. PROFICIENT IN FOREIGN LANGUAGE (X One) (If Yes, specify) [ ] YES [ ] NO 1st 2nd

14. VALID DRIVER'S LICENSE (X One) [ ] YES [ ] NO (If Yes, list State, number, and expiration date)

15. PLACE OF BIRTH (City, State, and Country)

16. APTITUDE:
- a. ASVAB REQUIRED TO ENLIST? (X One) [ ] YES [ ] NO
- b. ENLIST UNDER STUDENT TEST SCORES? (X One) - [ ] YES [ ] NO
- c. TEST TYPE [ ] INITIAL [ ] SPECIAL [ ] CONFIRMATION
- d. RETEST [ ] 1ST RETEST [ ] 6 MONTH RETEST [ ] 2ND RETEST [ ] IMMED RETEST AUTHORIZED
- e. PREVIOUS TEST VERSIONS 1. 2.
- f. PREVIOUS TEST DATES (YYYYMMDD) 1. 2.

17.a. RECRUITER ID/SSN **b. STATION ID**

18. TEST ADMINISTRATOR SSN/ID

19. TEST ADMINISTRATOR SIGNATURE

20. MEDICAL :
- a. MEPS MEDICAL EXAM REQUIRED TO ENLIST? (X One) [ ] YES [ ] NO
- b. EXAM TYPE [ ] FULL [ ] SPECIAL [ ] RE-EXAM [ ] INSPECT [ ] CONSULT [ ] OTHER
- c. DATE LAST FULL MEDICAL EXAM (YYYYMMDD)

21. APPLICANT'S SIGNATURE

22. MIRS CODING

WKID	ST	DATE	INT	DATE	INT

23. APPLICANT CERTIFICATION IN PRESENCE OF TEST ADMINISTRATOR
I certify that I am the person identified on this form:

Photo ID? (X One) [ ] YES [ ] NO

If yes, type/organization _____

ID Number _____

_____
(Signature of Applicant)

24. RIGHT THUMBPRINT

RIGHT THUMBPRINT, FIRST ATTEMPT
(AFFIX THUMBPRINT WITH THUMBNAIL POINTED TO THE LEFT)

25. APPLICANT CERTIFICATION IN PRESENCE OF RECRUITING PERSONNEL
I certify that I am the person identified on this form and that the information about me shown there, including my Social Security Number is all true and correct to the best of my knowledge. I also certify that:

a. [ ] I have never been tested ANYTIME or ANYWHERE with the ASVAB either for enlistment purposes or as a student under the ASVAB testing program.

b. [ ] I was tested with the ASVAB on or about _____ at _____
(Most Recent Date Tested)   (School, City, and State)

c. [ ] Request for student test scores (high school look-up) _____ at _____
(Most Recent Date Tested)   (School, City, and State)

d. [ ] Yes, I want to keep my AFQT scores from the student test listed in "c" above.

e. Current or last high school attended _____ / _____
(High School)   OR   (13 Digit Code)

f. _____ / _____ / _____
(Signature of Applicant)   (Social Security Number)   (Date)

IF SECOND ATTEMPT IS REQUIRED, TURN FORM OVER (TOP OF FORM ON THE BOTTOM) AFFIX RIGHT THUMBPRINT ON UPPER RIGHT CORNER, THUMBNAIL POINTED TO THE LEFT

MEDICAL RECORDS RELEASE AUTHORITY: I request and authorize individuals/organizations listed below to release to the MEPS a complete transcript of my medical records. This release is for the purpose of further evaluation of my medical acceptability under military medical fitness standards. The medical records are to be obtained by this examinee at no cost to the Government and made available for review during the pre-enlistment physical.

26. APPLICANT'S CURRENT MEDICAL INSURER NAME
(If none, sign your complete name to affirm that you have no current medical insurer):

27. APPLICANT'S CURRENT MEDICAL PROVIDER NAME
(If none, sign your complete name to affirm that you have no current medical provider):

28. MEDICAL INSURER ADDRESS (Street, City, State, Country, ZIP Code)

29. MEDICAL PROVIDER ADDRESS (Street, City, State, Country, ZIP Code)

30. CERTIFICATION BY RECRUITING PERSONNEL
I certify that I have properly identified this applicant in accordance with my service directives, have reviewed for completeness and accuracy the information provided on this form, and have witnessed the applicant's signature:

APPLICANT SSN

_____ / _____ / _____
(Signature of Recruiter (or rep, if auth))   (Printed/Typed Name of Recruiter or Rep)   (Date)

_____
(Printed/Typed Name of Recruiter (if not recorded above))

_____   _____   _____
(Recruiter ID/SSN)   (Local Recruiting Activity)   (Bn, NRD, Sq or RS Location)

USMEPCOM Form 680-3A-E, OCT 05

Replaces USMEPCOM Form 680-3A-E, DEC 03, which is obsolete

5 THE MILITARY ENTRANCE PROCESSING STATION (MEPS)

Perhaps the most traumatic and memorable experience in the entire enlistment process is the applicant's first trip to the MEPS. This chapter outlines the purpose of the MEPS and reassures you that the MEPS is not an indicator of what life is like in the military.

In 1978, I went to a place called the Armed Forces Examining and Entrance Station (AFEES) at Fort Hamilton in Brooklyn, New York, to process for enlistment. The AFEES's mission was to determine the physical, mental, and moral qualifications of each applicant. I spent the day filling out paperwork, answering questions, being probed and prodded, and rushing from place to place. Since 1978, some things have changed at AFEES; it is now the Military Entrance Processing Station (MEPS).

Besides dealing with a recruiter, the MEPS is the first contact most people have with the military. Although recent changes to MEPS staffing have increased the number of civilian personnel, the MEPS is also staffed by members of all the military branches, so no matter for which branch you are enlisting, you will interact with personnel from them all. At times, the MEPS may seem like an assembly plant to applicants, who go from station to station until they finally raise their hands for the oath of enlistment.

Because so many people go through the sixty-five MEPs each year, the MEPS system must be regimented to ensure that only qualified individuals enter the armed forces. Although from time-to-time individuals who are not qualified "slip through the cracks," the number would be much higher if every MEPS didn't abide by a stringent routine. In 2002, 262,324 (65 percent) of those 403,545 who processed through the MEPS passed the rigid standards for enlistment.

This chapter outlines the basic processes you will encounter at the MEPS. Although all MEPS follow standard procedures, there are some differences in the way each MEPS operates, so it is important to use this chapter as insight into the MEPS, not as a substitute for information or instructions from your recruiter.

I strongly suggest that you, and if applicable, your parents, watch the video, "**A Day at the MEPS**." You can view it at: www.mepcom.army.mil/video.html. If you do not have Internet access at home, try the public library, your school, or your recruiter's office. Of course, I urge you to read this chapter, but watching the video is essential. Additionally, you can find more information about MEPS processing at www.mepcom.army.mil/applicants.html, for applicants, and, www.mepcom.army.mil/parents.html, for parents.

Preparing for MEPS Processing

After you and your recruiter have worked out a day to do your MEPS processing, he or she will put you on the schedule, so the MEPs will be expecting you. If you have already taken the Armed Services Vocational Aptitude Battery (ASVAB) examination, chances are you will travel to the MEPS on the day you will be processed. However, depending on your circumstances, you may travel to a hotel near the MEPS the night before your processing.

TRANSPORTATION TO THE MEPS

If you are scheduled for "one-stop processing," which means taking the ASVAB and physical on the same day, you may be put up in a hotel (at government expense) near the MEPS the night before. You may also get to stay at a hotel, even if you've already taken the ASVAB, if you live a considerable distance from the MEPS; you should ask your recruiter about your options.

If you spend the night at the hotel, you will, more than likely, meet somewhere in the hotel lobby for a bus ride to the MEPS. Don't be late!

If you don't spend the night in the hotel, depending on the policy of the service you're joining, you'll probably be provided transportation to the MEPS. The type of transportation varies from service to service and location to location. Generally, there are several modes of transportation:

- your recruiter's government-owned vehicle (or in a van with other applicants)
- bus
- train
- possibly airplane

If you are required to take public transportation (again, depending on policy), you will be provided with the appropriate tickets. Because family members can witness the oath of enlistment, you may be allowed to provide your own source of transportation at your expense.

Applicants who spend the night in the hotel may take these same modes of transportation to get to the hotel the evening before MEPS processing.

Words of Wisdom If You Stay at a Hotel

If you spend the night before your MEPS processing in a hotel, there are a few things to remember. Because this is the first time many of the applicants have spent the night away from home, other than at a slumber party, applicants sometimes get into trouble at a hotel. Unlike a sleepover, this is not a time to party. The sole purpose for your being at the hotel is so that you will be rested when your processing begins the next day at around 5 a.m.!

In the past, I have had to deal with several applicants who did not understand, or otherwise disregarded, their reason for spending the night at the hotel. Often, those applicants went home without ever doing any MEPS processing and, therefore, never enlisted.

Here are a few things that will get you in trouble or cause you to be unfit to take the ASVAB and physical examination. Most of these are common sense, but for the sake of argument, I'll list them anyway:

- alcohol use of any kind, regardless of whether you are of legal age
- destruction of property (the hotel's or someone else's personal property)
- loud noise of any kind
- staying up all night (If you usually require eight hours of sleep, get to bed early enough to get it.)
- spending the night in someone else's room, or permitting someone to spend the night in your room
- stealing
- use of illegal drugs
- any other behavior that could be classified as disorderly conduct

Besides the military denying processing, some actions may result in criminal prosecution. As mentioned, the government will take care of all expenses, including meals. However, this does not include telephone calls.

CHECKING IN AT THE MEPS

Regardless of how you get to the MEPS, make sure you get there on time! If you are late, chances are you will not process that day. If you are traveling by public transportation, your recruiter should be able to provide you with the best times to leave to get there on time.

On your arrival, you will report to the check-in desk, where you will sign in and show proof of identity. Most of the time, there will be no problem with check-in; however, sometimes (usually because of an administrative error), your name may not be on the daily processing list. If this happens to you, MEPS will do everything possible to get you processed that day.

After you've checked in, you will be given a bar-coded label to wear that includes your name and the branch of service for which you are processing. You are now ready to begin your MEPS adventure!

THE MEPS LIAISON

Each branch of the military has one or more individuals from recruiting assigned to the MEPS. These individuals are your advocates at the MEPS. Their primary responsibilities include:

- ensuring that the applicants get through all stages of processing;
- job counseling (this is discussed later in this chapter);
- working through problems that applicants may encounter during processing;
- keeping the recruiters and recruiting staff informed of an applicant's processing progress; and
- intervening with the MEPS staff on the applicant's behalf.

Although you will undoubtedly see many individuals at the MEPS from the branch of service in which you are enlisting, only the MEPS liaison is a member of that branch's recruiting staff.

Applicants taking the CAT ASVAB.

MEPS Processing

MEPS processing contains five broad categories. They are in the order in which you encounter them:

- aptitude testing
- physical examination (medical screening)
- job search
- background screening
- oath of enlistment

Each step of the MEPS processing is important. These steps ensure that only qualified applicants enlist, and they also determine an applicant's suitability for specific military career fields. The following five processes establish the mental, physical, and moral qualifications for enlistment.

Rest assured that it's been quite awhile since this guy has worked at MEPS!

APTITUDE TESTING

Aptitude testing includes the ASVAB, which you may have already taken, as well as other specialty tests that you may be required to take, such as for some electronics specialties or for jobs requiring proficiency in foreign languages.

If you've already taken the ASVAB, you probably won't be taking it again unless you didn't achieve a satisfactory score the first time. If you are taking it again, you must ensure that enough time has elapsed since the previous test to make you eligible for a retest. Some people believe that they can get around the mandatory waiting period for retesting by going to another recruiter. A word of caution: if you've taken the test for another recruiter, even a recruiter for another branch, and you've decided to conceal this from your current recruiter, you will get caught and be denied processing. MEPS owns the ASVAB process—not the specific military branches. Therefore, if you've ever taken the ASVAB, the MEPS will know about it.

OTHER TESTING

In addition to the ASVAB, you may have to take other tests, depending on the branch of service and specific job or career field for which you are applying. If you've taken the ASVAB before the day of your MEPS processing, your recruiter may have talked to you about qualifying for a job that requires a specialized test. Or, if you've taken the ASVAB as part of your MEPS processing, the MEPS liaison will probably inform you of your eligibility to take a specialized test. In any case, taking one of the specialized tests can qualify you for more opportunities and, therefore, increase your number of job choices. Before going to MEPS, ask your recruiter if you will be required to take a specialized test.

PHYSICAL EXAMINATION

The physical examination you take at the MEPS will probably be one of the most thorough physicals you've ever taken. Because it is important that all individuals who are enlisting meet the physical fitness standards of the military branches, the MEPS personnel 'leave no stone unturned' in determining whether you meet those standards.

Basically, your physical examination will consist of:

- height and weight measurements;
- hearing and vision examinations;
- urine and blood tests;
- drug and alcohol tests;
- muscle group and joint maneuvers;
- complete physical examination and interview; and
- specialized tests, including strength tests, if required

Make sure you ask your recruiter if you will be required to undergo specialized tests.

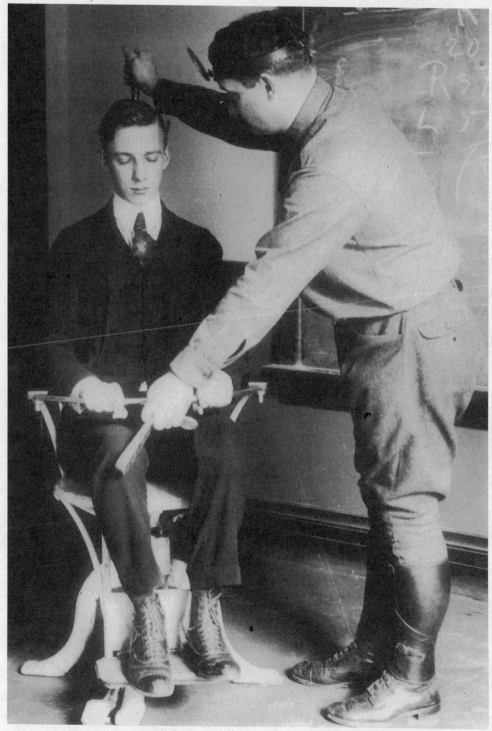

Some things have changed at MEPS since this WWI-era photo.

WOMEN APPLICANTS

Women applicants will be provided gowns to wear during their physical examination. They will also be examined by the MEPS physician in a private room. A female chaperone will be present during the portion of the examination that requires a woman to remove her clothing. All female applicants, even if they report that they are not sexually active, receive a pregnancy test.

DISCLOSURE OF YOUR MEDICAL HISTORY

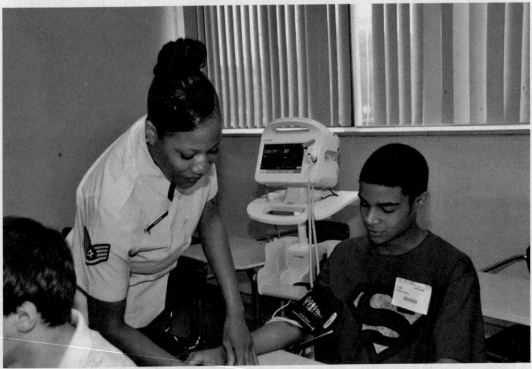

This is a part of a physical that we can publish.

As part of the recruiting process, your recruiter should have had you complete DD Form 2807-2, which includes questions about your past and current medical history. (I provide an example of this form in the Appendix.) Your recruiter will have used the information on this form to determine any potentially disqualifying medical problems. This form will also assist the MEPS medical personnel to understand your medical history better.

Let me reiterate that it is vital for you to be completely honest when completing this form. By honestly answering the questions, you may prevent problems. It is common for someone to conceal information that is discovered later during the medical examination or, even worse, during Basic Training.

By completing the DD Form 2807-2, you are agreeing to the following statement:

Warning: The information you have given constitutes an official statement. Federal law provides severe penalties (up to five years confinement or $10,000 fine or both), to anyone making a false statement. If you are selected for enlistment, commission, or entrance into a commissioning program based on a false statement, you can be tried by military court martial or meet an administrative board for discharge and could receive a less than honorable discharge, which would affect your future.

Although most people probably don't even read this statement before completing the DD Form 2807-2, it tells it all. Do not lie or conceal information about your medical history. Will you have to pay a fine or go to jail if MEPS personnel discover that you haven't been honest about your medical history? Probably not. However, if you somehow get through the physical, and then it's discovered in Basic Training that you weren't 100 percent truthful about your medical history, you may face severe penalties because you'll be an Active Duty service member by then.

Your long day at MEPS will start early in the morning.

Medical Waivers

Remember that there are certain "disqualifying" medical conditions that can be waived. Only the MEPS medical personnel can determine that on a case-by-case basis. In other words, a history of tumor removal, for example, may be waived in one case, but not in another. Certain conditions may never be waived; your recruiter will let you know if that is the case. I discuss this in more detail later in this section.

COMPLETING THE DD FORM 2807-2

More paperwork?

Before you complete the DD Form 2807-2, I would like to offer some advice on completing the form.

You are responsible for the answers to each and every question on the form—not your recruiter, not your parents—you! Therefore, no matter what anyone tells you, answer the form truthfully. I can't tell you how many times I've heard applicants say, "My recruiter told me not to say anything about . . . ." The truth is that some recruiters may ask applicants to conceal potentially disqualifying information; however, the bottom line is that it is your name on that form, not your recruiter's. When it comes down to it, it'll be your word against your recruiter's if it is found that you have lied on the DD Form 2807-2; who do you think they'll believe?

Another problem that occurs when completing this form is "phantom illnesses." These are medical conditions that the applicant never had, but either was told he or she did or were self-diagnosed. A common phantom illness is childhood asthma. Asthma, at any age, is a non-waiverable condition, yet every day applicants claim to have had asthma as a child when, in fact, they never did.

Quite often, parents tell their children they have asthma when they don't. It could be for one of several reasons. Mom doesn't want Johnny to play on the school football team, so she tells him he has asthma, or maybe, it's the infamous "trick" knee or a heart murmur. Chances are that if a doctor has never treated you for an illness, you've probably never had it.

Along the same lines, don't become so afraid of "lying" on the form that you start to self-diagnose and make yourself ineligible for enlistment. My own son almost fell into this trap. When filling out

DD Form 2807-2, he came to the question about "frequent trouble sleeping." He was about to answer "yes" when I asked him why. It turns out that for about two weeks before that time he was studying for finals, was worried about the upcoming SAT, and was anxious about college applications. This caused him to have some restless nights. This, however, did not warrant a "yes" response to the question about frequent trouble sleeping. Just as being out of breath after running three miles would not justify a "yes" to the question about "shortness of breath."

A good rule of thumb is that if you are about to answer "yes" to any question, ask for clarification. Review the sample DD Form 2807-2 contained in the Appendix with your parents or anyone else who may have knowledge of your medical history. If you can answer "yes" to any of the questions, ask your recruiter if it would help to provide documentation to explain your illness or injury. Providing documentation often will allow the MEPS medical personnel to clear you on that particular item without the need for further tests.

What to Do If You Do Not Qualify

Hopefully, you will be able to get through the MEPS physical without any problems; however, sometimes applicants become medically disqualified. You may be permanently disqualified (PDQ), which, as the name implies, is not a good thing, or you may receive temporary disqualification (TDQ), which, of course, is not good, but it is better than being PDQ.

There are several reasons why you may be disqualified temporarily. You may have a particular condition that requires you to wait until you are completely healed. For example, spontaneous pneumothorax (collapsed lung) is disqualifying for a period of three years following the incident. You may also temporarily be disqualified if more tests or documentation are needed before the MEPS physician can make a final determination. Therefore, the MEPS may send you for a consultation, you may be required to return to your own doctor for follow-up, or you may have to provide hospital and other medical records. Ultimately, the end-result will be either passing the physical or becoming PDQ.

Luckily, even if you are PDQ, there is a chance that you can receive a medical waiver. Waivers are the military's way of saying, "We know that you are not physically qualified, but in your case, we'll make an exception."

No one will offer you a medical waiver; you must request one. If you are PDQ on the MEPS physical, inform your recruiter that you would like consideration for a medical waiver. Asking for a waiver does not guarantee that you will get one. You may have to undergo more tests (at your own expense) or provide more documentation. Remember that there are certain illnesses and injuries that cannot be waived, no matter what.

Report of Medical Examination (DD Form 2808)

An example of the Report of Medical Examination (DD Form 2808) is in the Appendix. The DD Form 2808 is the actual form used as your physical report. I have provided an example so that you can see just how thorough the physical examination is. If you have any questions about the physical examination, ask your recruiter or the MEPS physical examination personnel.

BACKGROUND SCREENING

Fingerprinting is required for all applicants.

Your background screening began with your first meeting with your recruiter. More than likely, he or she asked you about any criminal offenses, including traffic infractions, that you might have committed. Depending on what you told him or her, he or she made a preliminary decision on your acceptability for enlistment. After you decided to move ahead with the enlistment process, your recruiter may have been required to run police checks to determine past and present criminal charges.

As discussed in Chapter 1, one mistake many people make is not disclosing offenses that occurred when they were juveniles. Most people don't intentionally deceive their recruiters, but rather they were told by the court that their records would be expunged after a certain period of time and that they would never have to report the offense to anyone. Unfortunately, this is not true.

In all likelihood, expunged offenses will not appear in checks reported by local police agencies; however, your background check will go way beyond the local agencies your recruiter contacted. The formal, in-depth, no-holds-barred background screening will begin at the MEPS.

When I was a recruiter, I would brief my applicants that the MEPS personnel would pull no punches when "asking" them about prior law violations. I would rather have dealt with a criminal offense that might have been taken care of with an enlistment waiver than have an applicant not tell me about the incident and then later admit to it at the MEPS. Unfortunately, not all recruiters will push their applicants this hard when asking about law violations. The old adage "ignorance is bliss" does not apply here.

Earlier in this chapter, I advised you never to allow anyone to influence the way you answer questions regarding your health; the same applies to questions regarding law violations. You alone are accountable if the MEPS finds that you lied about involvement with the law. If a recruiter tells you "Don't worry about mentioning it" or "That's not important enough to list" or makes any similar statement, find another recruiter.

You should go to the MEPS with a clear conscience; you should have nothing to hide. If your recruiter is doing his or her job properly, you will have any necessary waivers approved, if needed, before your MEPS processing. Therefore, you have nothing to worry about during the background-screening portion of your processing.

Your recruiter may not want to push you for answers regarding law violations, but I guarantee you that the MEPS personnel will. You will be threatened with fines and even jail time. They may even try to coerce you into "confessing" with statements like, "Everyone your age has at least one speeding ticket; do you expect me to believe that you don't even have one ticket?"

Don't take this line of questioning personally. Remember, the main purpose of the MEPS is to ensure that only qualified applicants enlist in the military. You may be the most honest and law-abiding applicant ever to go through MEPS processing, but the MEPS staff has no way of knowing that. Answer the questions fully and to the best of your ability, and you will have no problems. Remember that if you divulged all information regarding law violations to your recruiter and he or she determined you weren't morally qualified for enlistment, you wouldn't even be at MEPS.

The "investigation" into your background does not stop at the MEPS. Depending on the branch of service for which you enlist and the job you select, you will receive a more in-depth background check that may include agents interviewing friends, relatives, and teachers. My own experience with my background check was quite interesting, which you'll learn about in the next section.

Drug Involvement

Just as with law violations, your recruiter will have asked you about involvement with illegal drugs and improper use of prescribed drugs. Your recruiter should have briefed you on his or her particular service's policy on drug use. Whatever that service's policy on past drug use is, one thing is universal among all the services—there is zero tolerance for current drug use by its applicants.

Also as with law violations, the MEPS personnel will push you hard to disclose any drug involvement, past or present. Rest assured that you would not be at the MEPS if you disclosed anything disqualifying you concerning drugs to your recruiter.

Once again, if anyone tells you to withhold the truth, don't do it. You alone are responsible for the answers you give. A running joke among recruiters is how some recruiters ask applicants about previous drug use. Instead of asking "Have you ever or are you currently using any illegal drugs?" they may say, "You haven't ever taken any illegal drugs, have you?" Of course, the latter statement would lead an applicant to assume that he or she better say "no" or be disqualified. In this case, the recruiter hasn't told the applicant to lie, but he or she hasn't asked for the truth either.

You may think that you can outsmart the system by withholding information about prior drug usage. After all, if you've never been arrested on a drug charge, how will anyone ever know? Think again. Consider the following stories, the first of which is about my own background check that the Navy conducted when I enlisted. The job for which I was training required a "Top Secret" security clearance, which meant that agents would interview people from my past. One person they decided to interview was a friend of mine. When they asked him if he had ever known me to take any drugs, he thought it would be funny to say "yes." One thing you should know about these agents is that they have no sense of humor. Fortunately for me, my friend realized that in a hurry and told them he was only kidding. Had I been involved with drugs in the past, it is possible that someone would have told them.

The second story concerns a fellow recruit during Basic Training. Because the military wants to ensure that only qualified individuals become part of its team, you will be asked about your history throughout the enlistment process, and it doesn't stop at the MEPS. Because you are not fully a member of the military until your graduation from Basic Training, the questioning continues there.

If we were asked once, we were asked a thousand times about our use of drugs. One day a fellow recruit walked into the barracks, and he looked as if someone had shot his dog. I asked him what was wrong, and all he could say was, "They found out, somehow they found out." Of course, I had to ask, "They found out what?" "They found out that I once took a puff of a marijuana cigarette at a party."

How could they have possibly found out that information? As it turns out, they hadn't known a thing. They used the "technique" of coercing him by saying, "We know you tried marijuana at least once, everyone has." He packed his belongings, and we never saw him again. Had he told his recruiter about his one-time use of marijuana, odds are he would have been marching with the rest of us at graduation.

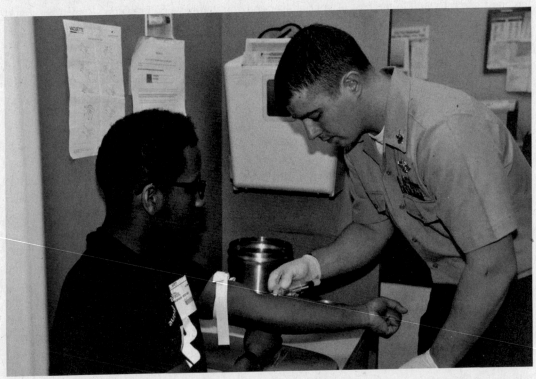

You will have to give a blood sample.

Drug Testing

You will be subjected to drug testing at the MEPS at initial processing and then again when you leave for Basic Training. Here is a sure-fire way to ensure that you don't come up positive on the drug test: Don't do drugs! As you are probably aware, the length of time that traces of a drug will stay in your system depends on the drug. Marijuana, for instance, can stay in your system for up to a month. I've heard of people doing all kinds of crazy things because they were told it would beat the drug test, like drinking enough water to fill a fish tank or, my favorite, drinking a bottle of vinegar. A word of advice about tricks to get around drug testing: they don't work!

One more thing about drug tests: get used to them. All military branches conduct random urinalysis tests to detect drugs. What that means is that at any time during your military career you will have to undergo drug testing. Would you want to fly in an airplane if there was a chance that the pilot or the mechanic who works on the plane used drugs?

THE JOB SEARCH

Depending on the branch of service, the purpose of the job search at MEPS may be to choose the actual job for which you will enlist or to choose one or more jobs for which you qualify. If it's the latter, you will be put on a waiting list. Either way, your service branch MEPS liaison will be the individual who conducts the search. Ultimately, the branch liaison will use the following criteria to determine for which jobs you qualify:

- physical profile
- ASVAB scores
- record of criminal offenses
- specialized test scores, if applicable,
- gender (until all military jobs are open to females)
- citizenship

Perhaps the best of all recruiters, the MEPS liaison will sit down with you to discuss your options. He or she must match your needs with those of the branch he or she represents. The key to getting the job you want is flexibility.

FLEXIBILITY IN THE JOB SEARCH

An Army applicant preparing for the job search.

The availability of jobs at any particular time depends on several factors, including:

- current and projected vacancies in the particular career field;
- the projected number of openings for classes; and
- the number of other applicants seeking particular career fields.

The military strives to ensure that all available technical school class seats are full. This makes filling those class seats one of the biggest factors in job availability. Therefore, you can increase the chances of getting the job you want by being flexible as to when you are available to leave for Basic Training. For example, by leaving in October instead of November, you may be able to get a particular job because of the availability of a technical school seat. Of course, there may be factors that would prevent you from being flexible in your availability, such as your current school commitments, especially for high school seniors. Because you may remain in the Delayed Entry Program (DEP) for a maximum of 365 days, it may be impossible for you to be flexible in your timing.

Another way you can increase your chances of getting a job you want is to be flexible to look for a job category rather than a specific job. In other words, you may be interested in mechanics, administrative work, or the medical field. Many jobs in the military are closely related to each other. By choosing a job in a particular "field," you will increase your chances of getting something you want.

Chapter 8 is entirely devoted to explaining the various "occupational fields" in each military branch. Spend some time reviewing the section pertaining to the branch for which you are enlisting before your MEPS processing. Highlight some of the fields that sound interesting to you even if you've never considered going into, or in some cases never heard of, that field.

Be open-minded. When I enlisted in the Navy, I chose electronics as my career category. Because I liked to work on cars, I wanted something to do with mechanics; I never even thought of electronics as an option. When I listened to what the MEPS liaison had to say about electronics, it sounded interesting to me and I decided to go for it. The ASVAB showed that I had the potential to excel in the electronics field, a career I would have never considered on my own. It's okay to go to the MEPS with a certain job or job category in mind, but also be flexible and consider other options.

Advanced Pay Grade

Most people enter the military at the lowest possible pay grade, or rank, E-1. As you'll see in Chapter 9, the E-1 is called by different names depending on the service; however, all services use the E-1 through E-9 scale to identify and pay their enlisted personnel.

Sometimes, however, individuals may enter the military at a higher pay grade, usually E-2 or E-3. Depending on the service, an individual may enter at a higher pay grade based on one of the following:

- college credits earned
- participation in organizations, such as high school Junior Officers' Training Corps (JROTC) or the sea cadets
- job selection

Even though you may qualify for a higher pay grade, everyone is treated the same at Basic Training; there is no rank distinction made. However, you will earn more at the higher pay level even during Basic Training, and you will be able to "sew on" the rank immediately after graduation. If you are entitled to enlist at a higher pay grade, make sure it is in your enlistment contract. See Chapter 9 for basic pay scales for each grade.

It's Okay to Say "No"

As I stated, it is the MEPS liaison's job to match applicants with available vacancies. Just as a car dealership will push its remaining year-end leftovers, MEPS liaisons will push their "leftovers."

Although you should be certain that the reason you came to the MEPS was to enlist that day, do not be pressured into taking a job choice with which you are not comfortable. Chances are that if you hold your ground, the MEPS liaison will offer a job that appeals to you. He or she tries to fill the vacancies that have been rejected by other applicants before the vacancies that he or she knows will fill with no problem.

Watch for the "impending doom" approach, such as, "If you don't leave by a certain date, you will not be able to get a particular job." Although I've told you to remain flexible, don't do anything that makes you feel uncomfortable. Therefore, if you requested to leave in two months and are told that the job you want is available only if you leave in one month, ask if it will be available if you leave in four months instead.

There may be times, however, when the impending doom approach may be legitimate. For instance, there may be an enlistment bonus for a limited time, and you may have to enlist by a specified date in order to qualify for it. Another example is what occurred in the 1980s: the military changed its method of calculating retirement pay to a less attractive method. At that time, there was a rush to get people enlisted so that they could enlist under the "old" retirement plan.

If all else fails and you are unable to get the job you want (assuming, of course, that you are qualified for that job), there is no shame in going home without enlisting. If this is the case, you may want to check with another service to see if it has a similar job available. Please note that I am not advocating going from branch to branch until you find what you want (you should have already decided which branch will best meet your needs), but in extreme cases, it may be the best solution.

However, you should keep in close contact with your recruiter in the event that an opening does come up. In most cases, you will find that something will become available, usually at the end of the month.

A MEPS TALE:

The following story is true, however, names have been changed to protect the innocent and not so innocent. In 2011, one of my daughters went to the local MEPS to process for enlistment. Before she went to the MEPS she let the recruiter know that although she was somewhat flexible, she would only enlist if she were offered a job in which she was interested. When she was offered only jobs in which she was not interested, she decided not to enlist; this is when the pressure and outright lies began. The service MEPS liaison told her that if she didn't enlist right then and there, she would never be able to enlist for that service and because all the services are connected, she would be barred from enlisting in any branch of the military! Of course, that was not true.

She called me not knowing what to do; I instructed her to come home... she never enlisted in the military. Not willing to let it go, I talked to the liaison and told him what I thought about his tactics. Not long after, I received a phone call from his boss explaining that my daughter probably misunderstood, although this was not likely.

This story is in no way an indictment of all MEPS liaison personnel, but it is an example of over-zealous military recruiting personnel; luckily, most are not like this and there are probably a hundred positive examples to every negative one.

A Word About Enlistment Bonuses

From time to time, the various services will offer enlistment bonuses for individuals who are willing to enlist in certain career fields. I encountered this a lot when I was a Navy recruiter. An applicant would tell me that the only thing holding him back was that the Army would give him a $5,000 enlistment bonus if he enlisted in "Field Artillery" for four years. Although there is nothing wrong with being in Field Artillery, I knew that I could offer certain applicants much more. I would approach those applicants by saying, "Are you willing to do something you really don't want to do for four years for an additional $1,250 per year? $104.17 a month? $3.36 a day? And don't forget the difference in the length of training and college credits by attending the more technical Navy schools." I never lost one applicant to the Army's enlistment bonus!

Are you willing to take a job you don't want for the enlistment bonus? You may, especially if you are joining the military for the experience more than specific training, or if you are joining just so you can qualify for the educational benefits.

NEGOTIATION IS KEY

Perhaps the most important part of the entire enlistment process, getting the job you want, may come down to how well you can negotiate with the MEPS liaison. By being flexible and holding your ground, you will be on your way to receiving the best training available!

THE OATH OF ENLISTMENT

Taking the oath of enlistment

After you've met all of the requirements for enlistment and have conducted your job search with the MEPS liaison, it will be time for you to do the one thing you came to the MEPS to do in the first place: enlist!

More than likely, you will enter the DEP, and, therefore, this will be the first of two enlistment oaths you will take prior to leaving for Basic Training. The first is an oath to enter the DEP, which puts you in a nonparticipating reserve status, the second is taken on the day you leave for Basic Training, which officially puts you on Active Duty.

The oath of enlistment is a solemn ceremony conducted by a military officer. It has a long tradition, and therefore, you should not enter into it lightly. You, as well as other applicants processing for all the different services, will assemble in a room. The officer will stand in front of you, with the U.S. flag in the background, and ask you to raise your right hand and repeat the following words:

I, [*state your name*], do solemnly swear (or affirm) that I will support and defend the Constitution of the United States against all enemies, foreign and domestic; that I will bear true faith and allegiance to the same; and that I will obey the orders of the President of the United States and the orders of the officers appointed over me, according to regulations and the Uniform Code of Military Justice. So help me God.

I invite you to read the oath again, and this time think about what its words mean to you. Most times, applicants are not given ample time to read and understand the meaning of the oath before they are asked to recite and sign it. This is understandable, considering the amount of paperwork that an applicant must review and sign during MEPS processing.

Can you get out of going into the military after taking the oath and "swearing into" the DEP? The answer is, without a doubt, absolutely "yes." However, I would urge you not to make a commitment you don't intend to keep. It's like proposing to your girlfriend when you have no intention of ever going through with the wedding. I'll cover this in depth in Chapter 6.

Processing for Reserve Components

MEPS processing differs somewhat for applicants enlisting in the reserve components. Depending on the branch of service, applicants may do their job search and oath of enlistment at their reserve unit instead of the MEPS. The following table outlines the procedure for each reserve branch. I must reiterate that policy and processes do change, so confirm the current procedures with your recruiter.

PROCEDURE PERFORMED AT MEPS

	Job Search	Oath of Enlistment
Air Force Reserve	No	No
Air National Guard	No	No
Army Reserve	Yes	No
Army National Guard	No	Yes
Coast Guard Reserve	No	Yes
Marine Reserve	No	Yes
Navy Reserve	No	No

Now What?

Once you've completed your oath of enlistment, you should be done for the day. It'll probably be late afternoon by then. You will return to your MEPS liaison, who will ensure that you have all the proper paperwork, and then you will be sent on your way. More than likely, you will be using the same form of transportation that you took to the MEPS; check with the MEPS liaison in case there's a change in plans.

If your recruiter is not picking you up at the MEPS and hasn't given you any other instructions, I suggest you phone him or her the next day if you haven't heard from him or her. Make sure that the information you received at the MEPS agrees with the information he or she was given. This includes:

- the job you received;
- the length of enlistment;
- ship date (the date you leave for Basic Training);
- amount of any enlistment bonus; and
- the pay grade or rank you were promised.

If for some reason the information does not match, take care of it immediately! Do not put off getting it taken care of, and do not allow your recruiter to put it off. If your recruiter does put it off, contact the MEPS liaison immediately (he or she should have given you his or her card during your MEPS processing). If it's not on the contract you received from the MEPS, it hasn't been promised to you. So, if you met the qualifications to enter the military as an E-2 and the MEPS liaison told you that you'll receive E-2, but for some reason it was left out of the contract, it needs to be fixed immediately. If your recruiter says, "They'll take care of it when you leave for Basic Training," he or she is 100 percent mistaken. The same goes for any discrepancies in your contract.

You will be required to keep in regular contact with your recruiter during the time you spend in DEP status (more about this in Chapter 6).

As I mentioned in the beginning of this chapter, the MEPS is in no way representative of military life. By now you have realized that I like to compare the enlistment processing to buying a car, and the MEPS is one case where it is completely the opposite. When you walk into a car dealership to purchase a car, usually the employees treat you well and everyone is willing to bend over backward to help you. It isn't until after the sale is made and you have to come back to have your car serviced that you are ignored and treated rudely. If you view the military applicant as a customer, just the opposite happens at the MEPS. The whole attitude changes once you've taken the oath of enlistment. It is then that you are officially a member of the "team" and will be treated as such. Before then, you are an outsider trying to gain membership and, of course, have to meet the membership requirements.

I don't want to give the impression that the MEPS personnel are all mean-spirited people who have nothing better to do than make your life miserable. However, most applicants have never been through an experience like MEPS processing, and to them their day at the MEPS will be one experience they most likely will never forget.

In addition to reading this chapter on MEPS processing and watching the video, "A Day at the MEPS," you should ask your recruiter questions about anything you are not 100 percent clear about, such as:

- How am I getting to the MEPS for processing and then home afterward?
- Will I be required to take additional tests at the MEPS?
- What time will the recruiter pick me up, or what time do I need to be at the MEPS?
- Will I be staying at a hotel overnight?
- Do I need to bring any medical records with me?

Dos and Don'ts

I would like to close this chapter with a few dos and don'ts concerning MEPS processing. Your recruiter hopefully should have discussed the following "rules" of the MEPS with you; if he or she did, then consider this a reminder. In most cases, not complying with these rules will result in the termination of your MEPS processing. Follow these rules:

- Bring your Social Security card, birth certificate, and driver's license.
- Remove earrings before going to the MEPS.
- Do not use profane or offensive language or have any offensive pictures or wording on your clothing.
- Do not wear a hat; they are not permitted inside the MEPS.
- If you wear either eyeglasses or contacts, bring them, along with your prescription and lens case.
- Bathe or shower either the morning of or the night before your processing.
- Wear clean underclothes.
- Wear neat, moderate, comfortable clothing.
- Don't bring stereo headphones, watches, jewelry, excessive cash, or any other valuables.
- Conduct yourself properly; don't use profanity and be polite.
- Report on time.

Chapter Summary

Now that you've made it over the biggest hurdle of the enlistment process, the MEPS, you'll want to make certain that nothing gets in your way before leaving for Basic Training. The next chapter helps prepare you to maintain your qualification to enter the military.

PART TWO

WHAT TO EXPECT AFTER ENLISTMENT

6 CONGRATULATIONS! YOU'VE ENLISTED: STAYING OUT OF TROUBLE UNTIL YOU'RE OFF TO BASIC TRAINING

Most applicants wind up in a Delayed Enlistment Program (DEP). In this status, the applicant has already sworn in and is awaiting his or her "ship date" to Basic Training. As an enlistee, you can remain in DEP status for up to a year. A lot can happen between the day you swear in and the day you ship. In this chapter, I discuss avoiding certain things, keeping in shape, and keeping the recruiter informed.

The Delayed Enlistment Program

Now that you have taken the oath of enlistment, you are no longer an applicant and but DEPer (pronounced *depper*). As a member of the Delayed Enlistment Program (DEP), you are technically a member of the military. You have taken an oath of enlistment and are therefore bound to maintain yourself physically, mentally, and morally.

Although you have already sworn in once, you will have to swear in one more time on the day you leave for Basic Training. However, there are many things that may stand in your way of getting to swear in that second time:

- medical problems that may arise, including injuries
- law violations (including traffic violations)
- weight gain that puts you over the maximum allowable weight (MAW)
- not graduating from high school (for those who enlisted as high school seniors)
- becoming pregnant while in the DEP
- becoming involved in a pending lawsuit
- drug usage while in the DEP

Although some of these disqualifiers may be out of the DEPer's control, you can avoid the majority of them.

Medical Problems

Although you cannot avoid most medical problems, you can avoid some. For instance, if you've never skydived before, don't wait until you are in the DEP to try it. A broken leg takes time to heal, and if you wind up having pins in your leg, you've just permanently disqualified yourself. On the other hand, you cannot avoid an emergency appendectomy.

In most cases, medical problems that arise while in the DEP are temporarily, rather than permanently, disqualifying. Many times, the military can postpone your "ship date" to accommodate the necessary healing period. However, remember that you can only remain in a DEP status for 365 days. Therefore, if the required healing period would put you over the maximum 365 days, the military will discharge you from the DEP. If this happens, you will be required to swear in to the DEP again once your condition has healed. More than likely, you will have also lost your job reservation and must go through the job counseling process again as well.

Another situation that may occur is the need for a medical waiver. Just as certain conditions require waiver approval for initial enlistment processing, those same conditions would require a waiver if they occur while you are in the DEP. The military may grant you a waiver and, depending on the reason for the waiver, may preclude you from working at certain jobs.

The key to ensuring that you will not encounter problems when it is time to "ship" to Basic Training is keeping your recruiter informed. If you were treated for pneumonia, for instance, don't wait six months—when it is time to leave for Basic Training—to tell your recruiter. Let him or her know as soon as possible so that he or she may take the necessary actions. He or she may require you to provide medical records or have tests performed before you are cleared for enlistment. In addition, you may be required to return to the MEPS for further evaluation. If you let your recruiter know early enough, it may not affect your original "ship" date. If you wait, you may find that you will be delayed by months.

KEEPING YOURSELF HEALTHY

To increase your chances of staying healthy while in the DEP, avoid any activity that may result in serious injury, such as skydiving. Also, avoid situations that may expose you to disease. For instance, if your little brother has measles, and you've never had them before, you should avoid contact with him. Maintain a healthy diet and exercise regularly; this will keep you in good shape and make you less susceptible to illness. Also, use common sense in your activities, use the appropriate protective gear when playing sports, wear a helmet while bicycling, use your car's seat belts, and, most of all, don't take risks with your personal safety.

Law Violations

Law violations keep many people from shipping to Basic Training and are perhaps the most easily avoided way to get disqualified while in the DEP.

A law violation as simple as a minor traffic ticket can disqualify you from enlistment, especially if you already have an enlistment waiver for previous law violations. Law violations while in the DEP may also make it necessary for you to obtain a waiver before enlistment. The course of action depends on the severity of the violation and on your history. For instance, if you had no history of previous law violations and receive a ticket for running a stop sign, your recruiter would more than likely just have you mention it at the MEPS before you swear for Active Duty. If, however, it was a more serious violation, he or she may have to initiate the waiver process.

As with medical problems, it is important that you let your recruiter know as soon as possible of any law violations that have occurred while you are in the DEP. If you fail to tell him or her, you may find yourself leaving the MEPS bound for home instead of Basic Training on ship day.

AVOIDING PROBLEMS

Although some law violations occur accidentally, such as absentmindedly changing lanes without signaling, most do not. Therefore, drive as if there is always a police car in your rearview mirror.

In addition to traffic violations, avoid committing other crimes as well. Shoplifting, fighting, and underage drinking will get you into trouble. Of course, more serious crimes also will cause problems for you and may permanently disqualify you from military service. Most important, if you are under twenty-one, don't consume alcohol. Sadly, many DEPers are charged with underage drinking while attending their own going-away parties.

PAYING FINES

If you find yourself in a situation that requires you to pay a fine, make sure that you pay the fine promptly. Unpaid fines will keep you from going to Basic Training. When I decided to enlist in the military, I had just received a traffic ticket (my first, but sadly not my last) and determined that I would go to court rather than pay the fine because I knew that I was not guilty. My recruiter put it this way, "Pay the fine, and you can leave for Basic Training, or you can wait and go to court, where you'll probably be found guilty anyway and have to pay the fine." I paid the fine.

WHAT IF I'M PERMANENTLY DISQUALIFIED?

If you find yourself permanently disqualified from enlisting based on law violations while in the DEP, you may still have a chance of getting into the military, depending on the severity of the violation. Although all the military branches have similar standards, they are not the same. Therefore, if you get discharged from the DEP, talk to the recruiters of the other branches and see what they can do for you. You may find that one service may waiver something another service can or will not.

Weight Gain

If you gain weight while in the DEP and wind up exceeding the maximum allowable weight (MAW) for your height, you really have only two choices: you can lose the weight or you can grow a few inches. Because you don't have much control over your height, the only solution is to lose the weight.

Because most people who end up exceeding their MAW while in DEP were close to the maximum weight when they went into the DEP, most recruiters will keep closer tabs on those individuals to ensure they stay within the standard. However, it is up to you, not your recruiter, to watch your weight. Maintaining a healthy diet and sticking to a regular exercise program will go a long way toward helping you remain within weight standards. Avoid overeating, and despite what your mother tells you, it's okay to leave some food on your plate.

Check your weight regularly, and use your recruiter's scale when you can. If you find you have gained weight and are either over or close to the MAW, let your recruiter know. Ideally, you should be seeing your recruiter from time-to-time while you are in the DEP, and he or she should be checking your weight regularly. If he or she doesn't, you need to let him or her know about your problem. If you arrive at the MEPS to ship and you are overweight, you will find yourself embarrassed and on your way back home instead of on your way to Basic Training.

To get an idea of the maximum (and minimum) allowable weights for your height and gender, review the following chart. Although it is a generic chart, all the services are more or less the same when it comes to weight standards.

TYPICAL MILITARY WEIGHT STANDARDS

(Please note that the Air Force now has a single chart, and requirements, for males and females.)

Height (in inches)	MALE		FEMALE	
	Minimum Weight	Maximum Weight	Minimum Weight	Maximum Weight
58	98	149	88	132
59	99	151	90	134
60	100	153	92	136
61	102	155	95	138
62	103	158	97	141
63	104	160	100	142
64	105	164	103	146
65	106	169	106	150
66	107	174	108	155
67	111	179	111	159
68	115	184	114	164
69	119	189	117	168
70	123	194	119	173
71	127	199	122	177

Height (in inches)	MALE		FEMALE	
	Minimum Weight	Maximum Weight	Minimum Weight	Maximum Weight
72	131	205	125	182
73	135	211	128	188
74	139	218	130	194
75	143	224	133	199
76	147	230	136	205
77	151	236	139	210
78	153	242	141	215
79	157	248	144	221
80	161	254	147	226

Note: Fractions of an inch are rounded to the closest inch.

Failure to Graduate from High School

Although some of the branches may take a non-high school graduate, depending on the Armed Services Vocational Aptitude Battery (ASVAB) scores, I recommend that you complete high school prior to enlisting, even if it means that you must be discharged from the DEP to do it. One reason for this recommendation is that non-graduates usually are not qualified to receive the same educational benefits that are afforded high school graduates. If the educational benefits were one of your motivators for enlisting, it becomes a nonissue if you fail to graduate from high school.

A recruiter who pressures you into enlisting without a high school diploma has only one person's best interests in mind, and I can assure you it's not yours!

If you enlisted as a high school senior and then fail to graduate, you may be able to remain in the DEP if you can complete summer school and then graduate. If that is not possible, you'll be discharged from the DEP and may go back into the DEP, depending on your chances of graduating the next school year.

AVOIDING PROBLEMS

You can avoid problems by doing your best in school, by not cutting classes, and by ensuring that you are taking enough classes to graduate. Get actively involved in your class schedule; do not assume that your guidance counselor will take care of you. If you are having problems in a particular subject, get help. Ask your teacher what you can do to improve your grades, and seek one-on-one tutoring if necessary. Inform your recruiter as soon as possible if there is a chance that you will not graduate so that he or she can determine the proper course of action.

Pregnancy While in DEP

Becoming pregnant while in DEP (a situation that happens all too often) will, of course, disqualify you for enlistment.

Terminating a pregnancy while in the DEP will require medical documentation and review by the MEPS physicians. Although some women try to conceal that they have terminated a pregnancy, it can easily be detected when you return to the MEPS for shipping to Basic Training. Once again, the key is to keep your recruiter informed. Of course, there are ways to prevent this situation from happening, but it is not the intent of this book to discuss the various methods of preventing unwanted pregnancy.

Although male DEPers do not have to worry about becoming pregnant while in the DEP, there is a chance that they may be the father in a paternity case, which will, in fact, disqualify them for enlistment.

Pending Lawsuits

There is not much that I can say about pending lawsuits other than if you become involved in one, you will become temporarily disqualified for enlistment. This applies to you not only if you have been named in a suit, but also if you are bringing the suit against someone else.

All you can do to protect yourself is to ensure that you are able to settle any matters without the need to go to court. If someone threatens to sue you, take him or her seriously and try to settle things before he or she files a lawsuit against you.

If you are the one threatening a lawsuit, consider bringing suit at a later date, because there is nothing barring you from initiating a lawsuit as a military member. Just ensure that there is no statute of limitations.

If you must go to court as a member of the DEP, try to get matters handled as quickly as possible. Ask for an early court date, if possible, and if an attorney is representing you, let him or her know of your situation.

If all else fails, you may need to be discharged from the DEP or have your ship date postponed. Whatever the case, let your recruiter know of a pending lawsuit as soon as possible so that he or she may determine a course of action.

Drug Use

If you want the military to discharge you from the DEP and probably be barred from enlisting again, then taking illegal drugs is the easiest way to do it. Drug use of any type is not acceptable in the DEP or on Active Duty, no matter what the circumstances.

Although not probable, you may be granted a waiver for drug use while in the DEP. More than likely, however, the military will discharge you from the DEP and permanently disqualify you.

Some branches of the service are more lenient than others, so it is possible that if one branch discharges you, another branch may be willing to grant you an enlistment waiver. There are no second chances, however, and after a branch grants you a waiver, if there is a "next time," it will be your last.

AVOIDING PROBLEMS

Because there is zero tolerance for drug use in all the military branches, you will be required to remain drug-free throughout your enlistment. If that is going to be a problem for you, then the military is not the place for you. If, however, you are not a drug user but your peers try to pressure you to use drugs while in DEP, I have one thing to say: **don't!**

You will be required to undergo drug testing before leaving for Basic Training, and because certain drugs can remain in your system for a while, there is a good chance they will show up in the drug screening. The bottom line is that you should not use illegal drugs while in the DEP, and, if you do, you must tell your recruiter.

What If I Keep My Mouth Shut?

Many people believe that they can beat the system by withholding information, whether about a medical problem, a law violation, or drug use. The truth is, many of these people do "cheat" the system and become members of the military despite problems they had while in the DEP.

One thing these people can and should count on, however, is that these problems have a good chance of catching up with them after they have become military members, whether it is disclosed during a background check, a routine physical examination, or a drug screening. The only difference is that if they had disclosed the information while in the DEP, the worst that would have happened would have been a discharge from the DEP. As members of the military, they are accountable under the Uniform Code of Military Justice (UCMJ), which can impose jail time, fines, and, of course, discharge under less-than-honorable conditions.

This section covered many of the potential problems that may occur while in the DEP that might keep a DEPer from going to Basic Training. Of course, I cannot address all situations; however, a good rule of thumb is that if you have contact with a doctor, a lawyer, a judge, the police, or drugs, you should contact your recruiter for guidance.

If your recruiter tells you to forget about it, ask him or her if it would be okay to reveal the information at the MEPS when you leave for Basic Training. If he or she says no, tell him or her that you are uncomfortable with concealing the information.

Getting Yourself Physically Conditioned for Basic Training

Although you may already be in good shape, chances are you could use a little help in preparing yourself physically for Basic Training. If you already maintain a rigorous workout routine, you can skip this section. However, if you are like most people, you'll want to read this section and put it into practice.

You'll want to get started early on conditioning yourself for Basic Training. Don't wait for the last minute to start exercising. It will be significantly less stressful for you to show up for Basic Training in good shape. You will be able to concentrate on the other aspects of Basic Training rather than worrying about whether you'll make the run or be able to do enough push-ups.

When you arrive at Basic Training, there will be minimum physical requirements that you must meet. Most people in reasonable shape can meet those requirements. With time, those requirements become more and more difficult.

This is the way you should work your exercise program: start slowly, and work your way up to a more stringent and demanding workout. You may have to modify your program depending on your current level of fitness and how much time you have until you leave for Basic Training.

At a minimum, you should work on:

- running;
- push-ups;
- sit-ups; and
- pull-ups.

RUNNING

You will do a lot of running in Basic Training. If you are not a runner now, you may begin by walking, which can progress into a jog and, finally, running. At first, you should strive for distance instead of speed. Although you will have to complete timed runs during Basic Training, it is important for you to build endurance.

Before you begin to run, you should buy a good pair of well-fitting running shoes. Running in shoes not designed for that purpose is a good way to cause discomfort, pain, and injury.

The best way to start running is to run with a partner, especially if that person regularly runs. Having someone with whom to run can push you along and will help you build the necessary endurance. If you are in high school or college, join the track or cross-country team. This is a good way for you to get the necessary practice.

You should use a track for running, if available. Running in the street poses many dangers, such as being struck by a vehicle, twisting your ankle or falling on uneven pavement, and, of course, getting chased by the occasional unfriendly dog. Although you could use a treadmill if the weather doesn't permit running outside you should not use it as a substitute for running on a track—they are just not the same thing.

You should plan on running about three times a week and gradually work up to the distance and time requirements for your particular branch of service you can find these in the next chapter.

PUSH-UPS

No doubt you will hear the following phrase more times than you could ever imagine while at Basic Training: "Get down and give me twenty!" That "twenty," of course, refers to twenty push-ups. Besides a form of exercise, the military uses push-ups as a form of punishment at Basic Training. Therefore, you will be required to do many push-ups in your short stay at Basic Training.

If you've never done push-ups, you should seek the help of someone who has, including gym teachers, if you are in high school; trainers at the health club; your recruiter; or friends. The key to doing more push-ups is practice. The more you practice, the more push-ups you will be able to do. It's that simple!

You should consult the next chapter for the minimum number of push-ups you'll have to do at Basic Training. Then shoot for doubling that number.

SIT-UPS

As with push-ups, you can significantly increase the number of sit-ups you can do by simple repetition. The more you practice, the more sit-ups you'll be able to do.

Do your sit-ups with a partner holding your feet down. Besides keeping you steady, your partner can help motivate you to do more sit-ups. Do as many sit-ups as you can, and then do five more!

Sit-ups have the added benefit of tightening the abdominal muscles. More than likely, you will be sore at first from doing sit-ups; therefore, you should alternate days between sit-ups.

PULL-UPS

Perhaps the most difficult exercise for most people, pull-ups will only become easier with practice.

When I went to Officer Training School (OTS) at age twenty-six, I had not done a single pull-up in at least eight years. To say it was difficult for me to do the required four pull-ups would be an understatement. However, at the end of the twelve weeks of OTS, after many hours of practice, I was doing many more than the minimum amount of pull-ups.

As with push-ups and sit-ups, the key to doing more pull-ups is practice, and as with sit-ups, the use of a partner to motivate you will help you achieve your desired goal. Besides offering verbal encouragement, you may want your partner to help support your legs while doing the pull-ups. To do this, bend your legs at the knees, and have your partner hold the bottom part of your legs and give you a little support. Do not have your partner do all the work for you, but instead have him or her give you an added boost.

You will find that, over time, you will be able to do many more pull-ups than you ever imagined.

Joining a Gym or Health Club

If you have the resources and the time, you may consider joining a local gym and doing your workouts there. Besides having a great deal of equipment, most gyms have trainers who are available for advice, guidance, encouragement, and instruction. If you cannot afford a health club membership, consider the local YMCA/YWCA, or if you are a high school student, consider asking your gym teacher for help and advice.

Wherever you do your workout, make sure that you maintain a routine of at least three days per week. The sooner you start your exercise program, the more you'll be physically prepared for Basic Training.

DEP Commander's Call

Most recruiters hold a monthly meeting with all of their DEPers, usually referred to as the DEP Commander's Call. These meetings have many purposes:

- exposing DEPers to marching (known as drill at Basic Training)
- helping DEPers get into physical shape for Basic Training
- teaching DEPers military and branch-specific history
- teaching DEPers about life in the military, including military terminology and rank structure
- keeping face-to-face contact with DEPers to ensure they are staying out of "trouble"

In the absence of DEP Commander's Calls, your recruiter should be requesting a face-to-face meeting with you at least once a month. If that isn't happening, I suggest that you make it happen! Visit your recruiter every month and let him or her know what is going on. If you have been close to your MAW, jump on the scale. If you need to make your recruiter aware of other things that are happening in your life, it's the perfect opportunity to do so.

Although your recruiter is responsible for making sure that you are ready to go to Basic Training and that you have not disqualified yourself during your time in the DEP, he or she is not a babysitter. You are ultimately responsible for your own actions.

I Want Out!

What happens if you've enlisted in the DEP, and while waiting to leave for Basic Training, you've decided that maybe this wasn't such a good idea after all. The simple answer is that you tell your recruiter, and he or she will get you discharged from the DEP.

No one would, or could, hold you to a commitment to enter Active Duty. However, as discussed in Chapter 5, you should have thought long and hard about enlisting in the military, and you should think long and hard about asking to be let out of your commitment.

Are you just getting "cold feet" (like most people), or is someone pressuring you not to go? Unless you've won the state lottery, landed a six-figure job, or been offered a free ride to an Ivy League college, I suggest that you review Chapter 2 and reevaluate why you enlisted.

After you've thought about it, meet with your recruiter and give him or her the chance to answer any concerns you may have. If your main concern is the military job you received, give him or her the chance to see if he or she can offer you something else.

If you decide not to enlist, be up front with your recruiter. Don't try to avoid him or her, and don't just fail to show up on your ship day.

On the other hand, if your recruiter becomes belligerent and tells you that you can't get out of your commitment, don't argue with him or her—just tell him you want to speak with his or her supervisor. If that doesn't work, contact the MEPS and ask to speak to the MEPS Commander. I can assure you that this will get your recruiter's attention. The bottom line is this: if you don't want to go, you won't go.

Although being "DEP Discharged" probably will not affect your chances of enlisting in the future, there is a chance that it may, so take your time when deciding whether you are doing the right thing.

Chapter Summary

As you now know, getting through the enlistment process does not end at the MEPS. You may have to remain in the DEP for up to 365 days. Although there are many obstacles that may prevent you from ever getting the chance to go to Basic Training, I hope that the guidance offered in this chapter will help you to avoid them or to deal with them effectively should they arise.

By following the physical fitness program presented, you should also be better able to prepare for the rigorous requirements at Basic Training. With the aid of this chapter, hopefully you will soon be ready to leave for Basic Training. I will discuss this in the next chapter. I describe each service's Basic Training in detail so that you will have a better understanding of what occurs there without having to rely on your recruiter for his or her "version" of what it's all about.

7 BASIC TRAINING AND BEYOND

This chapter outlines the Basic Training in each military branch. You will find sample training schedules as well as basic advice for getting through boot camp.

Although it was many years ago, some of my most vivid memories of my experiences in the military are of Basic Training, or as we called it back then, "Boot Camp." I learned and experienced things in those eight weeks that I will carry with me for the rest of my life.

No matter what the five military Basic Training mission statements are, the main objective of Basic Training is to transform civilians into well-disciplined military members in a matter of weeks. Performing such a monumental task takes a lot of hard work, both mentally and physically. For most people, Basic Training ends with a parade on graduation day. For some, it ends somewhere short of graduation. It is those "horror stories" that make Basic Training probably the one biggest fear, or anxiety, for those who are contemplating a military enlistment.

Unlike the boot camp you may have heard about from your Uncle Louie or seen on television, today's Basic Training is void of the verbal and physical abuse of yesterday. All of the military branches are ensuring that all new enlistees receive fair and dignified treatment. I'm not saying that enlistees aren't yelled at (because they are); however, the vulgarity and demeaning verbal attacks that once existed are a thing of the past. There are, from time to time, incidents involving instructors who contradict the military's policies. These violations receive a lot of attention because they are investigated thoroughly, and usually end up with disciplinary action taken against those involved in the abuses. Just as there are police officers who abuse their powers, there are Basic Training instructors who do the same. Luckily, however, they are few and far between.

I have divided this chapter by military branch. If you've already decided on a particular branch of the military, you might want to read only that section. However, I suggest that you at least skim through the other sections for some insight into the other military branches.

If you are still uncertain of which branch you'd like to join, I caution you to not allow what you read in this chapter to be your deciding factor. If, for example, the Marine Corps meets all your needs and is clearly your first choice, do not select the Air Force because its Basic Training seems easier. Conversely, if the Air Force is clearly your first choice, do not select the Marine Corps because it has the "toughest" Basic Training and you want to prove you are up to the challenge. Basic Training is a means to transform you from civilian life to military life. It happens in a relatively short time compared to the entire length of your enlistment. Do not base your choice of which branch to enter based on its Basic Training curriculum.

Some Words on Getting Through Basic Training

No matter what you may have heard or read elsewhere, there are no secrets to getting through Basic Training; only common sense and preparation will get you through. Here are some dos and don'ts that should help you survive Basic Training for any of the services.

Although following these guidelines will not ensure your success at Basic Training, your chances for success will be improved greatly by following them.

AUTHOR'S NOTE

After the release of the first edition of this book, I received an e-mail from someone who read it before joining the military. He wanted to let me know that the curriculum in the book did not exactly match the Basic Training curriculum. More specifically, he was not physically prepared to meet the time limits for the two-mile run. Please keep in mind that this book is a guide and everything is subject to change. It is important that you heed the advice in Chapter 6 regarding being conditioned physically for Basic Training. You should strive to arrive at Basic Training able to meet the initial physical requirements, and above all, check with your recruiter for any changes in the Basic Training curriculum.

BEFORE ARRIVING AT BASIC TRAINING

Do:

- start an exercise program before going to Basic Training;
- maintain a sensible diet;
- stay out of trouble (pay any traffic fines promptly before leaving for Basic Training);
- ensure that all of your financial obligations are in order;
- if you are married, ensure that your spouse has "Power of Attorney";
- bring the required items listed in the chart later in this chapter; and
- give up smoking!

Do Not:

- skip preparing yourself physically because you think that Basic Training will whip you into shape;
- abuse drugs and/or alcohol;
- have a big send-off party and get drunk the night before you leave for Basic Training;

- leave home with open tickets, summonses, warrants, etc.;
- get yourself into heavy debt (such as buying a new car because now you'll be making some serious money);
- bring any prohibited items listed in the chart later in this chapter;
- have your hair cut in a radical manner (this includes having your head shaved; men will receive a "very close" haircut shortly after arriving to Basic Training); and
- have any part of your body pierced, tattooed, or otherwise tainted.

I mention open law violations for a particular reason. Although some of the don'ts—such as body piercing and high blood alcohol content—can be detected at the MEPS and, in all likelihood, will keep you from ever going to Basic Training, open law violations could take weeks to uncover. There is nothing worse than getting through Basic Training only to be called in right before graduation and told that you have been eliminated from training and will be sent home.

FINANCIAL REQUIREMENTS

All military branches require that your pay be directly deposited to your checking account. Therefore, you must set-up a checking account and have a debit card before leaving for Basic Training. Ensure that you bring both your checks and debit card with you to Basic Training. Check with your recruiter for exact requirements.

ONCE YOU ARE AT BASIC TRAINING

Do:

- follow all instructions;
- speak up when called to do so;
- maintain a positive attitude (remember: Basic Training won't last forever);
- keep yourself well groomed;
- be a team player;
- look out for others;
- write home often;
- keep going to religious services (or think about going if you haven't been); and
- study course material.

Do Not:

- question authority;
- voice your opinion;
- assume you know everything (this is particularly important for those who were in high school Junior ROTC, the sea cadets, etc.);
- consider yourself better than anyone else (sure, you may have scored higher on the ASVAB and graduated high school with a 3.9 GPA, but that means nothing here; doing your best at Basic Training is all that counts);
- look for ways to cheat the system; and
- lose sight of why you came to Basic Training.

General Information About Basic Training

The information presented in this section pertains to all services' Basic Training. You may or may not hear about this information from your recruiter.

LIVING QUARTERS

In the movie *Private Benjamin*, the main character arrives at Basic Training to find that there is a terrible mistake. She is at the wrong boot camp—she signed up "for the Basic Training with the private condos and the swimming pools." She immediately finds out the truth about living conditions at boot camp. Although there may be swimming pools there, they are not for leisurely swims and sunbathing, and the living quarters are hardly private condos.

Although Basic Training recruits live in open barracks, each of which is composed of one large room, these rooms called dorms or barracks are, of course, segregated by gender. Each recruit sleeps in a single bed (in some cases, bunk beds are used) and is assigned a locker in which to store his or her belongings. It is the recruit's responsibility to keep his or her bed made and maintain his or her locker. Recruits learn how to fold their clothes and how to store their belongings, and they are expected to keep their locker exactly as instructed.

Bathroom and shower facilities are communal, similar to those found at the average high school gym. Recruits must get ready quickly in the morning and are allowed a short amount of time to take care of "business" in the bathroom (latrine or head, depending on the branch of service). If you are the type of person who likes to take long showers, you will not be doing that in Basic Training. One habit you will pick up, however, (again in no time) is cleaning up after yourself, because recruits are responsible for maintaining the cleanliness of the communal bathroom.

MEALS

When I graduated from high school, I weighed 138 pounds. As much as I tried to gain weight, I just couldn't do it. Shortly after graduation, I enlisted in the Navy and was off to boot camp in San Diego, California. In December, I graduated from Basic Training at 160 pounds! Although a lot of people lose weight at Basic Training, some gain weight, partly because of muscle gain and partly because of the three nutritious meals they eat every day.

Unlike in high school, when I never had time for breakfast, skipped lunch sometimes, and ate dinner on the run, meals at Basic Training were mandatory. At the same time each day, we would march to the chow hall and have our trays filled with food. It certainly wasn't home-style cooking, but it wasn't like fast food either; and it was edible and, at times, even good.

Unfortunately, the military does not offer special meals based on its recruits' dietary needs. Therefore, if you are a vegetarian, for example, you will have to eat everything except the meat—there will be no soy-based meat substitute foods. If you are a Muslim and have to avoid pork products or if you must eat only kosher foods, I can offer no suggestions.

One last comment about the meals at Basic Training: You'll be given little time to eat; meals are more inhaled than eaten. You'll be given approximately ten minutes for each meal.

OFF-DUTY TIME

Each branch of service allows its recruits some personal time each day. However, you will spend that time at the Basic Training facility. In most cases, you can not leave the Basic Training grounds until graduation.

Branch-Specific Information

The next sections are in alphabetical order by service branch. As I have mentioned, things change from time-to-time, and I have made every effort to keep up with those changes. However, this chapter is just a guide to Basic Training; you should not use it as a substitute for information given to you by your recruiter or information updated on official Basic Training websites.

Each of the following sections differs slightly in the detail of information. This is because each military branch has provided the information it believes is important for prospective recruits. In some cases, information comes from outside sources to help you see a more complete picture.

Air Force

BASIC MILITARY TRAINING (BMT)

In addition to the information contained in this section, there are two very useful resources to get you ready for Basic Training:

- The "Air Force Airman Fundamentals" app for i-Phone and Android smart phones not only contains information about Basic Training, it also contains videos to help you prepare physically. It is available for download free of charge.
- AFPAM 10-100 "Airman's Manual" is issued to all Airmen and is the A-Z guide to serving in the Air Force. It is available for free download as a PDF document at: http://static.e-publishing. af.mil/production/1/af_a3_5/publication/afpam10-100/afpam10-100.pdf.

There is one certainty you can count on if you decide to join the Air Force (including the Air Force Reserve or Air National Guard)—you will spend at least 8½ weeks in beautiful San Antonio, Texas!

The Air Force's only location for Basic Military Training (BMT), Lackland Air Force Base, has a long history of training some of the finest men and women ever to wear a military uniform. Each year, approximately 35,000 new enlistees enter through this "Gateway to the Air Force." Because policies and procedures change from time to time, you'll want to check with your recruiter to ensure the currency of the material presented in this section.

Temperatures in San Antonio range from mild to sizzling. Average daytime summer temperatures are in the 90s and mid-70s at night. Winter is a little cooler, with daytime temperatures in the 70s and nights in the 50s.

Recruits checking in at military reception at the San Antonio airport.

CURRICULUM OVERVIEW

On arrival at BMT, you will enter a Flight. A *Flight* is the smallest group of trainees; a group of Flights makes up a squadron. Every Flight is overseen by several Military Training Instructors (MTIs). Their sole purpose is to get you through BMT or to ensure that those not suited for service in the Air Force are identified. Your MTI will become your mentor, your friend, and, at times, seemingly, your enemy. Remember, though, that one of the "dos" to getting through BMT is to follow all of the instructions given to you. If you follow that one bit of advice, your experiences with your MTI will be a lot more pleasurable.

Following is an overview of what you can expect at BMT; you will find more detail later in this section.

BASIC MILITARY TRAINING CURRICULUM

Period	Activities
Zero Week: Orientation	In processing
	Haircuts
	Learn reporting statement
	Flight assignment
	Clothing and equipment issue
	Dorm and drill basics
	Individual duty assignment
	Entry control procedures
WEEK 1	Reporting and saluting
	Medical and dental appointments
	Fitness and nutrition
	Educational benefits briefing (MGIB/Post-9/11)
	ID card issue
	Individual drill
	Flight drill
	Dorm preparation
	Warrior role
	Law of armed conflict
	Chain of command
	Air Force rank insignia
	Weapon issue
	Weapon parts identification
	Human relations and cultural sensitivity
WEEK 2	Career guidance
	Weapon handling and maintenance
	Integrated defense
	Cover and concealment
	Tactical movement
	Firing positions
	FPCON (Force Protection Conditions)
	Defensive fighting positions
	SALUTE (Size/Activities/Location/Unit ID/Time/ Equipment) reporting
	Challenge procedures

Period	Activities
WEEK 3	SABC (Self Aid/Buddy Care) under fire
	Bleeding control
	Bandages and dressings
	Combat application tourniquet
	Blood clotting agents
	Splint fractures
	Internal bleeding
	Burn treatments
	Shock management
	Airway management
	Spinal injury
	Interview sessions
WEEK 4	CBRNE/chamber training
	Anti-terrorism/Force protection level I
	Cyber training
	Security programs
	Obstacle course
	Weapons evaluation (breakdown and assembly)
	Second clothing issue
	Dress and appearance (service uniform)
WEEK 5	Introduction to the Code of Conduct
	TEMPER (Tent Extensible Modular Personal) tents
	CPR
	CATM (Combat Arms Training and Maintenance)
	Mental preparation for combat
	Pugil stick application
	Basic leadership
	Basic situational awareness
	AEF (Air Expeditionary Force) prep
	Public relations
	Joint warfare
WEEK 6	SERE (Survival Evasion Resistance Escape)
	Deployment briefing
	Basic Expeditionary Airman Skills Training (BEAST)
WEEK 7	Air Force history
	Combat stress recovery
	Sexual assault prevention and reporting

Period	Activities
	Suicide awareness and prevention
	Financial management
	Sexually transmitted diseases
	Ethics
	Evaluation of drill, reporting, and courtesies
	PT (Physical Training) evaluation
	Written test
WEEK 8	Airmanship and core values
	Formal retreat/Airman's coin ceremony
	Haircuts
	Technical school briefing
	Commanders departure briefing
	Town pass briefing
	Graduation

In addition to the topics listed, you will participate in daily physical conditioning, periods of dorm cleanup, and individual study time. It all seems like a lot to cram into an 8½ week period, but don't worry—you'll have plenty of time, because your day will start at 5 a.m.!

ARRIVAL AT BMT

The BMT experience will begin with your arrival at the San Antonio International Airport. Once you've collected any luggage that you checked in, you'll report to the Air Force Receiving Station. Be sure to have a copy of your orders, which were given to you at the MEPS, ready to turn over to the MTI who greets you.

Next, you'll learn one of BMT's most notable sayings, "hurry up and wait," as you are directed to sit and wait for the bus that will take you on the hour-long ride to BMT. Because people will be arriving from all parts of the country, flight arrival times are varied, and you must wait until everyone arrives. Your official "in-processing" begins on your arrival at the Shipping and Receiving Center. With the preliminary processing completed, you'll get back on a bus and head for your dormitory.

Expect the orders to begin at the Shipping and Receiving Center. You will be told where to stand and how to stand, where to sit, and how to sit. In all likelihood, you will be chastised for something you did, or didn't, do. It will be during the time you spend in the Shipping and Receiving Center that you will ask yourself for the first time, "What did I get myself into?" Don't worry—everyone who has come before you and everyone who will come after goes through the same moment of doubt. Just remember the reasons why you joined the Air Force in the first place.

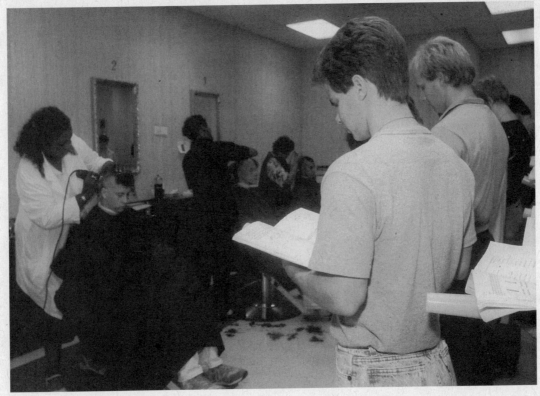

The first of many haircuts!

RESTRUCTURING OF BASIC TRAINING

In the past, Basic Training in the Air Force may have been referred to as, "the gentleman's boot, camp," in other words, it was the least physically challenging of all the services' Basic Training. Whether or not that was true for the BMT of the past, it is certainly not true of today's Air Force Basic Military Training. In November of 2005, besides being lengthened from six to 8½ weeks, Air Force Basic Training now focuses on the deployed, "Warrior," Airman. The 8½ weeks are split into three phases: Pre-Deployment, Deployment, and Post-Deployment. The first five weeks of training will focus on building those warrior skills, which will include intensive M-16 training and training hand-to-hand combat and pugil stick training, culminating in the week-six exercise, The Beast, which will be discussed later in this section.

Physical conditioning is a way of life at BMT.

PHYSICAL CONDITIONING

You will receive physical conditioning at least six times per week throughout your entire stay. Physical conditioning consists of running, stretching exercises, and circuit training, which includes deltoid lifts, bicep curls, tricep extensions, and other exercises.

In addition to your weekly physical conditioning schedule, you will have to pass a physical fitness test based on the criteria outlined below.

PHYSICAL FITNESS REQUIREMENTS

	1.5 Mile Run	Sit-ups	Push-ups
Males			
<30	11.57	42	33
30-39	11.57	39	27
Females			
<30	14.26	38	18
30-39	14.26	29	14

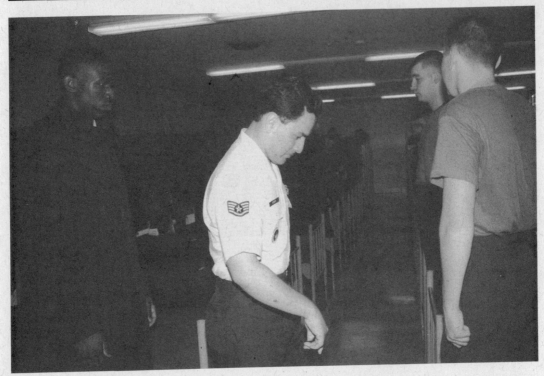

Dormitory inspection.

DAILY ROUTINE

You will be kept busy throughout your 8½ week stay at BMT;. there will be many activities. You will spend much of your time in classroom instruction studying topics such as military customs and courtesies, Air Force history, how to wear the Air Force uniform, and identifying military ranks. Some of the special topics covered include:

- Sexual Harassment—The Air Force has a zero-tolerance policy regarding sexual harassment.
- Religious Freedom—There is zero tolerance of discrimination based on religious beliefs and preference. In fact, you will be encouraged to attend the religious services of your choice while at BMT.

  The following religious services are offered:
  - Protestant
  - Roman Catholic
  - Eastern Orthodox
  - Jewish
  - Other: Muslim, Eckanar, Wicca, Baha'I, NSA Buddhist

DRILL

Your primary (well, your only) mode of transportation at BMT will be marching. You will begin to learn how to march even before you receive your uniform. From then on, you must know all aspects of *drill*. If you have had experience in Junior ROTC or similar organizations, you will have a distinct advantage in the beginning. However, in no time at all, everyone will learn how to drill like an expert. By the time graduation day arrives, even those who never marched before arriving at BMT will be marching with precision!

MARKSMANSHIP

One activity at BMT that some view as fun and others dread is Marksmanship Training—or, put in layman's terms, "shooting the guns." During BMT, you will be given the opportunity to fire an M-16 rifle on the firing range, but only after you have received thorough training on the safe handling of the weapon. Although individuals who have had experience dealing with firearms generally do better in this aspect of training, many people do well on the firing range after a minimum amount of instruction.

OBSTACLE COURSE

Another part of training loved by some and despised by others is the twenty-station obstacle course, known as the confidence course. This course will test your strength, stamina, willpower, and team spirit. Even though it's not dangerous, the confidence course is extremely challenging. Although completing the confidence course is an individual effort, getting through it is a team effort. You will have to support and cheer on your fellow trainees, and they may have to do the same for you.

THE BEAST

In the sixth week of Basic Training, Basic Expeditionary Airman Skills Training, or as it's better known, The Beast, is a five-day-long exercise that tests the warrior skills that you learned in the first five weeks of training. Trainees will live in a "deployed" environment and will handle scenarios they may encounter there. They will come under simulated attack and defend their position, will have to administer first-aid to "wounded" airmen, will have to identify and contain mock unexploded ordnance, and will have to negotiate a combat obstacle course. Additionally, trainees will take part in a CLAW (Creating Leader Airmen Warriors) mission. In this phase of the BEAST, trainees go on a simulated search-and-rescue mission for a downed Airman, or neutralize enemy positions.

A new airman celebrates with family after graduation.

GRADUATION

Although your last official moments as a trainee end with the graduation ceremony, there are two other significant events which precede it that are also open for your guests to observe. The first is the 2.5 mile Airman's Run, which will be your family and friends first chance to catch a glimpse of you in over eight weeks as you run by with your flight. The second is the Formal Retreat, after which you will be able to meet up with your guests. The graduation ceremony, the end of Basic Military Training, marks the beginning of your future in the Air Force. It is a proud and an emotional time for the graduates and their families. Your friends and family are welcome, and even encouraged, to attend BMT graduation. Because there is no leave between BMT and Technical Training, this may be the last chance you get to see them for a while.

Because minor things can cause setbacks in training and delay your graduation, I would suggest that anyone who is planning to fly in for graduation wait as long as possible before locking him- or herself into nonrefundable airline tickets.

SMOKING POLICY

You can not use any type of tobacco product during your entire stay at BMT. This includes, but is not limited to, cigarettes, cigars, any type of smokeless tobacco, and pipes. If you currently use any tobacco products, I recommend that you stop now instead of "going cold turkey" when you get to BMT. You will have enough stress adapting to military life; you don't need the added burden of nicotine withdrawal.

OTHER USEFUL INFORMATION

Here's some other information that you'll find useful before arriving at BMT.

Communication With Friends and Family

Even though your contact with the outside world will be limited during your stay at BMT, you will be able to stay in contact with friends and family members through letters and an occasional telephone call. You will be required to make contact with your family within seventy-two hours after arrival at BMT. If there is a family emergency, someone can reach you at any time.

Personal Effects

As mentioned in this chapter, there are certain items that you should bring with you to BMT and others that you should definitely leave at home. The following table lists those items. You'll be able to purchase many of the items on the "do bring list" once you reach BMT.

CLOTHING AND ACCESSORIES

Pack at least three days worth of comfortable, non-restricting civilian clothing. Do not pack or wear anything that might be unusual or draw unwanted attention.

- three to four days worth of civilian clothes*
- civilian eyeglasses
- boxers or briefs (male)
- underpants (female)
- white sports bra (female)
- hair bands, bobby pins (must be the same color as hair), etc.
- nylons/pantyhose
- simple watch

PERSONAL HYGIENE PRODUCTS

Be sure to bring only hygiene items that are easy to clean for inspection. These include: flip-top toothpaste, liquid soap dispensers, and square toothbrush trays.

- shampoo
- conditioner
- toothbrush, toothbrush tray, and toothpaste/powder
- liquid soap
- shower shoes (black)
- hairnet (female)
- deodorant
- shaving equipment
- brushes or combs
- sanitary napkins or tampons
- fingernail clippers

BANKING MATERIALS

The military requires all recruits to set up a direct deposit account. This will require a voided check to activate your account. You will need to provide:

• the name of your bank;
• your bank routing number;
• your account number; and
• your ATM card.

PAPERWORK

Make a copy of any important paperwork so you'll have backup if something is misplaced. This includes your:
• Social Security card;
• enlistment contract;
• college transcripts, Civil Air Patrol/JROTC certificates (if applicable);
• driver's license;
• Alien Card and/or naturalization certificates (if applicable); and
• marriage license and birth certificates for your dependents (if applicable).

MEDICAL MATERIALS

Bring any prescription medications in their pharmacy-issued containers with you to Basic Military Training. Once on base, a military doctor will examine your prescriptions and reissue necessary medication from the on-base pharmacy. Female recruits who are already taking birth control should continue doing so throughout the eight weeks of Basic Military Training.

OTHER ITEMS

• Social Security card (You'll need to memorize your Social Security number.)
• debit card
• contact lenses cases
• envelopes
• stationery
• stamps
• prepaid phone card
• ballpoint pen (black)
• notebook and paper
• active cell phone with charger (with minutes loaded, if pre-pay by minute phone)

THINGS NOT TO BRING

• cigarettes or tobacco of any kind
• personal running shoes
• makeup
• expensive jewelry
• food or candy
• magazines
• radio/CD/MP3 player

*Although you will not wear civilian clothes during BMT, you will wear them during technical school and your first assignment. Because you'll be leaving BMT with all of your newly issued Air Force gear, you'll want to limit the amount of civilian clothes you bring to one suitcase.

Uniform Issue

You will receive clothing items two times during Basic Military Training. You will be responsible for purchasing and maintaining all other clothing items thereafter; however, as an enlisted member of the Air Force, you will receive an annual clothing allowance. Although the clothing items you receive at BMT are of good quality, many people choose to replace these "issue" items with items of better quality and fit. You can purchase them at the Clothing Sales store on any Air Force base.

SUMMARY

I would like to close this section by, once again, saying that the information contained here is up-to-date at the time of this writing. Because things change from time-to-time, you should verify this information with your recruiter before departing for BMT. Your recruiter is required to have you view a video about BMT; in fact, you probably were asked to sign a statement indicating you have seen it. If you did not see this video, insist on seeing it as soon as possible. That being said, there are many videos available online, some excellent, some not so good. I encourage you to search for the good ones (start with airforce.com) and to download the Airman Fundamentals app. Additionally, I want to emphasize that this section gives only a glimpse into Air Force Basic Training. I could have written an entire book on the subject, but that would not be practical, and truthfully, few would read it. If nothing else, I hope that you've learned one important point, and one I can't emphasize enough; get prepared! The more prepared you are, both mentally, and physically, the easier and less stressful Basic Training will be.

Army

INITIAL ENTRY TRAINING (IET)

While this section gives you a brief look into Army Basic Training, the Army has two outstanding resources that give an incredible, in-depth, look into Basic Training, and the Army in general. If you are seriously considering the Army or have already decided to join it. I strongly encourage you to download the Army "Blue Book" app for smartphones, and download the 273-page "IET Soldier's Handbook" PDF document at: http://www.tradoc.army.mil/tpubs/pams/p600-4.pdf. If you enlist in the Army, you will go to one of five Initial Entry Training (IET) installations:

- Fort Benning, Georgia
- Fort Jackson, South Carolina
- Fort Knox, Kentucky
- Fort Leonard Wood, Missouri
- Fort Sill, Oklahoma

The Army, which is by far the largest of all the military branches, is unique because where you go for Basic Training depends on your Military Occupational Specialty (MOS). This allows the Army to train many of its soldiers at one location from Basic Training to Advanced Individual Training (AIT).

The Basic Training portion of Army IET is referred to as Basic Combat Training (BCT), whereas AIT refers to the job-specific training, which soldiers receive after completing BCT. The following table presents the specific BCT locations for each MOS category.

MILITARY OCCUPATIONAL SPECIALTIES

MOS Category	BCT Location
Infantry	Fort Benning, Georgia
Armor	Fort Knox, Kentucky
Combat Engineers	Fort Leonard Wood, Missouri
Field Artillery	Fort Sill, Oklahoma
All Others	Fort Jackson, South Carolina

Just a few words of advice (regardless of whether you want it or not): As I mentioned at the beginning of this chapter, it would be foolish for you to make a decision as to which military branch to join based solely on the Basic Training curriculum. It would also be equally foolish to choose an MOS based on the BCT location. Remember, don't make what could amount to be life-changing decisions based on where you receive nine weeks of training. If you decide the Army is the right choice for you, choose your MOS based on your needs and the factors discussed in this book.

According to the Army, IET is "the new soldier's introduction to the Army. The goal of IET is to transform civilians into technically and tactically competent soldiers." This training prepares soldiers for the Army's basic mission—to fight and win in combat. More than 75,000 men and women enter BCT every year!

The training you'll receive at BCT will be tough, challenging and, most of all, rewarding. Not everyone who enters BCT completes the training; however, those who do will go on to receive some of the finest training available anywhere.

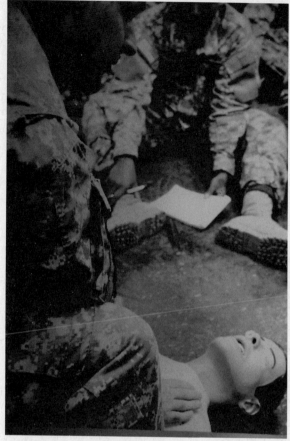

All soldiers learn CPR during Basic Training.

CURRICULUM OVERVIEW

BCT is nine weeks long and has three phases. They are referred to as the Red (Patriot), White (Gun-fighter), and Blue (Warrior) phases. The following table presents an overview of the aspects of each phase. You can find more details later in this section.

BASIC COMBAT TRAINING CURRICULUM—BY WEEK

Period	Activity
Red phase (weeks 1–2)	Begin instilling Army values
	Participate in physical training and testing
	Receive communications instruction
	Learn basic first aid

	Learn map-reading skills
	Practice drill and ceremony
	Learn military justice system
	Test skills and knowledge in phase testing
White phase (weeks 3–5)	Continue Army values training
	Improve fitness through physical training
	Learn, practice, and qualify in basic rifle marksmanship
	Tactical foot march
	Learn about chemical warfare and participate in gas chamber exercise
	Participate in bayonet training
	Negotiate obstacle course
	Test skills and knowledge in phase testing
	Engagement skills and situational training exercise
Blue phase (weeks 6–9)	Continue Army values training
	Participate in physical training
	Learn individual tactical techniques
	U.S. weapons training
	Perform 10K and 15K tactical foot marches
	Negotiate confidence course
	Execute obstacle course
	Test skills and knowledge in phase testing
	Field Training Exercise 3

Completing the low crawl portion of the obstacle course.

ARRIVAL AT BCT

Upon your arrival at BCT, your first stop will be the Reception Battalion. While there, you will:

- complete administrative and logistical processing;
- receive your first (of many) haircuts;
- receive your initial uniform issue;
- complete personnel file screening;
- complete medical screening;
- begin learning Army core values; and
- perform physical fitness screening.

You will stay at the Reception Battalion from three to fifteen days. You will not be released for BCT until you have passed a Physical Fitness Assessment composed of push-ups, sit-ups, and a one-mile run. Those not meeting physical fitness standards will go to a Fitness Training Unit (FTU) instead of proceeding directly to BCT.

You may remain in the FTU for up to four weeks. You will be released once you have successfully completed the exit criteria. This will occur if you do so before four weeks are up or, if you were unable to meet the criteria, at the end of the four weeks.

While assigned to the FTU, you will learn basic military skills, such as military knowledge, drill and ceremonies, and uniform appearance, to prepare you for BCT.

To pass the Physical Fitness Assessment, at a minimum you must meet the criteria presented in the following table:

PHYSICAL FITNESS REQUIREMENTS TO EXIT FTU

	Males	Females
Push-ups	13	3
Sit-ups	17	17
1-mile run	8 minutes 30 seconds	10 minutes 30 seconds

The following table shows an example of the physical fitness requirements necessary to graduate from Basic Training. This is an example because the Army uses a point system, with the trainee receiving points for each event. For a complete, and I mean complete, guide to becoming physically prepared for Army Basic Training, download the 118-page Army PT Guide at: www.goarmy.com/content/dam/goarmy/downloaded_assets/pt_guide/pocket_pt_guide.pdf.

SAMPLE PHYSICAL FITNESS REQUIREMENTS

Age	Gender	Push-ups*	Sit-ups*	2-Mile Run
17-21	Male	35	47	16:36
	Female	13	47	19:42
22-26	Male	31	43	17:30
	Female	11	43	20:36

* Performed in 2 minutes

Taking a break after completing the obstacle course.

Marching in formation on graduation day.

DAILY ROUTINE

You will be busy during your nine weeks at BCT. Besides the many hours you will spend involved in physical activities, you will spend countless hours in a classroom environment learning how to be a soldier. Here's an outline of a typical day at BCT:

TYPICAL DAY AT BASIC COMBAT TRAINING

Time	Activity
5:00 a.m.	Wake up
5:30 a.m.	Physical training
6:30 a.m.	Breakfast
8:30 a.m.	Training
12:00 p.m.	Lunch
1:00 p.m.	Training
5:00 p.m.	Dinner
6:00 p.m.	Drill Sergeant time
8:30 p.m.	Personal time
9:30 p.m.	Lights out

DRILL

If you learn nothing else in BCT, you'll learn to march! Besides getting soldiers from place-to-place in an orderly fashion, marching, also known as drill, helps soldiers learn coordination, teamwork, and discipline.

Those who've had some drill experience, such as in Junior ROTC, will find this aspect of training somewhat easier. However, with practice, even those with no experience will be marching like experts in no time. A word of caution to those who have JROTC (or similar) experience, do not, and I repeat, do not, utter words similar to; "but that's not how we did it in JROTC." Believe me, you will regret saying those words.

Checking targets during marksmanship training.

MARKSMANSHIP

One of the many graduation requirements for BCT is qualifying with the M-16A2 rifle. As a soldier, you must demonstrate proficiency with this weapon. Therefore, you will receive expert training on the handling, caring, and firing of this rifle.

Individuals with previous experience with firearms may find this part of BCT less challenging; however, these people, too, must learn the Army's way of handling weapons. Many individuals with no previous experience with firearms do well after receiving even minimum training.

PERSONAL TIME

Every soldier receives at least one hour of personal time each day. Although one hour may not seem like a lot, the rest of your day will be full of other activities, which you will usually do in a group setting. You will be grateful for any time that you have to yourself.

GRADUATION REQUIREMENTS AND GRADUATION DAY

There are certain minimum requirements that you must meet to graduate from BCT. The Army will do its best to prepare you to meet and perhaps exceed the requirements that are presented in the following table.

GRADUATION REQUIREMENTS FOR BCT

Qualify with the M-16A2 rifle

Complete 5K, 8K, 10K, and 15K foot marches

Pass the Army physical fitness test

Participate in buddy team live-fire exercise

Throw two live hand grenades and successfully complete the hand grenade qualification course

Negotiate the infiltration course

Pass all performance-oriented phase tests

Participate in hand-to-hand combat

Negotiate bayonet assault course and participate in pugil-stick training

Demonstrate understanding of and a willingness to live by the Army's seven core values

Negotiate all obstacles on the confidence course

Demonstrate the discipline, motivation, and adherence to Army standards of conduct of a soldier

Complete gas chamber exercise to standard

Your friends and family are welcome, and even encouraged, to attend your graduation from BCT. The graduation ceremony marks the beginning of your future in the Army. It is a proud and emotional time for the graduates, as well as their families. The Army will even grant you an off-post pass so that you may spend time with family members after the graduation ceremony. Since you will not be granted any time off between BCT and advanced training, this may be your last opportunity to see your loved ones for a while.

Because minor things can cause setbacks in training and delay your graduation, I would suggest that family members planning to fly in for graduation wait as long as possible before locking themselves into nonrefundable airline tickets.

SMOKING POLICY

You cannot use any type of tobacco products during your stay at BCT. This includes, but is not limited to, cigarettes, cigars, any type of smokeless tobacco, and pipes. If you currently use any tobacco products,

I would suggest that you stop now instead of "going cold turkey" when you get to BCT. You will have enough stress adapting to military life; you don't need the added burden of nicotine withdrawal.

Graduation parade.

RELIGIOUS WORSHIP SERVICES

Have you ever heard the expression "There are no atheists in foxholes"? To that end, the Army provides all its trainees the opportunity to attend weekly worship services. These can also be a good morale booster during BCT. Although not every religious denomination is represented, you are bound to find a service you will be comfortable attending.

OTHER USEFUL INFORMATION

Here are some other pieces of information that you'll find useful before arriving at BCT.

Communication with Friends and Family

Even though you will be extremely busy with day-to-day activities at BCT, you will be encouraged to maintain contact with your friends and family. You will be able to write regularly, and make an occasional telephone call. Take advantage of these opportunities; they will help keep your spirits up and reassure those at home that you are doing well. In the event of a family emergency, the Army will ensure that you are notified as soon as possible.

Personal Effects

As mentioned in this chapter, there are certain items that you should bring to BCT and others that would be best left at home. The following table lists the items that the Army recommends you bring . Even though the Army does not provide a list of items that should not be brought to Basic Training, the MEPS does, and that list is provided here.

WHAT TO BRING—AND NOT TO BRING—TO BCT

Bring These Items	Do NOT Bring These Items
Toothbrush/case	Guns
Toothpaste	Knives
Comb/hairbrush	Any weapons
Deodorant	Pornography
Soap/case	Tobacco products
Shampoo	Racist literature
Dental floss	Food/candy
Extra civilian clothing*	Magazines/books
Sport bras (white) (females only!)	Radio/CD/MP3 player
One pair calf-length white athletic socks	
Washcloth	
Towel	
Lock, combination or padlock	
Razor/shaving cream	

*Although you will not wear civilian clothes during BCT, you will get to wear them during technical school and your first assignment. Because you'll be leaving BCT with all of your newly issued Army gear, you'll want to limit the amount of civilian clothes you bring to BCT to one small suitcase.

SUMMARY

I would like to close this section by, once again, saying that the information contained here is up-to-date at the time of this writing. Because things change from time-to-time, you should verify this information with your recruiter before departing for Basic Combat Training.

Because "a picture is worth a thousand words" (and a video a million), I suggest that you view some of the many videos available online; begin with the videos you'll find at www.goarmy.com. Some of the videos you'll find online are excellent, others are not, but together with what you've learned from this book, you will be much better prepared to succeed in Basic Training. And, of course, don't forget those two valuable resources mentioned in the beginning of this section.

Coast Guard

The Coast Guard provides two excellent publications about Recruit Training, the first is a twenty-nine-page PDF document for download called, "Recruit Training Pocket Guide." This publication contains essential information for individuals preparing to attend Basic Training although it doesn't contain any information about physical conditioning. You can download it at: http://www.uscg.mil/hq/capemay/docs/pdf%20docs/RecruitTrainingPocketGuide.pdf

Another, perhaps more useful document is "The Helmsman," a brochure that outlines almost everything you need to know about Coast Guard Recruit Training. It's available at: http://www.gocoastguard.com/download-stuff/literature.

Additionally, the video produced by the Coast Guard, "It's just eight weeks: Coast Guard Basic Training" is a fantastic insight into basic training. The video is so good, in fact, that I recommend that everyone watch it, regardless of which branch you are interested in joining. You can see it at: http://www.youtube.com/watch?v=6i8PX3fyF0k. And by the way, watch all twenty minutes of it; you'll be glad you did.

RECRUIT TRAINING

If you've always had the desire to visit New Jersey, you'll be happy to know that since the closing of the Recruit Training Center at Alameda, California, in the early 1980s, the Coast Guard's only Basic Training facility is located in Cape May, New Jersey. The center opened on May 31, 1948, when all Coast Guard Recruit Training facilities were moved from Mayport, Florida.

According to the Coast Guard, the mission of Recruit Training Command is:

> To graduate motivated entry-level enlisted men and women ready and able to serve with a sense of pride and commitment in the world's premiere maritime service, and to proudly provide quality services to our people and others throughout the Coast Guard.

Furthermore, the stated training objectives of Training Center Cape May are:

> To prepare you for shipboard duty and stresses of daily life associated with emergency response situations. Our expert and professional training staff will work with you on Physical Fitness, Water Survival and Swim Qualifications, Wellness and Nutrition, Self-Discipline, Military Skill and Military Bearing. Your Vocational Skills and Academics will also be tested. We strive to instill a sense of Pride and Honor in every individual to bring you, along with your company, to a new level of excellence.

Earned, never given. A recruit receives her Coast Guard emblem.

CURRICULUM OVERVIEW

Coast Guard Recruit Training consists of many phases of training, each designed to ensure that, once you have graduated, you are ready and capable of joining the men and women serving in the Coast Guard. The training phases are:

- Forming
- Company formation
- Physical training
- Classroom training
- Drill
- Mid-Training
- The Final Phase

There are detailed descriptions of each phase in the following sections.

A recruit receives a little motivation from her company commander.

FORMING

You'll arrive at Recruit Training by bus on a trip that more than likely originated from the Philadelphia airport. The Forming process begins immediately on your arrival.

It is here that you will get your first military haircut, receive a medical screening, and get your first uniform issue. In addition, you will complete a ton of paperwork. It is in the Forming phase that you will probably question your decision to join the Coast Guard. You are not alone; you'll soon learn that just about everyone goes through the same self-doubt.

Recruits complete the obstacle course.

COMPANY FORMATION

Approximately three days after arriving at Recruit Training, you and others will be formed into a training unit called a Company. The responsibility of turning a group of civilians into a well-trained Recruit Company lies with your Company Commander (CC). Your CC is a senior enlisted Coast Guardsman who will become your coach, mentor, and, at times, surrogate parent.

PHYSICAL TRAINING

An important aspect of Recruit Training, Physical Fitnes Training will push you to your limits and beyond. You will participate in physical fitness throughout all phases of training.

To graduate from Recruit Training, you will have to meet the requirements presented in the following table:

PHYSICAL FITNESS REQUIREMENTS

Event	Male	Female
Push-ups	29 (in 1 minute)	15 (in 1 minute)
Bent Knee Sit-ups	38 (in 1 minute)	32 (in 1 minute)
1.5-mile run	12:51 minutes or less	15:26 minutes or less
Complete swim circuit	Jump off 6-foot platform into the pool, swim 100 yards, and tread water for 5 minutes*	Jump off 6-foot platform into the pool, swim 100 yards, and tread water for 5 minutes*

*Swimming on your back is not permitted.

If you aren't capable of meeting these requirements now, you must start an exercise program well before you leave for Recruit Training. Although you won't be expected to meet all the requirements immediately, showing up for Recruit Training prepared to meet them will tremendously reduce your stress level! If you are not immediately able to meet the swimming requirements, you will receive remedial training. Review the exercise instructions contained in the "Helmsman," however. I also suggest that you download the Air Force *Airman Fundamentals* "smartphone" app. Although its purpose is to prepare future Airmen, it contains excellent videos on properly performing exercises.

Recruits carry life rafts filled with sea bags while marching the parade field.

CLASSROOM TRAINING

Although much of Recruit Training is physical in nature, you will also spend many hours in a classroom environment. You will learn Coast Guard history, customs and courtesies, nautical terminology, the Coast Guard mission, and Coast Guard ranks. A word of advice: don't dare fall asleep!

DRILL

Drill is just another way of saying marching. If nothing else, before you graduate from Recruit Training you will have mastered the art of marching. Besides being an efficient way to get a group of people from place-to-place, drilling also serves to build confidence and to teach discipline and order. Some individuals may have an initial advantage because of prior marching experience, such as in Junior ROTC. However, marching is a team effort, so if one person is out of step, the entire company looks bad. Therefore, everyone works together to ensure that all members of the company become at least minimally competent in marching. Yet another word of advice: if you have JROTC, or similar experience, please do not tell the Company Commander, "that's not the way we did it in JROTC," or elsewhere.

Fire-fighting training.

MID-TRAINING

Mid-training begins with the end of the fourth week of training and the midterm examination. From then on, your training will be more hands-on and practical in nature. Of course, the physical and classroom training will continue; you will also receive instruction in:

- Fire fighting
- Marksmanship
- Line handling
- Seamanship

You may not think that you joined the Coast Guard to become a firefighter, but the truth is that everyone in the Coast Guard may be called at one time or another to fight a fire. That fire may be on your own Coast Guard vessel, or you may have to save a burning vessel at sea. When that call comes, you must be ready!

Marksmanship training is one aspect of Recruit Training that excites some and causes dread in others. You will receive expert instruction on the handling, firing, and care of firearms. Even those with no experience with firearms have done well in marksmanship training.

During Mid-training, you will also fill out your Assignment Data Card (ADC). The ADC lets the Coast Guard know where you would like to be assigned after training. The Air Force has a similar form, which is lovingly referred to as a "Dream Sheet." Although every effort will be made to match your desires with available openings, remember that the Coast Guard's needs come first. You will receive your assignment orders at the end of the fifth week of training.

Recruits field strip .40 cal. Pistols.

THE FINAL PHASE

During the Final Phase, you will continue with practical, physical, and classroom training. You will also practice for graduation and make travel arrangements.

GRADUATION

The graduation ceremony, the end of Recruit Training, marks the beginning of your future in the Coast Guard. It is a proud and emotional time for the graduates, as well as their families. Family and friends are welcome to attend the ceremony; your family will receive a package regarding graduation near the end of your training.

If you have excelled during Recruit Training, you may be one of the 3 percent of all graduates who receive the Honor Graduate Ribbon. Individuals who stood out during Recruit Training will receive other awards.

Because minor things can cause setbacks in training and delay your graduation, I would suggest that those planning to fly in for graduation wait as long as possible before locking themselves into nonrefundable airline tickets.

SMOKING POLICY

You cannot use of any type of tobacco products during your entire stay at Recruit Training. This includes, but is not limited to, cigarettes, cigars, any type of smokeless tobacco, and pipes. If you currently use any tobacco products, I recommend that you stop now instead of "going cold turkey" when you get to Recruit Training. You will have enough stress adapting to military life; you don't need the added burden of nicotine withdrawal.

RELIGIOUS WORSHIP SERVICES

A good source of morale during Recruit Training is attending weekly religious services. The Coast Guard conducts Sunday services for Catholic and Protestant recruits. However, you can make arrangements in the local community if you are of another faith.

OTHER USEFUL INFORMATION

Here are some other pieces of information that you'll find useful before arriving at Recruit Training.

Communication with Friends and Family

Even though your contact with the outside world will be limited during your stay at Recruit Training, you will be able to stay in contact with friends and family members. Besides the telephone call you will make on arrival to let everyone know you arrived safely, other telephone privileges will not come until near the end of training. If there is a family emergency, however, someone can reach you at any time.

Your primary source of communication will be through written communication. You will receive ample opportunity to write home and read letters from family and friends. Besides serving as a means to keep up with news from home, receiving letters serves as a morale booster.

Personal Effects

As mentioned in this chapter, there are certain items that you can, but are not required, to bring, and other items that would be best left at home. Additionally, you will receive many items at Basic Training; you will pay for them through your Coast Guard pay.

The following is a list of items that you will receive at Recruit Training. In addition, there are items listed that you may bring with you or that you may purchase at the Recruit Training Center. There also is a list of items that you should not bring with you to Recruit Training. Make sure you check with your recruiter if you have any questions regarding restricted items.

ISSUED ITEMS

1 Rucksack	1 Pkg. Band-Aids	12 Pens
1 Silver marker	1 Nail clipper	1 Highlighter
3 Bars of soap/1 soap dish	1 Pkg. razors	1 1" stencil
1 Antibacterial soap	1 Shaving cream	1 1/2" stencil
1 Deodorant	1 Blister kit	1 Black marker
1 Shampoo	1 Pkg. cotton balls	1 Sewing kit
1 Shower kit	1 Pkg. cotton swabs	1 Shoe shine kit
4 Towels	2 Locks	2 Ditty bags
1 Washcloth	3 Laundry pins	1 Canteen
1 Pair shower shoes	3 Laundry bags	1 Penlight
1 Lip balm	1 Bottle starch	2 Masking tape rolls
1 Dental floss	1 Notebook	1 Pair of running shoes
1 Toothpaste	1 3-ring binder	
1 Toothbrush/holder	1 Ruler	

Male Only Issue: 2 Athletic supporters
Female Only Issue: Small mesh laundry bag for delicates
Note: Insect repellent and sunscreen are issued May - Sept.

WHAT NOT TO BRING TO RECRUIT TRAINING

Alcohol beverages

All pornographic photos and materials

Any glass containers (plastic permitted)

Food or beverages

Magazines/newspapers

Narcotics and drug paraphernalia

All tobacco products and associated items

Weapons

You are not required, but can bring the items listed in the following table. They must be brought to Recruit Training in a small suitcase or duffle bag no larger than an airline carry-on bag. Many of these items are available for purchase while at Recruit Training.

WHAT YOU ARE PERMITTED (NOT REQUIRED) TO BRING TO RECRUIT TRAINING
All Enlistees Are Permitted to Bring

Address books

Aftershave lotion

All-white athletic socks (4 pair)

Black eyeglass retaining strap

Black pens/pencils

Cartridge-type razor

Comb/brush

Dental floss

Deodorant

Electric razor/clippers

Long underwear (white or navy blue only)

Manicure kit

Pen flashlight

Unframed family photos

Cellular phone

Religious materials

Religious medallion (with chain long enough so it cannot be seen under a V-neck T-shirt)

Shampoo (12 oz)

Soap (2)

Spray starch

Stationery, envelopes, stamps

Sunblock

Talcum powder

Toothbrush

Wallet

Watch

Wedding bands

Invisalign

Graduating company.

In Addition, Women Enlistees Are Permitted to Bring

Birth control pills (if already using them to maintain cycle)
Engagement rings
Feminine hygiene items
Gold ball earrings (1/4 inch, one set worn in lowest hole of ear)
Hair barrettes/bobby pins (hair color only)
Cloth covered elastic bands (matching hair color)
Hair dryer
Makeup (moderate amounts)

SUMMARY

I would like to close this section once again by saying that the information contained here is up-to-date at the time of this writing. Because things change, you should verify this information with your recruiter before departing for Recruit Training.

Remember to watch the video, "It's just 8 weeks: Coast Guard Basic Training" mentioned in the beginning of this section. Because "a picture is worth a thousand words" (and a video a million), I suggest that you view this video at least once. As mentioned in the beginning of this section the Coast Guard also has two publications called "Recruit Training Pocket Guide" and, "The Helmsman," which are essential downloads for anyone preparing to attend Coast Guard Recruit Training. Remember, above all, you are responsible for getting yourself prepared for basic training.

Marine Corps

RECRUIT TRAINING

Unlike the Air Force and Army, the Marine Corps does not offer any "smartphone apps" to help you prepare for Basic Training, although, once you enlist, your recruiter will give you a welcome kit that contains a DVD and other materials that will help you prepare for it. In the meantime, explore www.marines.com for more information or http://www.marines.com/becoming-a-marine/how-to-prepare/pft#, to go directly to the video that can help you prepare for the Physical Fitness Test. Additionally, there are a few "smartphone apps" available from third-party sources for a fee. I cannot endorse any of these apps, although they may be helpful. And, as an added note, it's pronounced "Marine Core" not "Corpse." I cringe when I hear it pronounced incorrectly.

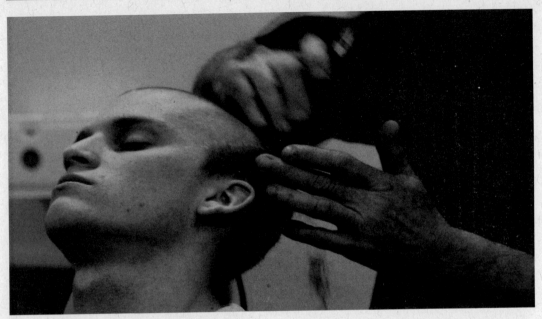

A recruit receiving his first "regulation" haircut.

The Marine Corps operates two locations for its Recruit Training. All males enlisting east of the Mississippi and all females nationwide go to Parris Island, South Carolina, whereas males enlisting west of the Mississippi go to the Marine Corps Recruit Depot in San Diego, California.

No matter which of the two Recruit Training sites you attend, you can count on twelve weeks of intense training. You will be challenged physically, mentally, and emotionally throughout your entire stay at Recruit Training. Although Recruit Training is officially twelve weeks long, that does not count the first week, which includes in-processing and orientation. Therefore, you will spend at least thirteen weeks in Recruit Training.

CURRICULUM OVERVIEW

Upon arrival at Recruit Training, you will make your first stop at Recruit Receiving. This is where you will spend your first few days in the Marine Corps. You will receive your first of many haircuts and your initial uniform issue, be given a thorough medical and dental screening, meet your senior drill instructor, and take your Initial Strength Test. The Strength Test consists of a 1.5-mile run, sit-ups, and pull-ups.

From Recruit Receiving, you will move on to the next phase of training, called Forming. In this phase, you will go to your training company where you will meet your drill instructor. During the three to five days of this phase, you'll learn the basics of marching and how to wear the uniform.

The following table lists the training events by week. You can view the specifics of the various Recruit Training activities later in this section. For a day-by-day schedule of activities, download the Training Matrix at: https://www.mcrdpi.usmc.mil/training/docs/MCRDPITrainingMatrix101001.pdf.

RECRUIT TRAINING CURRICULUM—BY WEEK

Processing:

Recruits arrive to Recruit Training, get the Welcome Aboard speech, receive clothing and gear issue, receive a medical screening, perform the Initial Strength Test, and meet their drill instructors.

Weeks 1-3:

Recruits receive instruction on military history, customs and courtesies, basic first aid, uniforms, leadership, and core values.

Recruits learn hand-to-hand combat skills through the Marine Corps Martial Arts Program (MC-MAP), which consists of various martial arts styles.

Week 4: Swim Qualification

There are four levels of swim/water survival qualification in recruit training. The Marines are an amphibious service, and water survival training is designed to increase their competence and survivability in an amphibious environment.

Week 5: Initial Written Testing and Initial Drill

Rappel Tower/Gas Chamber

Week 6: Grass Week (Rifle Range)

Recruits learn the fundamentals of Marine Corps marksmanship, sight in on the targets, and learn how to make adjustments to the M16 A2 service rifle.

Week 7: Firing Week (Rifle Range)

The recruits have three days to practice the KD course of fire, a pre-qualification day, and a qualification day, firing the M16 A2 service rifle.

Week 8: Team Week

The recruits will spend the week working in various areas of Recruit Training, maintaining the appearance of the Depot, and practicing for Final Drill.

Week 9: A-Line/Basic Warrior Training

The recruits will conduct various exercises to begin developing basic field and combat skills. Some of the events they will execute are:

Day Movement Course

Firing at multiple targets

Firing at targets from unknown distances

Combat Shooting

Combat Endurance Course

Week 10: Practical Application Evaluation

Week 11: Final Drill
Recruits and Drill Instructors receive an evaluation of their knowledge and application of Marine Corps drill and rifle manual.

Written testing: Recruits receive an evaluation of their knowledge of basic military education.

Week 12:
Ceremony practices
Liberty Brief
Graduation

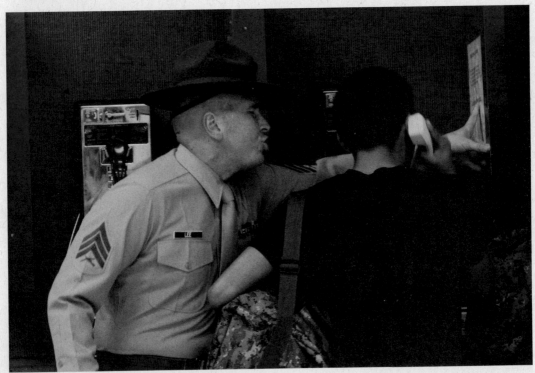

Calling home to let family know you've arrived.

Standing in formation.

Receiving Eagle, Globe, and Anchor during Emblem Ceremony.

DRILL

Some things about Basic Training never change, and Drill or marching is one of them. Besides getting platoons from place-to-place, drill instills discipline, team pride, and unit cohesion. Although individuals with marching experience will initially have an advantage over those with no experience, most people will become proficient with some practice.

Uniform inspection.

PHYSICAL TRAINING

Physical training (PT) is a way of life at Recruit Training. You will run, exercise, and participate in conditioning marches throughout your entire stay at Recruit Training. If you do not want physical challenges on a daily basis, maybe you should look elsewhere for a career. Do not show up for Marine Recruit Training if you are not physically fit. Your recruiter will, in all likelihood, ensure that doesn't happen. The charts below show the minimum requirements for the Initial Strength Test (IST) and the Physical Fitness Test (PFT), although the Marine Corps emphasizes that recruits should strive for more than the minimum requirements.

PHYSICAL FITNESS REQUIREMENTS—MALE RECRUITS

Event	IST	PFT
Pull-ups	2	3
Crunches	44	50
Run	13:30 minutes (1.5 miles)	28:00 (3 miles)

PHYSICAL FITNESS REQUIREMENTS—FEMALE RECRUITS

Event	IST	PFT
Flexed Arm Hang	12 seconds	15 seconds
Crunches	44	50
Run	15:00 minutes (1.5 miles)	31:00 minutes (3 miles)

Recruits practicing hand-to-hand combat.

ACADEMIC TRAINING

Besides facing physical challenges, you will also face mental challenges. Academic training will consist of subjects such as Marine Corps history, customs, courtesies, and basic lifesaving procedures.

CORE VALUES

As you can see in the Recruit Training Curriculum table presented, core values are important as they are the "bedrock" of a Marine's character. The core values are:

- honor;
- courage; and
- commitment.

In addition to these three core values, you also will learn integrity, discipline, teamwork, duty, and Esprit de Corps. Furthermore, these values will be reinforced throughout the entire time you'll spend in Recruit Training.

Negotiating the confidence course.

CLOSE COMBAT

Close-combat training teaches fighting techniques that Marines may need to employ in combat. Drill Instructors will teach the use of pugil sticks, and the practical application of bayonet fighting. You will also receive instruction on offensive and defensive skills.

CONFIDENCE COURSE

One aspect of Recruit Training that some love, and others love to hate, is the confidence course. As the name implies, its main purpose is to build recruits' confidence; the other purpose is to build upper-body strength. You will have two opportunities to navigate the eleven-station confidence course.

COMBAT WATER SURVIVAL

What is the exact opposite of skinny-dipping? The answer is combat water survival. All recruits will receive instruction on several water survival and swimming techniques, while they are dressed in full utility uniform!

After instruction, you must pass a minimum level of proficiency in combat water survival. Recruits exceeding the minimum level may go on to more advanced training, which requires them to train in full combat gear. This includes rifle, helmet, flak jacket, and pack. This definitely is not your average day at the beach! If you are a weak swimmer, I suggest that you get some practice, or swim instruction before reporting to Recruit Training; it will make your life a lot easier!

Learning basic water survival skills.

BASIC WARRIOR TRAINING

This phase of training introduces you to living in the field. During the three days you spend in this phase, you will learn everything from putting up a tent to field sanitation and camouflage. This is also when you will learn about the rappel tower and go through the gas chamber.

MARKSMANSHIP TRAINING

The proper handling, firing, and maintenance of the M-16A2 service rifle are essential for every Marine. You will receive two weeks of intense marksmanship training. During the first week of training, you will learn the four shooting positions, as well as how to fire and to adjust sites. During the second week, you will fire on a known-distance course, with ranges of 200, 300, and 500 yards. You will be required to qualify with the M-16A2 rifle.

Individuals with firearm experience may start with an advantage over those with no experience. However, after minimum training, beginners may outshoot experienced shooters. This is because experienced shooters may have to unlearn some bad habits, whereas beginners do not have to overcome this obstacle.

THE CRUCIBLE

Described by the Marine Corps as "Recruit Training's Defining Moment," the Crucible is a training event that tests your strength, endurance, will, team spirit, and determination.

For 54 hours, you will be subjected to physically and mentally challenging training. You can have a total of 8 hours of sleep during the entire 54 hours and are given 2½ MREs (Meals Ready to Eat). MREs (ready-made precooked meals) are packaged in foil wrappers that are almost impossible to open; the contents vary from spaghetti to hot dogs and my favorite, "Barbecue Meatballs."

The entire training event is conducted in the field where the little sleep you are allowed is done in a primitive wooden hut. The Crucible is an event that is, at the minimum, unpleasant, but when you've completed it, you will have a sense of accomplishment second only to the feeling you'll have on graduation day.

MARINE WEEK

The last week spent at Recruit Training known as Marine Week, you will spend completing final requirements such as the practical exam, physical fitness test, battalion commander's inspection, and final drill. This is the time that recruits transition to Marines. It is at this time that new Marines receive the "Eagle, Globe, and Anchor," the emblem of the Marine Corps, during a ceremony that can bring tears of pride to even the toughest of recruits.

FAMILY DAY AND GRADUATION

The last two days at Recruit Training are devoted to Family Day and graduation. New Marines receive on-base liberty to spend time with their family members. This may be the last chance you get to see them for a while. The following day, you graduate in an elaborate and impressive ceremony and parade. The ceremony marks the beginning of your future in the Marine Corps. It is a proud and an emotional time for the graduates as well as their families.

Because minor things can cause setbacks in training and delay your graduation, I would suggest that those planning to fly in for graduation wait as long as possible before locking themselves into nonrefundable airline tickets.

I just can't resist telling an amusing story about Family Week at Parris Island. At the beginning of every school-year, I take many of my JROTC Cadets to Parris Island for a day of "orientation." One particular year, I had the bright idea of having the cadets wear their gold colored physical-fitness t-shirts so we could readily recognize them in a crowd. What I didn't know was that all the newly graduated Marines' family members (and there was lots of them) would also be wearing gold t-shirts that day.

Graduation day.

SMOKING POLICY

You cannot use any type of tobacco products during your entire stay at Recruit Training. This includes, but is not limited to, cigarettes, cigars, any type of smokeless tobacco, and pipes. If you currently use any tobacco products, I would suggest that you stop now instead of "going cold turkey" when you get to Recruit Training. You will have enough stress adapting to military life; you don't need the added burden of nicotine withdrawal.

RELIGIOUS WORSHIP SERVICES

Although the Marines do not have chaplains of their own (they use Navy chaplains), you can attend the religious services of your choice. Although not all denominations are available at Recruit Training, you should be able to find services you feel comfortable attending.

OTHER USEFUL INFORMATION

Here are some other useful pieces of information for you to review before arriving at Recruit Training.

Communication with Friends and Family

Even though your contact with the outside world will be limited during your stay at Recruit Training, you will be able to stay in contact with friends and family members. You will be able to write home often. You will also be able to place one telephone call. If there is a family emergency, someone will be able to reach you at any time.

Personal Effects

Although the other branches of the military provide a list of things to bring and not to bring to Basic Training, the Marine Corps puts it quite simply: "Don't bring anything except yourself." You may be allowed to bring certain prescription drugs, so check with your recruiter before leaving for Recruit Training.

Graduating from recruit training.

SUMMARY

I would like to close this section by saying once again that the information contained here is up-to-date at the time of this writing. Because things change, you should verify this information with your recruiter before departing for Recruit Training.

As mentioned in the beginning of this section, once you've enlisted, your recruiter should have given you a welcome kit containing a wealth of information including a DVD about life as a Marine. Because "a picture is worth a thousand words" (and a video a million), I highly recommend that you view this DVD in its entirety and ask any questions you may have.

Navy

RECRUIT TRAINING

There are several valuable resources for future sailors:

1. The Navy has an excellent video about the Basic Training experience, which is a "must see" for all those who have decided to enlist, or are contemplating enlisting. The video is called, "Faces of Navy Boot Camp," and can be viewed at: http://www.youtube.com/watch?v=cQXXnMpJ6Ws.
2. The "Recruit Trainee Guide," is a 479-page complete guide to Navy Recruit Training and can be downloaded at: http://www.bootcamp.navy.mil/pdfs/recruit_trainee_guide_rev_a_july_2009.pdf.
3. If you'd like a more concise guide to get you ready for Recruit Training, you'll want to study the Standards-Transition-Acknowledgement-Requirements-Training, "START" guide which is provided to all Navy enlistees, but is also available at: http://www.cnrc.navy.mil/Graphic-Elements/PDFs/011-0144(Rev%202-13)-Start-Guide-Readerspread.pdf

I started my military career in October 1978 by enlisting in the Navy. At the time of my enlistment, I was given the choice of attending one of three Navy Recruit Training Centers: Orlando, Florida; San Diego, California; or Great Lakes, Illinois. It didn't take me long to figure out that I didn't want to be in Illinois in the winter. Because I had never been to the West Coast, I decided to go to San Diego. It was great returning to New York on leave in December with a suntan.

In late 1998, I once again traveled to San Diego, this time for a recruiting meeting. I figured it would be great to visit "Boot Camp" twenty years later. To my surprise, however, I discovered that the Navy no longer trained its recruits in San Diego. In fact, since 1994, Great Lakes, Illinois, has been the only location for Navy Recruit Training! I remember thinking that if I had chosen Great Lakes over San Diego, instead of a suntan, I would have been returning on leave with windburn. (Of course, that wouldn't actually happen—the Navy takes precautions to protect recruits from the sometimes-harsh Midwestern winters.)

CURRICULUM OVERVIEW

After arriving at Recruit Training, you will go to the Recruit In-Processing Center. This is your home for the next two hours, and it is here that your training begins. You will learn where to stand, when to stand, and how to stand. You will fill out more forms than you knew even existed and will be led around like a heard of cattle. To let the folks back home know you arrived safely, you can make one telephone call.

After you have completed all of the paperwork, you will be issued Navy Physical Training (PT) Gear (your first "official" uniform), and then you'll undergo urinalysis (they don't fool around about drugs). You'll then receive your first instructions on how to make your bed (and you thought your mom was tough) and will receive training on the fire safety requirements. By this point, you will have asked yourself (at least once) what you got yourself into. Don't panic: it's a kind of culture shock, buyer's remorse, and cold-feet feeling that everyone goes through, but most people overcome it.

On the first full day of Recruit Training, recruits are put into "divisions," which are headed up by a Recruit Division Commander (RDC). These RDCs are senior Petty Officers who are responsible for transforming a group of "clueless" civilians into a division of well-trained sailors.

Almost immediately, you will begin an eight-week journey that includes physical training, classroom instruction, hands-on training, and water survival courses.

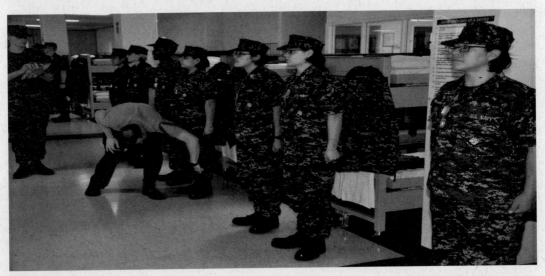

Uniform inspection.

DAILY ROUTINE

You will have a full schedule while attending Recruit Training. You may feel that it will be impossible to get all your daily activities accomplished, but you can put your worries to rest. You'll have plenty of time, because you'll start your day around 4 a.m.!

UNIFORM ISSUE

Perhaps one of the most interesting and memorable parts of Recruit Training is uniform issue. You'll be led through a huge facility where people issue and fit more than 35 million uniforms every year. For those who enjoy shopping and trying on clothes, this is like no other shopping trip you've ever experienced!

Uniform issue.

WATER SURVIVAL

Here's a surprise for you: If you join the Navy, chances are that sooner or later you'll be on a ship. Therefore, it's important for all sailors to receive at least a minimum amount of water survival training. You will receive instruction on water safety and survival techniques, and then receive a swim test to determine your skill level. If you are unable to meet the minimum swimming requirements, you will be given individual instruction twice a day until you are able to do so. I suggest, to make your life a whole lot easier at Basic Training, that if you cannot swim, or are a weak swimmer, you take lessons, or practice swimming, before leaving for Basic Training.

CONFIDENCE COURSE

The Navy's confidence course is unlike those found in Army, Air Force, and Marine Corps Basic Training programs. The Navy has created what it terms a "maritime obstacle course" to build your confidence, challenge you physically, familiarize you with shipboard equipment, and build team spirit.

Instead of rewarding individual effort, you successfully pass the confidence course only when every member of your team of four recruits completes the course. Some of the challenges of the confidence course are:

- wearing an oxygen-breathing apparatus (usually worn while fighting shipboard fires);
- carrying sandbags;
- tossing life rings; and
- climbing through a scuttle (a small circular door found on ships) with full seabags (known as duffel bags to most other military branches).

When you complete the confidence course, you will experience a sense of pride that can only come from being part of a team.

BATTLE STATIONS

Anyone who has ever watched an old World War II movie (or *Star Trek,* for that matter) knows the meaning of "Battle Stations!" Aboard ship, the call to battle stations means that everyone must come together as a crew to prepare for meeting the enemy. Everyone has his or her job to do, and there is no room for not doing that job to the best of one's ability.

The purpose of the Battle Stations event during Recruit Training is to instill in each recruit the confidence, dedication, and team spirit necessary for you to become a productive member of a ship's crew. All of the training you receive during your time at Recruit Training culminates in this event.

You'll work as a team to complete physically and mentally challenging tasks that will test your endurance and ability to work as a team. Battle Stations ends with a ceremony that can only be described as a rewarding experience. This is when recruits trade in their "Recruit" ball caps for caps that read "Navy." This is the recruit's first recognition as a Sailor.

Receiving the first of many Navy haircuts.

DRILL

One aspect of Recruit Training that every military branch has in common is Drill. Drill refers to the art of marching, and, if drill is an art, you will become an artist by the time you graduate from Recruit Training.

Although individuals who have had some experience with marching, such as those who belonged to high school Junior ROTC will have an initial advantage, everyone will soon become at least competent at marching. Here's a word of advice to those with JROTC, or similar, experience; never correct your RDC by saying, "that's not how we did it in JROTC," or elsewhere.

BARRACKS INSPECTIONS

Recruits live in barracks (called ships). Recruits must keep their barracks "shipshape." Besides making your own bed and ensuring that you fold your clothes just right, you and your fellow recruits will scrub, wash, wipe, and dust every inch of your barracks in preparation for barracks inspection.

Besides the obvious reasons for keeping your living quarters clean, working as a team cleaning the barracks and then doing well on an inspection helps build team spirit and pride in a job well done. If you're used to having your mother make your bed and pick up after you, I suggest that you get out of that habit before you get to Recruit Training.

CORE VALUES

You will find the core values of honor, courage, and commitment evident throughout all your training. These are the bedrock principles of naval service.

PHYSICAL TRAINING

A good part of Recruit Training is devoted to physical conditioning. You are expected to achieve minimum standards in running, push-ups, sit-ups, and pull-ups. You will receive three Physical Fitness Assessments while at Recruit Training. The chart below shows the minimum requirements for passing the assessments. If you are not currently involved in sports, or do not maintain a regular exercise program, start now, before you arrive at Recruit Training. Although most people, regardless of their physical fitness level, are able to work up to the minimum standards, life at Recruit Training is a whole lot easier if you show up ready to meet at least the minimum requirements.

PHYSICAL FITNESS REQUIREMENTS

Event	Male	Female
Push-ups	46 (in 2 minutes)	20 (in 2 minutes)
Curl-ups (Sit-ups)	54 (in 2 minutes)	54 (in 2 minutes)
1.5-mile run	12:15 minutes or less	14:45 minutes or less

The food must be good—they're lining up for it!

CLASSROOM TRAINING

Although a great deal of time is devoted to physical training, marching, and hands-on instruction, you will spend a lot of time in Recruit Training in the classroom. You'll receive instruction on such topics as naval history, sexual harassment, proper wear of the uniform, and basic seamanship. You will also be required to pass several written tests in order to graduate.

SMOKING POLICY

You cannot use any type of tobacco products during your entire stay at BMT. This includes, but is not limited to, cigarettes, cigars, any type of smokeless tobacco, and pipes. If you currently use any tobacco products, I would suggest that you stop now instead of "going cold turkey" when you get to Recruit Training. You will have enough stress adapting to military life; you don't need the added burden of nicotine withdrawal.

GRADUATION

Graduation from Recruit Training is known as "Pass-in-Review." An elaborate and emotional ceremony, it marks the end of Recruit Training and the beginning of the future of those individuals who nine weeks earlier were civilians, became Recruits, and now are Sailors. Family and friends are welcome and are encouraged to attend graduation ceremonies. This may be the last chance you get to see them for a while.

Because minor things can cause setbacks in training and delay your graduation, I would suggest that those planning to fly in for graduation wait as long as possible before locking into nonrefundable airline tickets.

One of the unique things about Navy Recruit Training graduation is that it is streamed live on the Internet! That means that those friends and family unable to attend your graduation are able to view it live from almost anywhere in the world. To access the live-stream go to: http://navylive. dodlive.mil/.

Graduation

RELIGIOUS WORSHIP SERVICES

An activity that can help ease the stresses of Recruit Training is attending religious services. You will be able to attend the services of your choice throughout Recruit Training. Although there isn't a service available for every religious denomination, you are bound to find a service that you are comfortable attending.

Things have changed a little since this recruiting poster.

OTHER USEFUL INFORMATION

Here are some other pieces of information that you'll find useful before arriving at Recruit Training.

Communication with Friends and Family

Even though your contact with the outside world will be limited during your stay at Recruit Training, you will be able to stay in contact with friends and family members. Besides the one telephone call you were able to make when you first arrived at Recruit Training, you will get few chances to make any others. If there is a family emergency, however, someone will be able to reach you at any time.

Your primary source of communication will be through written correspondence. You will be able to write home and read letters from family and friends. Besides serving as a means to keep up with news from home, receiving letters serves as a morale booster.

Personal Effects

As mentioned in this chapter, there are certain items that you must bring to Recruit Training, items that you are permitted but not required to bring, and other items that would be best left at home.

The following is a list of items you must bring with you. Make sure you check with your recruiter if you have any questions regarding these items. Additionally, cell phones and civilian clothes brought with you to basic training will be mailed home in a small box, so pack accordingly.

WHAT YOU ARE REQUIRED TO BRING TO RECRUIT TRAINING

All Recruits Must Bring

1. Photo identification/driver's license
2. Social Security Card
3. Marriage certificate/Divorce decree (if applicable)
4. Copies of dependent birth certificates (if applicable)
5. Immunization records
6. Direct deposit system form with bank account and routing number information

WHAT YOU ARE PERMITTED—NOT REQUIRED—TO BRING TO RECRUIT TRAINING

All Recruits Are Permitted to Bring

1. Wrist watch, wedding ring
2. Religious medallion no larger than the size of a dog tag
3. Writing material (NO bottled ink)
4. Pocket dictionary
5. Pocket bible
6. Small address book
7. Hairbrush and comb
8. Pre-paid phone cards

9. One pair of prescription glasses, reading glasses, or contacts (with one week of cleaning solution)
10. A small amount of cash (i.e., less than $10)

Female recruits may retain the following personal items:

1. Feminine sanitary items
2. Conservative cosmetics. Female/one of each: face powder, blush, lipstick, eye shadow and mascara (non-aerosol or glass); recruits can wear make-up for division photos and graduation weekend only.
3. Barrettes (female/must match hair color)
4. Birth control medications

Note: Female recruits may not bring a swimsuit, underwear, or bras. They will receive these upon arrival.

WHAT YOU ARE NOT PERMITTED TO BRING TO RECRUIT TRAINING
Do Not Bring

1. Large cans of shaving cream (12 oz. or larger)
2. Aerosol containers
3. After shave/cologne
4. Lighter fluid
5. Disposable lighters (the fluid cartridge of a "Zippo" lighter will be confiscated, and the casing will be retained)
6. Magazines, books (non-navy)
7. Playing cards, dice, gambling paraphernalia
8. Large stationery
9. Large hair combs/afro pics, rakes, or anything made of metal
10. Anything in glass containers including mirrors
11. Double edge razors, blades
12. Cigarettes, cigars, pipes, tobacco, chewing tobacco
13. Large deodorants (larger than 4 oz.)
14. Alcohol-based health & comfort items
15. Portable electronics (cell phones, pagers, PDAs, CD/cassette players, radios, MP3 players, hand-held video games)
16. Civilian clothing
17. Cameras
18. Electric razors
19. Large hair dryers
20. Curling irons.
21. Other electrical items deemed unnecessary by the RTC's staff
22. Food items (gums, candy, chip, etc.)
23. Any non-prescription drugs and medications
24. Weapons of any type
25. Scissors
26. Narcotics/illegal drugs or any paraphernalia

SUMMARY

I would like to close this section by saying once again that the information contained here is up-to-date at the time of this writing. Because things change, you should verify this information with your recruiter before departing for Recruit Training.

The video, mentioned at the beginning of this section, "Faces of Navy Boot Camp," is an excellent resource. Because "a picture is worth a thousand words" (and a video a million), I highly recommend that you view this video in its entirety and ask any questions you may have. Additionally, the two publications mentioned in the beginning of this section, should also be studied to prepare yourself for basic training. Remember, you ultimately are responsible for getting yourself prepared for basic training.

PART THREE

MILITARY BASICS

MILITARY OCCUPATIONS

This chapter lists the occupational groups each branch of the armed forces offers. These are not specific jobs but rather "fields," such as electronics or mechanics.

As you learned in Chapter 5, which dealt with the Military Entrance Processing Station (MEPS), being flexible in your job selection is a good idea. By focusing on a broad field rather than a specific job, your chances of getting a job and training in something that interests you and makes you happy are much greater.

I encourage you to read through all the job categories for all the services As also mentioned in Chapter 5, there may be a career field that you have never heard of that might interest you.

Ultimately, the results of the Armed Forces Aptitude Battery (ASVAB) examination and the physical examination will determine the career fields for which you are best suited. However, it helps if you also have some interest in that field.

Go through the following tables and (unless you've borrowed this book) highlight all the job categories that interest you. Once you've compiled your list of job categories, ask your recruiter for information about the jobs that are included in those categories.

Also, take your list with you to the MEPS and share it with the MEPS Liaison. Keeping flexibility in mind, go prepared to discuss two or more job categories. Rank order them, and start by talking about your number one choice.

If you cannot find a job category that interests you from the these tables, perhaps you need to look elsewhere for a career.

Air Force Occupations

VEHICLE/MACHINERY MECHANICS

Aircraft Maintenance

Duties and Responsibilities

Performs the mechanical functions of maintenance; repair and modification of helicopters, turboprops, reciprocating engines, and jet aircraft

Qualifications

This requires considerable mechanical or electrical aptitude and manual dexterity. Physics , hydraulics, electronics, mathematics, and mechanics desirable

Examples of Civilian Jobs

Aircraft Mechanic and Airframe Inspector

Aircraft Systems Maintenance

Duties and Responsibilities

Performs maintenance on aircraft accessory systems and propulsion systems; fabrication of metal and fabric materials used in aircraft structural repair and inspection and preservation of aircraft parts and materials

Qualifications

Electrical or mechanical aptitude and manual dexterity. Electronics, mathematics, hydraulics, mechanics, chemistry, metalworking, and mechanical drafting desirable

Examples of Civilian Jobs

Aircraft mechanic, aircraft electrician, sheet metal worker, welder, and machinist

Intricate Equipment Maintenance

Duties and Responsibilities

Overhauls and modifies photographic equipment; works with fine precision tools, testing devices, and schematic drawings

Qualifications

Considerable mechanical ability and manual dexterity; algebra and physics desirable. Must have normal color vision

Examples of Civilian Jobs

Camera repairer, statistical machine, and medical equipment service person

Mechanical/Electrical

Duties and Responsibilities

Performs installation, operation, maintenance, and repairs of base direct support systems and equipment

Qualifications

Physics, mathematics, blueprint reading, and electricity

Examples of Civilian Jobs

Elevator repairer, electrician, lineman, powerhouse repairer, diesel mechanic, pipefitter, steamfitter, and heating and ventilation worker

Vehicle Maintenance

Duties and Responsibilities

Overhauls and maintains powered ground vehicles and mechanical equipment for transporting personnel and supplies

Qualifications

Machine shop, mathematics, and training in the use of tools and blueprints helpful

Examples of Civilian Jobs

Automobile accessories installer and automobile and truck mechanic

ELECTRONIC/ELECTRICAL SYSTEMS

Avionics Systems

Duties and Responsibilities

Installs, maintains, and repairs airborne bomb navigation, fire control, weapons control, automatic flight control systems, and radio and navigational equipment and maintains associated test and precision measurement equipment

Qualifications

Electronic aptitude, manual dexterity, and normal vision. Mathematics, physics, chemistry, electronics, and trigonometry desirable

Examples of Civilian Jobs

Radar, television, and precision instrument maintenance technician

Communications—Electronics Systems

Duties and Responsibilities

Installs, modifies, maintains, repairs, and overhauls airborne and ground television equipment, high-speed general and special purpose data processing equipment, automatic communications and cryptographic machine systems, teletypewriter, tele-autographic equipment, telecommunications systems control, and associated electronic test equipment

Qualifications

Basic knowledge of electronic theory. Mathematics and physics desirable. Normal color vision mandatory

Examples of Civilian Jobs

Communications, electronics technician, radio and television repairer, meteorological, and teletype equipment repairer

LOGISTICS AND SUPPLY

Aircrew Operations

Duties and Responsibilities

Primary duties require frequent and regular flight. In-flight refueling operator performs duties associated with in-flight refueling of aircraft. Defensive aerial gunner is a B-52 integrated crewmember with responsibility for defense of aircraft. Aircraft loadmaster supervises loading of cargo and passengers and operates aircraft equipment. Pararescue/recovery personnel perform aircrew protection skills. Flight engineers ensure mechanical condition of the aircraft and monitor in-flight aircraft systems

Qualifications

High electrical and mechanical aptitude, manual dexterity, normal vision, and good physical condition. Mathematics, physics, general science, English, typing, computer principles, and shop work desirable

Examples of Civilian Jobs

Aircraft mechanic, electrician, hydraulic tester, oxygen system tester, cargo handler, dispatcher, and shipping clerk, depending on the area in which training and experience is received

Fuels

Duties and Responsibilities

Receives, stores, dispenses, tests, and inspects propellants, petroleum fuels, and products

Qualifications

Chemistry, math, and general science desirable

Examples of Civilian Jobs

Petroleum industry supervisor and bulk plant manager

Munitions and Weapons Maintenance

Duties and Responsibilities

Maintains and repairs aircraft armament. Assembles, maintains, loads, unloads, and stores munitions and nuclear weapons. Disposes of bombs, missiles, and rockets and operates detection instruments

Qualifications

Mechanical or electrical aptitude, manual dexterity, and normal color vision and depth perception Mathematics, mechanics, and physics desirable

Examples of Civilian Jobs

Aircraft armament mechanic, armorer, ammunition inspector, and munitions handler

Supply

Duties and Responsibilities

Designs, analyzes, and operates supply data systems. Responsible for operation and management of material facilities

Qualifications

Accounting and business administration

Examples of Civilian Jobs

Junior accountant, machine recourse section supervisor and receiving, shipping, and stock clerk

PERSONNEL/BASE SUPPORT

Accounting, Finance, and Auditing

Duties and Responsibilities

Prepares documents required to account for and disburse funds, including budgeting, allocation, disbursing, auditing, and preparing cost analysis records

Qualifications

Dexterity in the operation of business machines. Typing, mathematics, statistics, and accounting desirable. High administrative aptitude mandatory

Examples of Civilian Jobs

Public accountant, auditor, bookkeeper, budget clerk, and paymaster

Administration

Duties and Responsibilities

Prepares correspondence and statistical summaries, arranges priority and distribution systems, maintains files, prepares and consolidates reports, and arranges graphic presentations

Qualifications

Business, English, typing, and mathematics courses desirable

Examples of Civilian Jobs

Clerk typist, file secretary, stenographer, and receptionist

Band

Duties and Responsibilities

Plays musical instruments or sings in concert bands and orchestras, repairs and maintains instruments; performs as drums major, arranges music, and maintains music libraries

Qualifications

Knowledge of elementary theory of music and orchestration desirable

Examples of Civilian Jobs

Orchestrator, music librarian, music teacher, and instrumental musician

Dental

Duties and Responsibilities

Operates dental facilities and provides paraprofessional dental care and preventive dental services, treats oral tissues, and fabricates prosthetic devices

Qualifications

Knowledge of oral and dental anatomy, biology, and chemistry

Examples of Civilian Jobs

Dental Hygienist and Dental Assistant

Education and Training

Duties and Responsibilities

Conducts formal classes of instruction, uses training aids, develops material for various courses of instruction, teaches classes in general academic subjects and military matters, and administers educational programs

Qualifications

English composition and speech desirable

Examples of Civilian Jobs

Vocational training instructor, counselor, educational consultant, and administrator

Fire Protection

Duties and Responsibilities

Operates fire-fighting equipment, prevents and extinguishes aircraft and structural fires; rescues and renders first aid; maintains fire-fighting and fire-prevention equipment

Qualifications

Good physical condition. No allergies to oil and fire extinguishing solution. General science and chemistry desirable

Examples of Civilian Jobs

Fire chief, fire extinguisher service person, firefighter, and fire marshal

Legal

Duties and Responsibilities

Takes and transcribes verbal accordings of legal proceedings; uses a stenomask; performs office administrative tasks; processes claims

Qualifications

Knowledge of stenomask, typing, legal terminology, and military processing of claims. English grammar and composition. Ability to speak clearly and distinctly

Examples of Civilian Jobs

Law librarian, court clerk, and shorthand reporter

Medical

Duties and Responsibilities

Operates medical facilities; works with professional medical staff as they provide care and treatment. May specialize in such medical services as nuclear medicine, cardiopulmonary techniques, physical and occupational therapy, and administrative services

Qualifications

Knowledge of first aid; ability to help professional medical personnel. Anatomy, biology, zoology, high school algebra, and chemistry desirable in most specialties and are mandatory requirements for some

Examples of Civilian Jobs

X-ray and medical records technician, medical laboratory and pharmacist assistant, respiratory therapy technician, and surgical technologist

Morale, Welfare, and Recreation

Duties and Responsibilities

Conducts physical conditioning, coaches sports programs and administers recreation, entertainment, sports, and club activities

Qualifications

Good muscular coordination. English, business math, and physical education desirable

Examples of Civilian Jobs

Athletic or playground director, physical education instructor, and manager of a recreational establishment

Public Affairs

Duties and Responsibilities

Interviews people, reports news, composes, proofreads, writes, and edits news copy; provides public affairs advice

Qualifications

High general aptitude. English grammar and composition, speech, journalism, radio/television, and history

Examples of Civilian Jobs

Reporter, copyreader, historian, public relations representative, editorial assistant, broadcast or program director, and announcer

Safety

Duties and Responsibilities

Performs functions related to the conduct of both safety and disaster preparedness programs; conducts safety programs; surveys areas and activities to eliminate hazards; analyzes accident causes and trends; trains personnel to accomplish the primary mission under the handicaps imposed by enemy attack or natural disaster

Qualifications

Knowledge of industrial hygiene, safety education, safety psychology, and blueprint interpretation Typing, English, public speaking, mathematics, and science desirable

Examples of Civilian Jobs

Safety inspector and instructor

Sanitation

Duties and Responsibilities

Operates and maintains water- and waste-processing plant systems and equipment and performs pest and rodent control functions

Qualifications

Physics, biology, chemistry, and blueprint reading desirable

Examples of Civilian Jobs

Purification plant operator, sanitary inspector, exterminator, and entomologist

Security Police

Duties and Responsibilities

Provides security for classified information and material; enforces law and order; controls traffic and protects lives and property, and organizes as local ground defense force

Qualifications

Good physical condition, vision, and hearing; civics and social sciences desirable

Examples of Civilian Jobs

Guard, police inspector, police officer, and police superintendent

Transportation

Duties and Responsibilities

Ensures service and efficiency of transportation of supplies and personnel by aircraft, train, motor vehicle, and ship

Qualifications

Driver training, operation of office machines, and business math

Examples of Civilian Jobs

Cargo handler, motor vehicle dispatcher, shipping or traffic rate clerk, trailer truck driver, and ticket agent

Visual Information

Duties and Responsibilities

Operates aerial and ground cameras, motion picture, and other photographic equipment, processes photographs and film, edits motion pictures, and performs photographic instrumentations, and operates airborne, field, and precision processing laboratories

Qualifications

Considerable dexterity on small precision equipment; excellent eyesight. Mathematics, physics, chemistry, public speaking, commercial art, drafting, photography, drama, communicative arts, and computer science desirable

Examples of Civilian Jobs

Photographer, darkroom technician, film editor, aerial commercial photograph finisher, sound mixer, and motion picture camera operator

ENGINEERING, SCIENCE, AND TECHNICAL

Aircrew Protection

Duties and Responsibilities

Performs functions involved in the instruction of aircrew and other designated personnel on the principles, procedures, and techniques of global survival. This includes life-support equipment, recovery, evasion, captivity, resistance to exploitation, and escape

Qualifications

Good physical condition required; knowledge of pioneering and woodsman activities helpful. Courses in communication, science, and education desirable

Examples of Civilian Jobs

No civilian job covers the scope of the jobs in this career field, but a related job is that of hunting or fishing guide

Communications—Computers

Duties and Responsibilities

Operates radio and wire communications systems, automatic digital switching equipment, cryptographic devices, airborne and ground electronic countermeasures equipment, all kinds of communications equipment, and the management of radio frequencies

Qualifications

Knowledge of telecommunications functions and operations of electronic communications equipment; typing or keyboard experience and clear speaking voice desirable in many specialties. Business math, algebra, and geometry desirable

Examples of Civilian Jobs

Central Office Operator (telephone and telegraph), cryptographer, radio operator, telephone supervisor, and photo-radio operator; card-type converter or computer operator, data typist, data-processing control clerk, high-speed printer operator, and programmer

Control Systems Operations

Duties and Responsibilities

Operates control towers; directs aircraft landings with radar landing control equipment, and operates ground radar equipment, aircraft control centers, airborne radar equipment, space tracking, and missile warning systems

Qualifications

Equipment dexterity, clear voice, speech ability, and excellent vision. English desirable

Examples of Civilian Jobs

Aircraft log clerk, airport control operator, and air traffic controller

Geodetics

Duties and Responsibilities

Procures, compiles, computes, and uses topographic, photogrammetric, and cartographic data in preparing aeronautical charts, topographic maps, and target folders

Qualifications

Ability to use precision instruments required in measuring and drafting. Algebra, geometry, trigonometry, and physics necessary

Examples of Civilian Jobs

Cartographer and Topographical Drafter

Intelligence

Duties and Responsibilities

Collects, produces, and disseminates data of strategic, tactical, or technical value from an intelligence viewpoint, and maintains information security

Qualifications

Knowledge of techniques of evaluation, analysis, interpretation, and reporting. Foreign languages, English composition, photography, mathematics, and typing desirable

Examples of Civilian Jobs

Crypto-analyst, draftsperson, interpreter, investigator, statistician, radio operator, and translator

Structural/Pavements

Duties and Responsibilities

Constructs and maintains structural facilities and pavement areas; maintains pavements, railroads, and soil bases; performs erosion control; operates heavy equipment; performs site development, general maintenance, cost and real-property accounting, work control functions, and metal fabricating

Qualifications

Blueprint reading, mechanical drawing, mathematics, physics, and chemistry are desirable

Examples of Civilian Jobs

Plumber, bricklayer, carpenter, stonesman, painter, construction worker, welder, and sheet metal worker

Weather

Duties and Responsibilities

Collects, records, and analyzes meteorological data; makes visual and instrument weather observations; and forecasts immediate and long-range weather conditions

Qualifications

Visual acuity correctable to 20/20. Physics, mathematics and geography desirable

Examples of Civilian Jobs

Meteorologist, weather forecaster, and weather observer

Army Occupations

COMBAT SPECIALTIES

Air Defense Artillery

Duties and Responsibilities

Operates and maintains electrical systems, uses technical diagrams to locate and replace defective parts, conducts communications with air traffic controllers, supervises or assists in repairing electronic or radar equipment, and monitors computers and telemetry display systems

Qualifications

Basic mechanical, electronic, and mathematical abilities; emotional stability; and a high degree of observational and reasoning ability

Examples of Civilian Jobs

Systems specialist and radar operator and data-processing equipment, electronic instruments, and systems, radar, radio equipment, and teletype repairer

Armor

Duties and Responsibilities

Operates and maintains heavy equipment over rough terrain; serves as a member of a reconnaissance, security, or special operations force; and interprets maps and operational data

Qualifications

High state of physical fitness and possess a high degree of ability in leadership, communications, mathematics, and mechanical maintenance

Examples of Civilian Jobs

Supervisor, heavy equipment operator or repairman, truck mechanic, and armament machinist and operator

Combat Engineering

Duties and Responsibilities

Constructs, repairs, and maintains roads; fixes bridges, port facilities, pipelines, supply tanks, and related facilities; and performs as a team leader and supervisor in construction and demolition

Qualifications

Mathematical reasoning ability, auto mechanics, carpentry, woodworking, mechanical drawing, and drafting courses

Examples of Civilian Jobs

Construction worker, supervisor, heavy equipment operator, drafter, rigger, bridge repairer, lumber worker, and blaster

Field Artillery

Duties and Responsibilities

Serves or supervises in the operation/intelligence, fire support, and target acquisition activities of a highly specialized organization; operates unique rocket launching computers that assist cannons and rockets in obtaining maximum accuracy; and operates and maintains radar, meteorological, and survey equipment

Qualifications

Mathematical reasoning, abilities in mechanical maintenance, meteorology, communications, and a high state of physical fitness

Examples of Civilian Jobs

Supervisor, surveyor, topographical drafter, cartographer, meteorologist, and radio operator

Infantry

Duties and Responsibilities

Serves in closely coordinated teams organized for highly unified action. As a supervisor, provides effective leadership and management of a highly motivated organization

Qualifications

Highest state of physical fitness. Organizational maintenance, leadership, and communications abilities. Mechanical aptitude

Examples of Civilian Jobs

Supervisor, human relations counselor, physical education instructor, supply clerk, computer operator, dispatcher, and security officer

VEHICLE/MACHINERY MECHANICS

Aircraft Maintenance

Duties and Responsibilities

Performs the mechanical functions of maintenance, repair, and modification of helicopters and turboprop engine aircraft

Qualifications

Considerable mechanical or electrical aptitude and manual dexterity. Shop mathematics and physics desirable

Examples of Civilian Jobs

Aircraft mechanic and plane inspector

Aircraft System Maintenance

Duties and Responsibilities

Performs maintenance of aircraft accessory systems, propulsion systems, armament systems, and fabrication of metal materials used in aircraft structural repair and inspection and preservation

Qualifications

Electrical and mechanical aptitude. Shop mathematics and shop work desirable

Examples of Civilian Jobs

Aircraft mechanic, aircraft electrician, and sheet metal machinist

Mechanical Maintenance

Duties and Responsibilities

Services and repairs land and amphibious wheel and track vehicles, ranging from cars and light trucks to tanks and self-propelled weapons, and installs and repairs refrigeration, bakery, and laundry equipment

Qualifications

Automotive mechanics, electricity, blueprint reading, machine shop, and physics

Examples of Civilian Jobs

Automotive mechanic, motor analyst, bakery or refrigeration equipment repairer, frames, wheel alignment, and tractor mechanic

ELECTRONIC/ELECTRICAL SYSTEMS

Air Defense Missile Maintenance

Duties and Responsibilities

Inspects, tests, maintains, and repairs guided missile fire control equipment and related radar installations that guide missiles to the targets

Qualifications

Mathematics, physics, electricity, and electronics

Examples of Civilian Jobs

Radio installation and repair inspector, electronic equipment technician, and radio and television repairer

Aviation Communications—Electronic Systems Maintenance

Duties and Responsibilities

Repairs and maintains navigation, flight control, and associated communications equipment

Qualifications

Electrical/electronic theory and repair

Examples of Civilian Jobs

Electronics technician, radar repairer, and electrical instrument mechanic/repairer

Aviation Operations

Duties and Responsibilities

Maintains, installs, and repairs aviation communication radar systems used for aircraft navigation and landing and performs air traffic control duties

Qualifications

Mathematics and shop courses in electricity and electronics useful

Examples of Civilian Jobs

Radio and television or electrical instrument repairer, communications, electrical and electronics engineer, and radio engineer

Ballistic/Land Combat Missile and Light Air Defense Weapons Systems Maintenance

Duties and Responsibilities

Inspects, tests, maintains, and repairs tactical missile systems and related test equipment and trainers

Qualifications

Mathematics, physics, electricity, electronics (radio and television), and blueprint reading

Examples of Civilian Jobs

Radio control room technician, radio mechanic, transmitter, and radio and television repairer

Communications—Electronic Maintenance

Duties and Responsibilities

Installs and maintains radar and radio receiving, transmitting, carrier, and terminal equipment

Qualifications

Electricity, mathematics, electronics, and blueprint reading.

Examples of Civilian Jobs

Radio control room technician, radio mechanic, transmitter, and radio and television repairer

Electronics Warfare Intercept Systems Maintenance

Duties and Responsibilities

Installs, operates, and maintains intercept, electronic measuring, and testing equipment

Qualifications

Physics, mathematics, electricity, electronics (radio and television), and blueprint reading

Examples of Civilian Jobs

Electrical instrument repairer and electronic equipment inspector

PERSONNEL/BASE SUPPORT

Administration

Duties and Responsibilities

Performs general administrative duties, such as typing, stenography, and postal functions, and specific administrative duties, such as personnel, legal, equal opportunity, and chapel activities

Qualifications

Basic clerical and communication abilities, typing, bookkeeping, stenography, or office management skills desirable

Examples of Civilian Jobs

Clerk, typist, secretary, employment interviewer, postal clerk, recreation specialist, office manager, personnel clerk, bookkeeper, cashier, payroll clerk and court clerk

Audiovisual

Duties and Responsibilities

Operates radio and television equipment, still/motion picture photography, audiovisual equipment repair, and graphic illustration

Qualifications

Normal color vision, verbal ability, clear speech, and attentiveness

Examples of Civilian Jobs

Cameraman, camera repairer, photographer, illustrator, and video editor

Band

Duties and Responsibilities

Plays brass, woodwind, or percussion instruments in marching, concert, dance, stage, and show bands, combos, or instrumental ensembles; sings in vocal groups, writes and arranges music

Qualifications

Vocal audition or instrumental audition with bass, woodwind, or percussion instrument

Examples of Civilian Jobs

Bandsman, bandmaster, musician, accompanist, arranger, music director, orchestrator, music teacher, orchestra leader, and vocalist

Finance and Accounting

Duties and Responsibilities

Maintains pay records for military personnel; prepares vouchers for payment; prepares reports; disburses funds; accounts for funds to include budgeting, allocation, and auditing; compiles and analyzes statistical data; and prepares cost analysis records

Qualifications

Dexterity in the operation of business machines. Typing, mathematics, statistics, and basic principles of accounting desirable. High administrative aptitude mandatory

Examples of Civilian Jobs

Paymaster, cashier, statistical or audit clerk, accountant, budget clerk, and bookkeeper

Food Service

Duties and Responsibilities

Plans regular and special diet menus and cooks and bakes food in dining facilities and during field exercises. May serve as aide and cook on personal staff for general officer

Qualifications

Home economics, restaurant worker, bake shop, or meat market

Examples of Civilian Jobs

Cook, chef, caterer, baker, butcher, kitchen supervisor, and cafeteria manager

Healthcare

Duties and Responsibilities

Assists or supports physicians, surgeons, nurses, dentists, psychologists, social workers, and veterinarians in 32 separate job classifications; some provide direct patient care in hospitals and clinics; and others make and repair eyeglasses, dentures, or orthomedical equipment or maintain medical records

Qualifications

Biology, chemistry, hygiene, sociology, general math, algebra, animal care, knowledge of mechanics, electronics, and general clerical skills

Examples of Civilian Jobs

Social Worker (case aide), practical nurse, nurse aide, dental assistant, surgeon assistant, psychological aide, hospital attendant or orderly, veterinary assistant, food quality control, medical or dental laboratory technician, physical therapist assistant, and dietetic technician

Military Police

Duties and Responsibilities

Enforces military regulations; protects facilities, roads, designated sensitive areas, and personnel; controls traffic movement; and guards military prisoners and enemy prisoners of war

Qualifications

Sociology and demonstrated leadership in athletics and other group work helpful

Examples of Civilian Jobs

Police officer, plant guard, detective, investigator, crime detection laboratory assistant and ballistics expert

Public Affairs

Duties and Responsibilities

Prepares and disseminates news releases on military activities and prepares scripts and newsletters, announcements, and public-speaking engagements

Qualifications

Clerical aptitude, verbal ability, clear speech, and attentiveness

Examples of Civilian Jobs

Newspaper editor, editorial assistant, public information specialist, and photojournalist

LOGISTICS AND SUPPLY

Ammunition

Duties and Responsibilities

Handles, stores, reconditions, and salvages ammunition, explosives, and components and locates, removes, and destroys or salvages unexploded bombs and missiles

Qualifications

Mechanical aptitude, attentiveness, good close vision, normal color discrimination, manual dexterity, and hand-eye coordination

Examples of Civilian Jobs

Toxic chemical handler, ammunition inspector, and acid plant operator

Petroleum

Duties and Responsibilities

Receives, stores, preserves, and distributes bulk-packaged petroleum products; performs standard physical and chemical tests of petroleum products; and storage and distribution of purified water

Qualifications

Hygiene, biology, physics, chemistry, and mathematics

Examples of Civilian Jobs

Biological laboratory assistant, petroleum tester, and chemical laboratory assistant

Supply and Service

Duties and Responsibilities

Receives, stores, and issues individual, organizational, and expendable supplies, equipment, and spare parts; establishes, posts, and maintains stock records; repairs and alters textile, canvas, and leather supplies; rigs parachutes; decontaminates materials; and performs mortuary and grave registration functions

Qualifications

Mathematical ability and perceptual speed in scanning and checking supply documents. Verbal ability; courses in bookkeeping, typing, and office machine operation

Examples of Civilian Jobs

Inventory clerk, stock control clerk or supervisor, shipping or parts clerk, warehouse manager, and parachute rigger

Transportation

Duties and Responsibilities

Operates and performs preventive maintenance on personnel, light, medium, and heavy cargo vehicles; operates and maintains marine harbor craft; and performs as air traffic controller

Qualifications

Mechanical aptitude, manual dexterity, hand-eye coordination, FAA certification for air traffic control, and license for vehicle operation

Examples of Civilian Jobs

Truck driver and FAA air traffic controller

ENGINEERING, SCIENCE, AND TECHNICAL

Automatic Data Processing

Duties and Responsibilities

Operates several electrical accounting and automatic data processing equipment to produce personnel, supply, fiscal, medical, intelligence, and other reports

Qualifications

Reasoning and verbal ability, clerical aptitude, manual dexterity, and hand-eye coordination. Knowledge of typing and office machines

Examples of Civilian Jobs

Coding clerk; keypunch, computer, and sorting machine operator, and machine records unit supervisor

Chemical

Duties and Responsibilities

Provides decontamination service after chemical, biological, or radiological attacks; produces smoke for battlefield concealment; repairs chemical equipment; and assists in overall planning of chemical, biological, or radiological activities

Qualifications

Biology, chemistry, and electricity

Examples of Civilian Jobs

Laboratory assistant (biological, chemical, or radiological), pumper and repairer (chemical), and exterminator

Communications—Cryptologic Operations

Duties and Responsibilities

Installs and maintains field telephone switchboards and field radio communications equipment

Qualifications

Mathematics, physics, and shop courses in electricity

Examples of Civilian Jobs

Communications engineer assistant, plant electrician, and radio electrician or operator

Electronic Warfare—Cryptologic Operations

Duties and Responsibilities

Collects and analyzes electromagnetic warfare duties in fixed or mobile operations

Qualifications

Verbal and reasoning ability and perceptual speed; hearing and visual acuity

Examples of Civilian Jobs

Radio and telegraph operator, navigator, intelligence research analyst, statistician, and signal collection technician

General Engineering

Duties and Responsibilities

Provides utilities and engineering services, such as electric power production, building and roadway construction and maintenance, salvage activities, airstrip construction, and fire-fighting and crash rescue operations

Qualifications

Mechanical aptitude, emotional stability, and ability to visualize spatial relationships. Carpentry, woodworking, or mechanical drawing

Examples of Civilian Jobs

Carpenter, construction equipment operator, electrician, firefighter, driver, plumber, welder, and bricklayer

Military Intelligence

Duties and Responsibilities

Gathers, translates, correlates, and interprets information, including imagery, associated with military plans and operations

Qualifications

English composition, typing, foreign languages, mathematics, and geography

Examples of Civilian Jobs

Investigator, interpreter, records analyst, research worker, and intelligence analyst (government)

Topographic Engineering

Duties and Responsibilities

Performs land surveys; produces construction drawings and plans, maps, charts, and diagrams and illustrates material; constructs scale models of terrain and structures; and operates offset duplicators, presses, and bindery equipment

Qualifications

Mechanical drawing and drafting, blueprint reading, commercial art, fine arts, geography, and mathematics

Examples of Civilian Jobs

Drafting (structural, mechanical, and topographical), cartographic and art layout, model maker, and commercial artist

Coast Guard Occupations

VEHICLE/MACHINERY MECHANICS

Aviation Maintenance Technician

Duties and Responsibilities

Inspects, services, maintains, troubleshoots, and repairs aircraft power plant, power train, and structural systems; maintains metal, composite, and fiberglass materials; fabricates cables, wire harnesses, and structural components; and performs aircraft corrosion control, nondestructive testing, basic electrical troubleshooting, and record keeping. Also, hold an aircrew position in specific Coast Guard aircraft

Qualifications

Automobile or aircraft engine work; algebra and geometry helpful. High degree of mechanical aptitude. Metal shop, woodworking, algebra, plane geometry, physics, and experience in automobile bodywork desirable

Examples of Civilian Jobs

Airport serviceperson, aircraft engine test mechanic, small appliance repairer, mechanic, machinist, and flight engineer; welder, sheet metal repairer, hydraulics technician, and aircraft repairer

Machinery Technician

Duties and Responsibilities

Operates, maintains, and repairs ship's propulsion, auxiliary equipment, and outside equipment, such as steering, engineering, refrigeration/air conditioning and steam

Qualifications

Aptitude for mechanical work. Practical or shop mathematics, machine shop, electricity, and physics valuable

Examples of Civilian Jobs

Boiler house repairer, engineer maintenance, machinist, marine engineer, turbine operator, and engineer repairer, air-conditioning and refrigeration repairer

ELECTRONIC/ELECTRICAL SYSTEMS

Avionics Technician

Duties and Responsibilities

Inspects, services, maintains, troubleshoots, and repairs aircraft power, communications, navigation, auto flight, and sensor systems; performs minimum performance checks, system alignments, avionics corrosion control, and recordkeeping; and holds an aircrew position in specific Coast Guard aircraft

Qualifications

Algebra, trigonometry, physics, and shop experience in electrical work are desirable. High degree of aptitude for electrical work

Examples of Civilian Jobs

Aircraft electrician, electrician, substation operator, instrument inspector and electrical consultant, radio mechanic, electronics technician, radio repairman/technician, and television repairer

Electrician's Mate

Duties and Responsibilities

Tests, maintains, and repairs aviation electronics equipment, including navigation, identification, detection, reconnaissance, and special-purpose equipment, and operates warfare equipment

Qualifications

Aptitude for electrical and mechanical work. Electrical, practical, and shop mathematics and physics are useful

Examples of Civilian Jobs

Electrician, electric motor and electrical equipment repairer, armature winder, and radio/television repairer

Electronics Technician

Duties and Responsibilities

Maintains all electronic equipment used for communications, detection ranging, recognition and countermeasures, worldwide navigational systems, computers, and sonars

Qualifications

Aptitude for detailed mechanical work. Radio, electricity, physics, algebra, trigonometry, and shop valuable

Examples of Civilian Jobs

Electronics technician, radar and radio repairer, instrument and electronics mechanic, and telephone repairperson

Telephone Technician

Duties and Responsibilities

Installs and maintains telecommunications equipment, ranging from towers, antennas, pole lines, and underground cables to computer-based data communications and processing systems, telephone and data switching systems and networks, and public address, security, and remote control systems

Qualifications

An interest in electrical equipment and an above-average ability to solve mathematical problems. School courses in algebra, physics, trigonometry, electricity, and communications useful. Experience with electronics, electrical, or communications equipment helpful

Examples of Civilian Jobs

Electronics technician, telephone installer, telephone lineperson, data/computer equipment technician, and telephone repair

LOGISTICS AND SUPPLY

Aviation Survival Technician

Duties and Responsibilities

Inspects, services, maintains, troubleshoots, and repairs aircraft and aircrew survival equipment and rescue devices; performs the duties of a rescue swimmer; and provides aircrew survival training to all aviators

Qualifications

Must perform extremely careful and accurate work. General shop, math, and sewing desirable. Experience in use and repair of sewing machines

Examples of Civilian Jobs

Parachute packer, inspector, repairer, and tester; sailmaker, ammunition foreman; and rescue gear specialist

Boatswain's Mate

Duties and Responsibilities

Operates small boats, stores cargo, handles ropes and lines, and directs work of deck force

Qualifications

Must be physically strong. Practical mathematics desirable. Algebra, geometry, and physics

Examples of Civilian Jobs

Motorboat operator, pier superintendent, able seaman, rigger, cargo wincher, longshoreman, marina operator, and heavy equipment operator

Storekeeper

Duties and Responsibilities

Orders, receives, stores, inventories, and issues clothing, food, mechanical equipment, and other items; serves as a payroll clerk

Qualifications

Typing, bookkeeping, accounting and commercial mathematics, general business and English helpful

Examples of Civilian Jobs

Sales or shipping clerk, warehouse worker, buyer, invoice control clerk, purchasing agent, and accountant

PERSONNEL/BASE SUPPORT

Food Service Specialist

Duties and Responsibilities

Cooks and bakes, prepares menus, keeps cost accounts, assists in ordering provisions, and inspects food

Qualifications

Experience or course in food preparation, dietetics, and recordkeeping helpful

Examples of Civilian Jobs

Cook, steward, butcher, chef, and restaurant manager

Health Services Technician

Duties and Responsibilities

Administers medicine, applies first aid, assists in operating room, nurses patients, assists dental officers

Qualifications

Hygiene, biology, first aid, physiology, chemistry, typing, and public speaking helpful

Examples of Civilian Jobs

Practical nurse and medical, dental, or X-ray technician

Public Affairs Specialist

Duties and Responsibilities

Reports and edits news; publishes information about servicemembers and activities through newspapers, magazines, radio, and television; and shoots and develops film and photographs

Qualifications

High degree of clerical aptitude; English, journalism, typing, and writing experience helpful

Examples of Civilian Jobs

News editor, copyreader, script writer, reporter, freelance writer, rewrite or art layout person, producer, public relations advertising specialist, and photographer

Yeoman

Duties and Responsibilities

Performs typing and filing duties, operates office equipment, prepares and routes correspondence and reports, and maintains personnel records and publications

Qualifications

Same qualifications required of secretaries and typists in private industry. English, business, stenography, and typing are helpful

Examples of Civilian Jobs

Office manager, secretary, general office clerk, administrative assistant, legal clerk, personnel manager, and court reporter

ENGINEERING, SCIENCE, AND TECHNICAL

Damage Controlman

Duties and Responsibilities

Fabricates, installs, and repairs shipboard structures, plumbing, and piping systems; uses damage control in firefighting; operates nuclear, biological, chemical, and radiological defense equipment; and construction work

Qualifications

High mechanical aptitude. Sheet metal foundry, pipefitting, carpentry, mathematics, geometry, and chemistry

Examples of Civilian Jobs

Firefighter, welder, plumber, ship-fitter, blacksmith, metallurgical technician, and carpenter

Fire Control Technician

Duties and Responsibilities

Operates, tests, maintains, and repairs weapons control systems and tele-metering equipment used to compute accuracy of naval guns and missiles

Qualifications

Ability to perform fine, detailed work. Extensive training in mathematics, electronics, electricity, and mechanics useful

Examples of Civilian Jobs

Radar or electronics technician, test range tracker, instrument repairer, and electrician

Gunner's Mate

Duties and Responsibilities

Operates and performs maintenance on guided missile-launching systems, rocket launchers, guns, and gun mounts; and inspects/repairs electrical, electronic, pneumatic, mechanical, and hydraulic systems

Qualifications

Prolonged attention and mental alertness, ability to perform detailed work. High aptitude for electrical and mechanical work. Arithmetic, shop math, electricity, electronics, physics, machine shop, and welding are helpful

Examples of Civilian Jobs

Gunsmith, locksmith, machinist, instrument repairer, hydraulics, pneumatic or mechanical technician, small appliance, and test equipment repairer

Marine Science Technician

Duties and Responsibilities

Makes visual/instrumental weather and oceanographic observations; conducts chemical analysis; enters data on appropriate logs, charts, and forms; and analyzes/interprets weather and sea conditions

Qualifications

Ability to use numbers in practical problems. Algebra, geometry, trigonometry, physics, physiology, chemistry, typing, meteorology, astronomy, and oceanography helpful

Examples of Civilian Jobs

Oceanographic technician, weather observer, meteorologist, chart maker, statistical clerk, and inspector of weather and oceanographic instruments

Quartermaster

Duties and Responsibilities

Performs navigation of ship's steering; lookout supervision, ship control, bridge watch duties, visual communication, and maintenance of navigational aids

Qualifications

Good vision and hearing and ability to express oneself clearly in writing and speaking. Public speaking, grammar, geometry, and physics helpful

Examples of Civilian Jobs

Barge, motorboat or yacht captain, quartermaster, harbor pilot aboard merchant ships, navigator, and chart maker

Radar Technician

Duties and Responsibilities

Operates surveillance and search radar, electronic recognition and identification equipment, controlled approach devices, and electronic aids to navigation; and serves as plotter and status board keeper

Qualifications

Prolonged attention and mental alertness. Physics, mathematics, and shop courses in radio and electricity helpful. Experience in radio repair valuable

Examples of Civilian Jobs

Radio operator (aircraft, ship, government service, radio broadcasting) and radar equipment supervisor

Telecommunications Specialist

Duties and Responsibilities

Operates communication equipment; and transmits, receives, and processes all forms of military record and voice communications

Qualifications

Good hearing and manual dexterity. Mathematics, physics, and electricity desirable. Experience as amateur radio operator is helpful

Examples of Civilian Jobs

Telegrapher, radio dispatcher, radio/telephone operator, and computer operator

Marine Corps Occupations

COMBAT SPECIALTIES

Field Artillery

Duties and Responsibilities

Maintains 155-mm, 8-inch, and 105-mm howitzers and self-propelled 8-inch and 105-mm howitzers

Qualifications

Mathematical reasoning, mechanical aptitude, good vision, and stamina; mechanics, electricity, and meteorology

Examples of Civilian Jobs

Surveyor, meteorologist, radio operator, recording engineer, and ordnance inspector

Infantry

Duties and Responsibilities

Performs as rifleman, machine gunner or grenadier, and infantry unit leader; supervises training and operations of infantry units

Qualifications

Verbal and mathematical reasoning, good vision and stamina; general mathematics, mechanical drafting, geography, and mechanical drawing

Examples of Civilian Jobs

Firearms assembler, gunsmith, policeman, immigration inspector, and plant security policeman

Tank and Amphibian Tractor

Duties and Responsibilities

Performs as driver, gunner, and loader in tanks, armored amphibious tractors

Qualifications

Mechanical ability and stamina; auto mechanics, machine shop, electricity, and mechanical drawing

Examples of Civilian Jobs

Automotive mechanic, bulldozer operator or repairman, armament machinist-mechanic, and gunsmith assistant

VEHICLE/MACHINERY MECHANICS

Aircraft Maintenance

Duties and Responsibilities

Performs the mechanical functions of maintenance, repair, and modification of Marine air and ground support equipment

Qualifications

Mechanical or electrical aptitude with manual dexterity; shop mathematics desirable

Examples of Civilian Jobs

Aircraft mechanic, electrician or hydraulics specialist, aviation machinist, sheet metal worker, and aircraft instrument maker or repairer

Motor Transport

Duties and Responsibilities

Performs auto mechanics and body repair, motor vehicle, and amphibian truck operations

Qualifications

Automotive mechanics, machine shop, electricity, and blueprint reading useful

Examples of Civilian Jobs

Automobile mechanic, electrical systems repairer, truck driver, motor vehicle dispatcher, and motor transport

ELECTRONIC/ELECTRICAL SYSTEMS

Avionics

Duties and Responsibilities

Installs and repairs aircraft electrical, communications/navigation, and fire control equipment and air-launched guided missiles; and serves as electrician and instrument repairman

Qualifications

Mathematics and shop course in electricity, hydraulics, and electronics useful

Examples of Civilian Jobs

Radio and television or electrical instrument repairer, communications, electrical or electronics engineer, and radio operator

Data/Communications Maintenance

Duties and Responsibilities

Installs, inspects, and repairs telephone, teletype, and cryptographic equipment and cables and calibrates precision electronic, mechanical, dimensional, and optical test instruments

Qualifications

Mathematics, electricity, and blueprint reading courses helpful

Examples of Civilian Jobs

Telephone installer and troubleshooter

Electronics Maintenance

Duties and Responsibilities

Installs, tests, and repairs air search radar, radio, radio relay, missile fire control, and guidance systems

Qualifications

Electronics, mathematics, electricity, and blueprint reading useful

Examples of Civilian Jobs

Radio and television repair, radio engineer, electrical instrument repairer, recording communications, and electrical engineer

Training and Audiovisual Support

Duties and Responsibilities

Operates still, motion picture, and aerial cameras; develops film and prints; repairs cameras; edits motion picture films; and performs as illustrator or draftsman

Qualifications

Mathematics, chemistry, and shop courses in electricity; normal color perception desirable

Examples of Civilian Jobs

Commercial illustrator, photographer, cinematographer, copy camera operator, motion picture film editor, camera, and instrument repairer

PERSONNEL/BASE SUPPORT

Airfield Services

Duties and Responsibilities

Maintains aircraft log books, publications, and flight operations records; prepares reports and schedules; and installs and repairs aircraft launching and recovery equipment

Qualifications

Typing, geography, and mechanical drawing useful

Examples of Civilian Jobs

Airplane dispatch clerk, flight dispatcher, timekeeper, and airport crash truck driver

Auditing, Finance, and Accounting

Duties and Responsibilities

Prepares and audits personnel pay records, processes public vouchers, and administers and audits unit fiscal accounts

Qualifications

Computational work and attention to detail; typing, bookkeeping, office machine, and mathematics useful

Examples of Civilian Jobs

Payroll or cost clerk, bookkeeper, cashier, bank teller, accounting and audit clerk, and accountant

Food Service

Duties and Responsibilities

Performs as cook, baker, or meat cutter

Qualifications

Hygiene, biology, chemistry, home economics, and bookkeeping courses useful

Examples of Civilian Jobs

Cook, chef, baker, meat cutter or butcher, caterer, executive chef, dietician, and restaurant manager

Legal Services

Duties and Responsibilities

Prepares legal documents, operates stenotype machines

Qualifications

Manual dexterity, English

Examples of Civilian Jobs

Law clerk, court reporter, chief clerk, and stenotype operator

Marine Corps Exchange

Duties and Responsibilities

Keeps and audits books and financial records, performs sales and merchandise stock control duties

Qualifications

Typing, bookkeeping, business, arithmetic, office machine operations, and accounting useful

Examples of Civilian Jobs

Salesman, stock control supervisor, buyer, bookkeeper, accounting clerk, accountant, and auditor

Military Police and Corrections

Duties and Responsibilities

Enforces military orders, guards military and war prisoners, and controls traffic

Qualifications

Sociology and athletic ability helpful

Examples of Civilian Jobs

Policeman, ballistics expert, and investigator

Musician

Duties and Responsibilities

Performs in Marine Corps Band, unit bands, and Drum and Bugle Corps; repairs musical instruments

Qualifications

Music experience as a member of a high school band or orchestra

Examples of Civilian Jobs

Musician, music librarian, music teacher, bandmaster, orchestra or music director, and musical instrument repairer

Personnel and Administration

Duties and Responsibilities

Performs as personnel classification clerk, administrative specialist, and postal clerk

Qualifications

Reasoning, verbal ability, and clerical aptitude. English composition, typing shorthand, and social studies helpful

Examples of Civilian Jobs

Secretary, typist, vocational advisor, employment interviewer, manager, office manager, job analyst, and postal clerk

Printing and Reproduction

Duties and Responsibilities

Performs letterpress and lithographic offset printing; sets type; and operates linotype machines, presses, process cameras, and bookbinding equipment

Qualifications

General mathematics, printing, and other graphic arts useful

Examples of Civilian Jobs

Printing, compositor, linotype operator, photo lithographer, press operator, printing bookbinder, printing plant makeup worker, and proofreader

Public Affairs

Duties and Responsibilities

Serves as liaison between the marine corps and the public and media. Gathers material for and writes and edits news stories and historical reports; gathers material for, prepares, and edits radio and television broadcast scripts. Conducts community-relations projects. Assists in operations of armed forces radio and television service detachments worldwide

Qualifications

English grammar and composition, typing aptitude required, and speech, journalism, and photography helpful

Examples of Civilian Jobs

Public relations, television news reporter/anchor, radio disc jockey, news reporter correspondent, columnist, copyreader, copy or news editor, radio television announcer, and script writer. Television/radio station programmer/traffic director, video editor and producer, television news cameraman, and print journalism photographer

LOGISTICS AND SUPPLY

Ammunition and Explosive Ordnance Disposal

Duties and Responsibilities

Inspects, issues, and supervises storage of ammunition and explosives; locates, disarms, detonates, or salvages unexploded bombs

Qualifications

Mechanics, general science, and chemistry useful

Examples of Civilian Jobs

Firearms and ammunition proof director, ordnance technician (government), and powder and explosives inspector

Logistics

Duties and Responsibilities

Performs administrative duties involving the supply, quartering, movement, and transport of Marine units by land, sea, and air

Qualifications

Clerical aptitude, knowledge of verbal and math reasoning; ability to operate office machines and read maps useful

Examples of Civilian Jobs

Inventory or shipping clerk, pier superintendent, stock control clerk or supervisor, and warehouse manager

Supply Administration and Operations

Duties and Responsibilities

Administration procurement, subsistence, packaging, and warehousing; requisitions, purchases, receipts, and accounts; classifies, stores, issues, sells, packages, preserves and inspects new scrap, salvage, waste material, supplies, and equipment

Qualifications

Typing, bookkeeping, office machine operation, and commercial subjects helpful

Examples of Civilian Jobs

Shipping, receiving, stock and inventory clerk, stock control supervisor, warehouse manager, and parts and purchasing agent

Transportation

Duties and Responsibilities

Handles cargo and transacts business of freight shipping and receiving and passenger transportation

Qualifications

Typing, bookkeeping, business, arithmetic, office machine operation, and commercial subjects beneficial

Examples of Civilian Jobs

Shipping clerk, cargo handler, freight traffic clerk, passenger, and railroad station agent

ENGINEERING, SCIENCE, AND TECHNICAL

Air Traffic Control and Enlisted Flight Crew/Air Support/ Anti-Warfare

Duties and Responsibilities

Operates airfield control tower and radio-radar air traffic control systems; serves as navigator, radio and radar operator, and intercept controller anti-air warfare missile batteryman

Qualifications

Clear speaking voice, good hearing, and better-than-average eyesight; speech, mathematics, and electricity and experience as a ham radio operator helpful

Examples of Civilian Jobs

Airport control tower or flight radio operator, navigator, instrument-landing truck operator, and radio or television studio engineer

Aviation Ordnance

Duties and Responsibilities

Maintains and repairs aircraft armament systems, gun pods, machine guns, bomb racks, and rocket/missile launcher equipment

Qualifications

Electricity, hydraulics, and mechanics shop courses useful

Examples of Civilian Jobs

Firearms assembler, gunsmith, armament mechanic, and aircraft accessories repairer

Construction Equipment and Shore Party

Duties and Responsibilities

Performs metalworking operation and maintenance of fuel storage, heavy engineering equipment, construction, and repair of military facilities

Qualifications

Automotive mechanics, sheet metal working, machine shop, carpentry, and mechanical drafting useful

Examples of Civilian Jobs

Sheet metal worker, engineering equipment mechanic, carpenter, road machinery operator, rigger, and construction superintendent

Data Systems

Duties and Responsibilities

Operates and programs data-processing equipment

Qualifications

Clerical aptitude, manual dexterity, and hand-eye coordination, mathematics, accounting, and English useful

Examples of Civilian Jobs

Computer operator or programmer and data control coordinator

Drafting, Surveying, and Mapping

Duties and Responsibilities

Makes architectural and mechanical drawings, prepares military maps, and creates or copies articles of illustrative materials

Qualifications

Mathematics, mechanical drawing and drafting, geography, and commercial art helpful

Examples of Civilian Jobs

Architectural or mechanical drafting, surveyor or cartographer, illustrator, and commercial artist

Intelligence

Duties and Responsibilities

Records and interprets information, makes study of aerial photographs, conducts interrogations in foreign languages, and translates written material and interprets conversations

Qualifications

Geography, history, government, economics, English, foreign languages, typing, mechanical drafting, and mathematics useful

Examples of Civilian Jobs

Investigator, research worker, intelligence analyst (government), map drafter, cartographic aide, and records analyst

Nuclear, Biological, and Chemical

Duties and Responsibilities

Performs routine duties to apply detection, emergency, and decontamination measures to gassed or radioactive areas; inspects and performs preventive maintenance on chemical warfare protection equipment

Qualifications

Must not have any known hypersensitivity to the wearing of protective clothing; be emotionally stable; biology and chemistry background useful

Examples of Civilian Jobs

Laboratory assistant (nuclear, biological, or chemical), exterminator, and decontaminator

Operational Communications

Duties and Responsibilities

Lays communication wire; installs and operates radio, radio telegraph, and radio relay equipment; and encodes and decodes messages

Qualifications

Mathematics, typing, and courses in electricity and electronics useful

Examples of Civilian Jobs

Radio operator, telephone lineperson, radio broadcaster, traffic manager, and communications engineer

Ordnance

Duties and Responsibilities

Inspects, maintains, and repairs infantry, artillery, and anti-aircraft weapons; handles fire control optical instruments; operates machine tools; and modifies metal parts

Qualifications

Mathematics, mechanics, machine shop and blueprint reading, welding, and heat treatment or metal electricity

Examples of Civilian Jobs

Armament mechanic, gunsmith, time-recording equipment service person, electrician, optical instrument inspector, and electrical engineer

Signals Intelligence/Ground Electronic Warfare

Duties and Responsibilities

Performs routine duties for collecting, translating, recording, and disseminating information associated with military plans and operations

Qualifications

English composition, geography, and mathematics useful

Examples of Civilian Jobs

Radio intelligence operator, intelligence analyst, investigator, and records analyst

Utilities

Duties and Responsibilities

Installs, operates, and maintains electrical, water supply, heating, plumbing, sewage, refrigeration, hygiene, and air-conditioning equipment

Qualifications

Mechanical aptitude and manual dexterity important; vocational school shop course in industrial arts and crafts beneficial

Examples of Civilian Jobs

Electrician, plumber, steam fitter, refrigeration mechanic, electric motor repairer, and stationary engineer

Weather Service

Duties and Responsibilities

Collects, records, and analyzes meteorological data; makes visual and instrumental observations

Qualifications

Visual acuity correctable to 20/20, normal color perception; mathematics desirable, meteorology and astronomy helpful

Examples of Civilian Jobs

Meteorologist and weather forecaster/observer

Navy Occupations

COMBAT SPECIALTIES

Aviation/Anti-Submarine Warfare (ASW) Operator

Duties and Responsibilities

Performs general flight crew duties; operates ASW sensor systems; performs diagnostic functions to effect fault isolation and optimize system performance

Qualifications

High degree of electrical and mechanical aptitude. Must pass flight physical and be able to swim. Courses in algebra, trigonometry, physics, and electricity

Examples of Civilian Jobs

Radar technician and oil well sounding device operator

Electronic Warfare Technician

Duties and Responsibilities

Operates and maintains electronic equipment used for detection, analysis, and identification of emissions in electromagnetic spectrums, as well as deception and jamming of enemy electronic sensors

Qualifications

Good arithmetic and recordkeeping ability. Competence with tools, equipment, and machines

Examples of Civilian Jobs

Electronics intelligence operations specialist and electronics mechanic

Fire Control Technician

Duties and Responsibilities

Operates, tests, maintains, and repairs weapons control systems and telemetering equipment used to compute and resolve factors that influence accuracy of torpedoes and missiles

Qualifications

Perform fine, detailed work. Extensive training in mathematics, electronics, electricity, and mechanics

Examples of Civilian Jobs

Radar or electronics technician, test range tracker, instrument repairer, and electrician

Gas Turbine Systems Technician

Duties and Responsibilities

Operates, repairs, and maintains gas turbine engines, main propulsion machinery, including gears, shafts, controllable pitch propellers, related electric and electronic equipment, and propulsion

Qualifications

Mechanical ability. Experience in electricity/electronics repair, blueprint reading, mathematics, and physics

Examples of Civilian Jobs

Electronics technician and power plant operator

Gunner's Mate

Duties and Responsibilities

Operates and performs maintenance on guided missile-launching systems, rocket launchers, guns, gun mounts; inspects/repairs electrical, electronic, pneumatic, mechanical, and hydraulic systems

Qualifications

Prolonged attention and mental alertness, ability to perform detailed work. High aptitude for electrical and mechanical work. Arithmetic, shop math, electricity, electronics, physics, machine shop, and shop work

Examples of Civilian Jobs

Electronics mechanic, missile facilities repairer, gunsmith, rocket engine component mechanic, and marksmanship instructor

Sonar Technician

Duties and Responsibilities

Operates underwater detection and attack apparatus; obtains and interprets information for tactical purposes; maintains and repairs electronic underwater sound-detection equipment

Qualifications

Normal hearing and clear speaking voice. Algebra, geometry, physics, electricity, and shop work desirable. Aptitude for electrical and mechanical work

Examples of Civilian Jobs

Oil well sound device operator, radio operator, inspector of electronic assemblies; electronic technician, electrical repairer, and fire control mechanic

Aviation Structural Mechanic

Duties and Responsibilities

Maintains and repairs aircraft, airframe, structural components, hydraulic controls, utility systems, and egress systems

Qualifications

High degree of mechanical aptitude. Metal shop, algebra, plane geometry, physics; experience in automobile bodywork

Examples of Civilian Jobs

Welder, sheet metal repairer, hydraulics technician, radiographer, and aircraft plumbing systems mechanic

Aviation Support Equipment Technician

Duties and Responsibilities

Services, tests, and repairs gasoline and diesel engines, gas turbine compressors, power generating equipment, liquid and gaseous oxygen and nitrogen servicing equipment, electrical systems, and air-conditioning systems

Qualifications

High mechanical aptitude, physical strength, manual dexterity, and ability to work well with others

Examples of Civilian Jobs

Automobile mechanic for diesel and gasoline engines, air-conditioning systems, ignition systems, hydraulic systems, and electrical systems for aviation support equipment

Construction Mechanic

Duties and Responsibilities

Maintains, repairs, and overhauls automotive and heavy construction equipment

Qualifications

High mechanical aptitude. Electrical or machine shop, shop mathematics, and physics helpful

Examples of Civilian Jobs

Machinist or auto mechanic work; automotive or diesel engine mechanic, construction equipment mechanic, automotive electrician, and automobile body repairer

Engineman

Duties and Responsibilities

Operates, services, and repairs internal combustion engines, ship propulsion machinery, refrigeration and air-conditioning systems, air compressors, and related electro-hydraulic equipment

Qualifications

Clear speech, physical stamina, and manual dexterity. Knowledge of arithmetic and internal combustion engines is desirable

Examples of Civilian Jobs

Diesel plant engine operator, diesel mechanic, automobile engine mechanic, marine engine machinist, stationary engineer, fuel system maintenance worker, and power plant operator

Instrumentman

Duties and Responsibilities

Installs, services, adjusts, calibrates, and repairs a variety of small instruments. Responsible for the repair and calibration of precision measuring devices, which include pressure and vacuum gauges, thermometers, micrometers, tachometers, pressure/flow regulating devices, and watches and clocks

Qualifications

Manual dexterity, ability to do detailed work and repetitive tasks, good memory, and competence in mathematics

Examples of Civilian Jobs

Office machine repairer, electrical instrument repairer, watch repairer, and instrument mechanic

Machinery Repairer

Duties and Responsibilities

Makes replacement parts and repairs or overhauls ship's engine auxiliary

Qualifications

Experience in practical or shop mathematics, machine shop, electricity, mechanical drawing, and foundry desirable

Examples of Civilian Jobs

Engine lathe operator, machinist tool clerk, bench machinist, turret and milling machine operator, and toolmaker

Machinist's Mate

Duties and Responsibilities

Operates, maintains, and repairs steam turbines used for ship's propulsion and auxiliary equipment, such as turbo generators, pumps, refrigeration/air-conditioning, and laundry equipment

Qualifications

Aptitude for mechanical work. Practical or shop mathematics, machine shop, electricity, and physics valuable. Physical stamina and ability to work well with others

Examples of Civilian Jobs

Power plant operator, oxygen plant operator, marine mechanic, diesel mechanic, stationary engineer/mechanic, and refrigeration mechanic

ELECTRONIC/ELECTRICAL SYSTEMS

Aviation Electronics Technician

Duties and Responsibilities

Tests, maintains, and repairs aviation electronics equipment, including navigation, identification, detection, reconnaissance, weapons systems, weapon-control radar, computers, computer sights, gyroscopes, guided missiles equipment, and anti-submarine warfare equipment. Source rating for aircrew as in-flight technician; debriefs flight crews

Qualifications

High degree of electronic, electrical, mechanical, and mathematical aptitude. Ability to do detailed work, a good memory, resourcefulness, and curiosity

Examples of Civilian Jobs

Aircraft electrician, radio mechanic, electrical repairer, instrument repairer, electronics technician, radar computer repairer, and television repairer

Construction Electrician

Duties and Responsibilities

Installs, operates, maintains, and repairs electrical generating and distribution systems, transformers, switchboards, motors, and controllers

Qualifications

Interest in mechanical and electrical work. Electricity, shop mathematics, and physics helpful; ability to work alone

Examples of Civilian Jobs

Powerhouse or construction electrician, electrical and telephone repairer, power plant operator and diesel-plant operator

Electrician's Mate

Duties and Responsibilities

Maintains power and lighting equipment, generators, motors, power distribution systems, and other electrical equipment; rebuilds electrical equipment

Qualifications

Aptitude for electrical and mechanical work. Electrical and shop mathematics and physics valuable

Examples of Civilian Jobs

Electrician, electric motor and electrical equipment repairer, and power reactor operator

Electronics Technician

Duties and Responsibilities

Maintains all electronic equipment used for communications, detection, navigation, ranging, recognition, and countermeasures

Qualifications

Aptitude for detailed electrical and mechanical work. Radio, electricity, physics, algebra, trigonometry, and shop valuable

Examples of Civilian Jobs

Computer-peripheral equipment operator or electronics mechanic

PERSONNEL/BASE SUPPORT

Dental Technician

Duties and Responsibilities

Assists dental officers, administers dental hygiene, makes dental X-rays, and performs administrative duties. Some qualify for dental prosthetical laboratory techniques and maintenance, and repair of dental equipment

Qualifications

Scientific background or interests, normal color vision; competence with tools; good communication skills; and ability to perform repetitive tasks without losing interest

Examples of Civilian Jobs

Dental assistant, dental records clerk, dental laboratory technician, dental X-ray technician, dental hygienist, dental equipment, and repairman/technical representative

Disbursing Clerk

Duties and Responsibilities

Maintains military pay records; prepares payrolls and maintains related fiscal records and reports

Qualifications

Typing, bookkeeping, accounting, business mathematics and office practices

Examples of Civilian Jobs

Paymaster, cashier, statistical or audit clerk, bookkeeper, bookkeeping machine operator, and cost accountant

Hospital Corpsman

Duties and Responsibilities

Assists in the prevention and treatment of disease and injuries. May function within more than forty specialties, technician healthcare, or special operational fields. May specialize as a healthcare provider who performs independent of a physician in the air, ashore or at sea, or aboard surface ships or submarines. May attain additional specialty training for assignment with Navy SEALS, USMC reconnaissance, or deep-sea diving

Qualifications

Scientific background or interest in providing healthcare is extremely important. Good communication skills, writing, and arithmetic abilities are necessary

Examples of Civilian Jobs

Technician fields of pharmacy, nuclear medicine, laboratory specialties, surgery/operating room, emergency medicine, medical photography, industrial health and safety, radiology/X-ray, EEG, orthopedics/cast room, cardiopulmonary, respiratory therapy, optician/ocular, and physical/occupational therapy

Illustrator Draftsman

Duties and Responsibilities

Designs, sketches, does layouts, and makes signs, charts, and training aids; operates visual presentation equipment; uses art media, computer reproduction systems, and graphic arts equipment

Qualifications

Experience as draftsman, tracer, or surveyor valuable. Art, mechanical drawing, and blueprint reading valuable. Creativity, manual dexterity, and competence in mathematics

Examples of Civilian Jobs

Structural or electrical draftsman, technical illustrator, specification writer, and graphic artist

Lithographer

Duties and Responsibilities

Operates print shops, which produce Navy publications, such as newspapers, forms, manuals, magazines, and training materials

Qualifications

Work with machinery and chemicals. Printing, physics, chemistry, English, and shop mathematics valuable

Examples of Civilian Jobs

Lithographic and plate press operator, bookbinder, engraver, camera operator, photolithographer, printer, and composing room machinist

Mess Management Specialist

Duties and Responsibilities

Orders, prepares, and serves food; prepares menus; maintains records for food supplies and financial budgets; manages personnel living quarters

Qualifications

Ability in arithmetic, recordkeeping, and detail work; interest in nutrition and culinary arts valuable

Examples of Civilian Jobs

Baker, cook, butcher, nightclub manager, cake decorator, chef, and restaurant manager

Musician

Duties and Responsibilities

Provides music for military ceremonies, religious services, concerts, parades, various recreational activities; plays one or more musical instruments

Qualifications

Proficiency on standard band or orchestral instruments

Examples of Civilian Jobs

Music teacher, instrument musician, orchestra leader, music arranger, instrument repairer, and music librarian

Photographer's Mate

Duties and Responsibilities

Operates and maintains various types of cameras for several uses; performs duties as member of flight crew; develops motion picture film and microfilm prints; takes news photographs; and operates laboratory and darkroom equipment for film processing

Qualifications

Ability to relate to people and speaking and writing skills; ability to do detailed work and keep records; good color vision; ability to work as part of a team; manual dexterity; physical strength; a knowledge of mathematics

Examples of Civilian Jobs

Photographer, camera repairer, screen writer, camera operator, photojournalist, film editor, photofinisher, and sound mixer

Photojournalist

Duties and Responsibilities

Gathers facts and writes articles for publication in civilian and Navy communities; prepares stories for hometown news outlets; gathers facts, photos, writes, edits, and proofreads news for radio and television outlets; prepares layouts for base papers

Qualifications

Writing and speaking skills, creativity, typing, an interest in people, maturity, and manual dexterity

Examples of Civilian Jobs

News editor, screenwriter, reporter, producer, announcer, production manager, and photographer

Postal Clerk

Duties and Responsibilities

Processes mail, sells stamps and money orders, maintains mail directories, and handles correspondence concerning postal operations

Qualifications

Bookkeeping, accounting, business math, typing, and office practices

Examples of Civilian Jobs

Parcel post or mail clerk, mail room manager, stock clerk, and cashier

Religious Program

Duties and Responsibilities

Supports chaplains of all faiths and religious activities of the command; assists in management and development of the command's religious programs and determinations of resources; maintains records of various funds, ecclesiastical documents, and references

Qualifications

Typing; ability to express ideas, do detailed work, and keep accurate records; good moral character; interest in people, initiative; and writing skills

Examples of Civilian Jobs

Church business administrator, religious facilities manager, and administrative assistant

LOGISTICS AND SUPPLY

Aircrews Survival Equipment Man

Duties and Responsibilities

Maintains and packs parachutes, survival equipment, flight and protective clothing, and life jackets; tests and services pressure suits

Qualifications

Must perform extremely careful and accurate work. General shop and sewing desirable. Experience in use and repair of sewing machines

Examples of Civilian Jobs

Parachute packer, inspector, repairer, and tester; sailmaker

Boatswain's Mate

Duties and Responsibilities

Performs seamanship tasks, operates small boats, stores cargo, handles ropes and lines, and directs work of deck force personnel

Qualifications

Must be physically strong. Practical math desirable; algebra, geometry, and physics

Examples of Civilian Jobs

Motorboat operator, pier superintendent, able seaman, canvas worker, rigger, cargo wincher, mate, longshore worker, and quartermaster

Storekeeper

Duties and Responsibilities

Orders, receives, stores, inventories and issues clothing, foodstuffs, mechanical equipment, and general supplies

Qualifications

Typing, bookkeeping, accounting, commercial mathematics, general business studies, and English

Examples of Civilian Jobs

Sales or shipping clerk, warehouse worker, buyer, invoice control clerk, purchasing agent, travel clerk, accounting clerk, bookkeeper, and stock control clerk

ENGINEERING, SCIENCE, AND TECHNICAL

Aerographer's Mate

Duties and Responsibilities

Collects, records, and analyzes meteorological and oceanographic data; enters information on appropriate charts; forecasts from visual and instrumental weather observations; operates and maintains computers

Qualifications

Skills in mathematics, speaking, writing, recordkeeping, and ability to perform repetitive work

Examples of Civilian Jobs

Weather observer, meteorologist, chart maker, oceanographer's assistant, and computer programmer

Air Traffic Controller

Duties and Responsibilities

Controls air traffic, operates radar air traffic control ashore and afloat; uses radio and light signals; directs aircraft under visual flight and instrument flight conditions; assists in preparation of flight plans

Qualifications

High degree of accuracy, precision, self-reliance, and calmness under stress. Experience in radio broadcasting and good vision

Examples of Civilian Jobs

Air traffic controller, control tower operator, radio telephone operator, flight operations specialist, and aircraft log clerk

Boiler Technician

Duties and Responsibilities

Operates equipment that produces steam for propulsion engines and steam-driven electric power generator; tests and inventories supplies for fuel and water; maintains boilers, pumps, and associated machinery

Qualifications

Working knowledge of common hand and power tools. Strong interest in mechanical work. Shop courses and practical mathematics are valuable

Examples of Civilian Jobs

Marine firefighter, boiler inspector, boilermaker, stationary engineer, boiler or heating plant technician, and fuel system maintenance worker

Builder

Duties and Responsibilities

Constructs, maintains, and repairs wood, concrete, and masonry structures; erects and repairs waterfront structures

Qualifications

High mechanical aptitude. Carpentry and shop mathematics desirable. Experience with hand and power tools valuable

Examples of Civilian Jobs

Plasterer, roofer, mason, painter, construction worker, carpenter, and estimator

Cryptologic Technician

Duties and Responsibilities

Operates and maintains sophisticated electronic equipment in a high-tech environment. Consists of six separate career fields: administration, maintenance, linguistics, communications, and collection (manual and electronic)

Qualifications

Individual and immediate family must be U.S. citizens of excellent character. Individual must be motivated, speak and write clearly, and work well with others

Examples of Civilian Jobs

Administrative/security specialist, electromechanical technician, interpreter/translator, computer programmer, and radio-telegraphic operator

Damage Controlman

Duties and Responsibilities

Operates, maintains, and repairs fire-fighting equipment, damage control equipment, and chemical, biological, and radiological defense equipment

Qualifications

Good vision and color perception, manual dexterity, a good memory, and resourcefulness

Examples of Civilian Jobs

Firefighter, plumber, welder, shipfitter, blacksmith, and sheet metal worker

Data-Processing Technician

Duties and Responsibilities

Operates data-processing equipment, including sorters, collators, reproducers, tabulating printers, and computers

Qualifications

High clerical aptitude. Typing, bookkeeping, and operating business machines desirable. Experience in mechanical work

Examples of Civilian Jobs

Keypunch operator, systems analyst, verifier, and tabulating machine operator

Equipment Operator

Duties and Responsibilities

Operates automotive and heavy construction equipment

Qualifications

Good physical strength and normal color perception. Experience in construction work, automotive or electrical shop

Examples of Civilian Jobs

Bulldozer operator, power shovel or motor grader operator, excavation foreperson, truck driver, asphalt paving machine operator, and blaster

Hull Maintenance Technician

Duties and Responsibilities

Fabricates, installs, repairs shipboard structures and plumbing and piping systems; conducts nondestructive metal tests

Qualifications

High mechanical aptitude. Sheet metal foundry, pipefitting, carpentry, mathematics, geometry, and chemistry are useful

Examples of Civilian Jobs

High-pressure and nuclear welder, plumber, shipfitter, blacksmith, and metallurgic technician

Intelligence Specialist

Duties and Responsibilities

Assembles and analyzes multisource operations intelligence; prepares maps, graphics, mosaics, and charts; extracts information from aerial photos; prepares intelligence reports

Qualifications

Individual and immediate family must be U.S. citizens of excellent character. Ability to write, speak clearly, and work well with others. Mathematics, geography, and photography skills valuable

Examples of Civilian Jobs

Aerial photographer, intelligence clerk, and intelligence specialist

Mineman

Duties and Responsibilities

Tests, maintains, and repairs mines, components, and mine-laying equipment

Qualifications

Manual dexterity, mechanical inclination, and ability to work as a team member

Examples of Civilian Jobs

Electromechanical technician, ammunition inspector, and electronics mechanic

Operations Specialist

Duties and Responsibilities

Operates surveillance and search radar, electronic recognition and identification equipment, controlled approach devices, and electronic aids to navigation; serves as plotter and status board keeper; coordinates aircraft operations at sea

Qualifications

Prolonged attention and mental alertness. Physics, mathematics, and courses in radio and electricity helpful. Experience in radio repair helpful

Examples of Civilian Jobs

Radio operator (aircraft, ship, government service, radio broadcasting), radar equipment supervisor, control tower operator, air traffic controller, and computer equipment operator

Opticalman

Duties and Responsibilities

Maintains scientifically accurate optical tools used for visual aids and required for navigation and weapons systems; manufactures optical parts, such as lens cells

Qualifications

Orientation toward fine tools and precision equipment and machinery; manual dexterity and resourcefulness; physics, shop mathematics, and machine shop/tools helpful

Examples of Civilian Jobs

Precision instrument technician, toolmaker, locksmith, instrument mechanic, optical instrument assembler, and camera repairer

Quartermaster

Duties and Responsibilities

Performs navigation of ships, steering, lookout supervision, ship control, bridge watch duties, visual communication, and maintenance of navigational aids

Qualifications

Good vision and hearing and ability to express oneself clearly in writing and speaking; geometry and physics helpful

Examples of Civilian Jobs

Barge, motorboat, yacht captain, quartermaster, and harbor pilot aboard merchant ships

Radioman

Duties and Responsibilities

Operates communication, transmission, reception, and terminal equipment; transmits, receives, and processes all forms of military record and voice communications

Qualifications

Good hearing and manual dexterity; mathematics, physics, and electricity desirable; experience as amateur radio operator and personal computer utilization helpful

Examples of Civilian Jobs

Telegrapher, radio dispatcher, radio/telephone operator, and copy writer

Utilitiesman

Duties and Responsibilities

Installs, maintains, and repairs plumbing, heating, steam, and compressed-air systems; fuel storage, collection, and disposal facilities and water purification units

Qualifications

High mechanical aptitude; apprentice training in plumbing and related fields and mathematics helpful

Examples of Civilian Jobs

Stationary engineer, plumber, pipe fitter, and water plant or boiler operator; boiler house supervisor; furnace installer; welder; and refrigeration mechanic

---

SEARCH MILITARY JOBS

After you've spoken to your recruiter about specific military jobs I recommend that you visit www.onetonline.org/crosswalk/MOC/ (the address is case sensitive). There you will be able to input specific job specialty numbers and get more detailed information than what may be available through your recruiter. Additionally, you will obtain information about related civilian jobs and the prospect of employment in those jobs.

---

9 BENEFITS

Besides the "basic" military pay, there are lots of other benefits that add up to an attractive compensation package. This chapter outlines those, as well as the various forms of military pay, allowances, and educational opportunities.

Military pay has never been great. Few people, if any, have ever said, "I want to get rich, so I'd better join the military!" However, military pay has increased significantly during the years. I remember stories from veterans who used to be paid $50 a month, and I vividly remember that my first military paychecks were $201 every two weeks.

It is not the intention of this chapter to list and explain every military benefit, because benefits change, and certain benefits apply to only a select few. If you have any questions about pay and benefits, you should ask your recruiter for the latest information. Another resource for pay information is the Defense Finance and Accounting Service (DFAS). You can get up-to-date pay information on its website: www.dfas.mil.

Because of the many changes occurring on such a frequent basis, it would be impossible to list all the programs here . This chapter covers the programs that are in place at the time of this writing and describes their features. Check with your recruiter to get an up-to-date list of all the benefits, including educational opportunities, for which you may qualify.

Basic Pay

As the name implies, basic military pay is the base pay you'll receive without any of the allowances to which you may be entitled. The amount of basic pay is based on your rank (when it relates to pay, it is referred to as "pay grade") and the amount of time you've been in the military. Unlike most civilian jobs, where pay raises are sporadic and often based on the mood of management, military pay raises will occur:

- on promotion to the next higher pay grade;
- at regular intervals based on longevity; and
- when granted by Congress (usually on January 1 of each year).

Most new military members begin at the lowest level of the military pay scale. However, as mentioned in this book, there may be ways in which you can enter the military at a higher pay grade. The following pay charts are current at the time of this writing; however, remember that there is usually an increase in basic pay every year.

Longevity, or years of service, is presented from top to bottom in ascending order starting with less than two years (< 2) and going up to twenty-six years. The pay grades are presented left to right in descending order from the highest enlisted grade, E-9, to the lowest grade, E-1. To determine the base pay for a particular grade and length of service, find the intersection of the years-of-service row and the pay-grade column. If you have put in four years of active-duty service, for example, and your rank is E-3, your base pay would be $2014.80 per month.

MONTHLY BASIC PAY CHART – EFFECTIVE JANUARY 1, 2013

Years of Service	Pay Grade								
	E-1	E-2	E-3	E-4	E-5	E-6	E-7	E-8	E-9
<2	1516.20	1699.80	1787.40	1979.70	2159.40	2357.10	2725.20		
2		1699.80	1899.90	2081.10	2304.30	2593.80	2974.50		
3		1699.80	2014.80	2193.90	2415.90	2708.10	3088.20		
4		1699.80	2014.80	2304.90	2529.90	2819.40	3239.10		
6		1699.80	2014.80	2403.30	2707.50	2935.50	3357.00		
8		1699.80	2014.80	2403.30	2893.50	3196.50	3559.20	3920.10	
10		1699.80	2014.80	2403.30	3045.60	3298.50	3673.20	4093.50	4788.90
12		1699.80	2014.80	2403.30	3064.20	3495.30	3875.70	4200.90	4897.50
14		1699.80	2014.80	2403.30	3064.20	3555.60	4043.70	4329.60	5034.30
16		1699.80	2014.80	2403.30	3064.20	3599.70	4158.60	4469.10	5194.80
18		1699.80	2014.80	2403.30	3064.20	3650.70	4281.00	4720.50	5357.40
20		1699.80	2014.80	2403.30	3064.20	3650.70	4328.40	4847.70	5617.50
22		1699.80	2014.80	2403.30	3064.20	3650.70	4487.40	5064.60	5837.10
24		1699.80	2014.80	2403.30	3064.20	3650.70	4572.90	5184.90	6068.70
26		1699.80	2014.80	2403.30	3064.20	3650.70	4897.80	5481.00	6422.70

Note: E-1 with less than four months of service = $1402.20

RESERVE DRILL BASIC PAY CHART – EFFECTIVE JANUARY 1, 2013
REFLECTS PAY FOR ONE DRILL WEEKEND

Years of Service	E-9	E-8	E-7	E-6	E-5	E-4	E-3	E-2	E-1
<2			363.36	314.28	287.92	263.96	238.32	226.64	202.16
2			396.60	345.84	307.24	277.48	253.32	226.64	
3			411.76	361.08	322.12	292.52	268.64	226.64	
4			431.88	375.92	337.32	307.32	268.64	226.64	
6			447.60	391.40	361.00	320.44	268.64	226.64	
8		522.68	474.56	426.20	385.80	320.44	268.64	226.64	
10	638.52	545.80	489.76	439.80	406.08	320.44	268.64	226.64	
12	653.00	560.12	516.76	466.04	408.56	320.44	268.64	226.64	
14	671.24	577.28	539.16	474.08	408.56	320.44	268.64	226.64	
16	692.64	595.88	554.48	479.96	408.56	320.44	268.64	226.64	
18	714.32	629.40	570.80	486.76	408.56	320.44	268.64	226.64	
20	749.00	646.36	577.12	486.76	408.56	320.44	268.64	226.64	
22	778.28	675.28	598.32	486.76	408.56	320.44	268.64	226.64	
24	809.16	691.32	609.72	486.76	408.56	320.44	268.64	226.64	
26	856.36	730.80	653.04	486.76	408.56	320.44	268.64	226.64	

Pay Grade

Note: E-1 with less than four months = 186.96

Housing Allowance

Whether you will receive a housing allowance depends on two things: your marital status (married couples, as well as single members with minor dependents, are usually authorized housing allowance) and the availability of government-owned quarters, which are for service members either not married or without dependents.

Most single people will find themselves living in government-owned quarters and, therefore, not entitled to a housing allowance. During Basic Training and technical school, however, all personnel are housed in government-owned quarters.

The amount of the housing allowance depends on three things: pay grade, whether the service member has any dependents, and location of the base.

Housing allowances are generally larger in areas with a higher cost of living. The location used for determining the housing allowance is the zip code of the base at which the service member is stationed, not the location of his or her dependents. Therefore, if a member is stationed in North Carolina in an area with a relatively low cost of living and his or her dependents are living in New York in an area with a high cost of living, the member's housing allowance will be based on the North Carolina rate.

Consult the DFAS website for up-to-date housing allowances. You can search the site using zip codes to find the rates for any area of the United States.

MILITARY HOUSING

Another alternative for members with dependents is military family housing. Military family housing, or "base housing," is exactly what the name implies—it is housing units owned by the government and occupied by service members and their families. To live in base housing, military members forfeit their housing allowance; however, there are a few advantages to living in base housing:

- no utility bills
- a secure environment (entrance to most bases is usually restricted to military members and other authorized personnel)
- all maintenance done by the government
- expenses often less than those incurred living off base (especially in high cost-of-living areas)

Along with benefits, there are also some disadvantages to living in on-base housing:

- Weekly yard inspections—There is no putting off getting the lawn mowed or raking the leaves; you are required to maintain the outside of your base house. Of course, this can also be looked at positively because you do not have to deal with neighbors who never take care of their lawns (every neighborhood has them).
- On-base houses typically are smaller than those available off-base—Because housing is assigned based on rank and number of dependents, you will usually receive a house that "fits" your family. Generally, this means no spare rooms (although this does not apply to married couples with no children).

- Waiting list—At times, based on a higher demand for on-base housing than the number of available houses, you may be required to go on a waiting list. If this is the case, you will probably have to rent a house or apartment off base until military housing becomes available.

Some military bases offer contracted quarters which are a hybrid of on-base housing and off-base housing. These quarters offer the benefits of on-base housing but housing management, rather than the service member, handles most landscaping.

ON-BASE SINGLE QUARTERS

Single enlisted members, in what are known as the "junior pay grades," will, in most cases, be required to live in barracks or dormitories.

There have been tremendous improvements in single enlisted quarters during the years. When I first entered Active Duty, we lived in "open bay" barracks. These facilities housed everyone in one large room with one communal bathroom. Eventually, they upgraded our facilities to dormitory-style rooms, with three people to a room and with each room having one bathroom.

Today, most facilities are at least at the dormitory-style room level, and others are at a much higher standard, with private rooms and private bathrooms. Most rooms are equipped with a dorm-sized refrigerator. Military members can often install their own stereo systems and televisions.

Navy and coastguardsmen assigned to shipboard duty, however, will experience different living conditions. More than likely, they will live onboard the ship in what are known as berthing compartments. The quality and comfort of these berthing compartments depends on the type and age of the ship.

Basic Allowance for Subsistence

In addition to Basic Pay and Housing Allowance, most military members who live off base also receive what is known as Basic Allowance for Subsistence (BAS). This allowance provides enlisted members $352.27 per month to offset the cost of food.

Single enlisted personnel who live on base generally receive a "meal card" that enables them to eat in government-run dining facilities free of charge.

Partial BAS was started because the value of being able to eat free of charge at on-base dining facilities is often less than the Full BAS rate. Therefore, Partial BAS makes up the difference.

Clothing Allowance

All enlisted personnel receive an annual clothing allowance to cover the cost of purchasing and maintaining uniforms. The amount of the annual clothing allowance depends on the branch of service and the member's gender. Currently, the allowances range from $327.60 to $612.00.

Enlisted members of the Guard and Reserve do not receive an annual clothing allowance. However, they are entitled to free replacement of worn or damaged uniforms on an as-needed basis.

Other Pay and Allowances

There are many other types of special pay and allowances that military members may receive. These include:

- Cost of Living Allowance (COLA)—This is paid to members who are living in high cost-of-living areas as well as to military members who are stationed overseas.
- Dislocation Allowance—This is designed to offset some of the extra expenses associated with moving.
- Per Diem—Literally translated, this means "per day." The military pays this allowance to its members when serving on temporary duty and is used to offset the cost of lodging and food.
- Diving Pay—This is paid monthly to all military members who are performing diving duties.
- Flight Pay—This is paid monthly to military aircrew members.
- Foreign Language Proficiency Pay—This is paid monthly to members who have qualified in and remain proficient in a language considered critical to the military; these members may be called on to act as interpreters or translators.
- Hazardous Duty Pay—As the name implies, this is paid to members who are serving in certain "dangerous" jobs.
- Sea Pay—This monthly pay is intended to offset the hardship of having to serve at sea.
- Special Duty Pay—Certain enlisted members may receive Special Duty Pay (SDP). For example, recruiters receive a monthly SDP.
- Submarine Pay—Sailors serving on board submarines receive "Sub Pay" in addition to their Sea Pay.

As a rule, any benefit designated as "pay" is taxable, whereas those benefits designated as "allowances" are not. Depending on the amount of your total allowances, your tax savings may be considerable.

On-Base Facilities

One of the greatest benefits to military members is the various on-base facilities. Although many of these facilities are provided free of charge to military personnel and their families, some are provided at a nominal cost. As you'll see from the following list, military bases are their own self-contained towns. Facilities available include:

- Fitness Centers—These are the on-base equivalent to health clubs. They feature modern fitness equipment and basketball courts. Some have indoor pools, tracks, racquetball courts, and saunas. There is no charge for using the fitness centers.
- Swimming Pools—Most bases have at least one swimming pool that is open (weather permitting) to all military personnel and their dependents. There is no cost to use the pools.
- Golf Courses—Just about every base has its own golf course. Just like private golf clubs, you may pay for a membership or you may choose to pay on a per-use basis. Courses have driving

ranges, pro shops, and restaurants or snack bars. Golf courses are open to military personnel, their families, and guests.

- Bowling Alleys—Most bases have a bowling center. These facilities usually, in my experience, provide the best option for lunch on the base. Besides the snack bar, base bowling alleys usually contain state-of-the-art equipment. There are usually adult and children's bowling leagues on most bases.

- Other Sports—Most bases have many other facilities for various sports for both adults and children, such as soccer, baseball, softball, track, tennis, football, basketball, and volleyball. Quite often there are adult and children leagues in many of these sports, depending on the season.

- Auto Hobby Shops—If you like working on your own car, the auto hobby shop is where you'll find the facilities to accommodate you. Whether it's something as simple as an oil change or as complex as a complete engine rebuild, you'll find what you need there. Auto hobby shops have lifts, hand tools, specialty tools, and almost anything you'll need when working on your car. The auto hobby shops charge by the hour.

- Youth Centers—These facilities provide a safe environment for minor dependents to enjoy themselves. Most youth centers have game rooms, video games, and basketball courts. They also sponsor events such as dances.

- Recreation Centers—More commonly called "Rec Centers," these are basically the adult versions of the youth centers.

- Aero Clubs—Most Air Force Bases have an Aero Club, where you can learn to fly and rent small airplanes.

- Camping—Many bases offer on-base camping as well as a recreational vehicle (RV) park. These facilities often offer boating and fishing activities. Some bases also have their own private beaches available for use by military members and their families.

- Rental Centers—Here you can rent anything from camping equipment to small boats, as well as lawn mowers, log splitters, bicycles, sporting equipment, and many other items.

- Arts and Crafts—Various arts and crafts activities are available at these centers. These include woodworking, ceramics, picture framing, and others. Arts and crafts lessons are usually available, as are necessary supplies.

- On-Base Lodging—Intended to house visiting military members who are on official business, these motel-like accommodations may be used on a space-available basis for vacationing service members. In some locations, the military also runs on-base lodging facilities whose sole purpose is for the recreation of military members and their families.

- Libraries—On-base libraries are no different from any other public library.

- Nightclubs—Military clubs are similar to nightclubs that you would find in the civilian community. The main difference is that they also usually offer an array of dining facilities. In addition, "membership" in the club usually provides you with discounts on meals.

- Department Stores—The name of the store depends on the branch of service (Base Exchange for the Air Force, Post Exchange for the Army, Navy Exchange, and Marine Exchange). These stores offer discounts on items from clothing to garden supplies, household products to computers, shampoo to CDs, and everything in between. The main benefit of these "department stores" is that there is no sales tax.

- Grocery Stores—Called commissaries, these stores offer substantial savings over grocery stores located in the civilian community. They don't charge any tax, although there is a surcharge of 5 percent on all purchases.
- Ticket Offices—Tickets for theme parks and other recreational activities are available at discount rates to military members.
- Movie Theaters—Although you won't find any multi-screen theaters on military bases, base movie theaters do show current features at discount prices.
- Fast Food—Most military bases have at least one nationally known fast-food restaurant. In addition, most also have several snack bars and other eating establishments.
- Service Stations—These not only sell gasoline but also offer car repair, auto parts, and tires. Besides selling at lower prices, there is no sales tax on your purchases.
- Chapels—If you choose to attend religious services, base chapels usually accommodate most religions.
- Horse Stables—Many bases have facilities for military members who own horses.
- Day-Care Centers—Facilities are available for all-day care to hourly care. Rates are set according to family income.

Healthcare Benefits

Active Duty members receive free medical treatment provided by military as well as civilian healthcare professionals. Unlike their civilian counterparts, there are no such things as "sick days" in the military. For instance, if you have a cold and must miss work for a few days, you may be put on "quarters," which means you are excused from work until you are well enough to be cleared to go back. The good part about this is that you do not have to worry about using up your sick days; however, you can't call in sick because you wake up and decide it would be a good day to go to the beach. Another advantage is that if you become temporarily disabled, you do not have to worry about losing wages or your job. You will continue to receive full pay and allowances while you are recuperating.

DEPENDENT CARE

Military dependents are also entitled to healthcare and often receive treatment through the military's "insurance" program, TRICARE.

TRICARE has been the military's attempt to privatize military dependent healthcare. Military members may choose the "TRICARE Option" that best meets their needs. There are three TRICARE options from which to choose:

- TRICARE Extra—A Preferred Provider Organization (PPO), TRICARE Extra contracts with healthcare providers to offer its beneficiaries discounted fees. Although there are no fees for enrollment in TRICARE Extra, there are standard deductibles that must be met before insurance benefits are paid. These deductibles are based on the military sponsor's rank.
- TRICARE Prime—The military's version of a health maintenance organization (HMO), TRICARE Prime requires its members to enroll with a Primary Care Manager (PCM), who, in effect, "man-

ages" the beneficiaries' care. All care must be pre-approved and referrals issued before patients can be seen by either on-base or approved off-base healthcare providers. There are no deductibles; however, small co-pays may be required.

- TRICARE Standard—Based loosely on the traditional "Fee-for-Service" concept, TRICARE Standard offers patients more of a choice in choosing their healthcare providers. Providers receive a set fee based on a fee schedule. Patients are required to meet a standard deductible, pay co-pays, and, in some instances, receive authorization before treatment.

More information about TRICARE can be found at: www.tricare.mil.

Dependent Dental Care

Although military members are entitled to free dental care, their dependents are not. However, there is a low-cost dental insurance plan available to offset some of the expenses associated with dependent dental care. The cost of the plan comes directly out of the military member's pay.

Vacation

Every military member receives thirty days of vacation, or leave, each year. One accrues leave at a rate of 2 1/2 days per month. At times, the member may receive advance leave depending on the circumstances.

The main difference between military leave and "ordinary vacation" is that weekends and holidays usually are counted as leave if they fall during the leave period. For example, say that you wanted to take leave the week of Thanksgiving and also the entire next week—even though you would have had Thanksgiving off as a holiday, it would count as leave, as would the weekend after the holiday.

Moving

Periodic moves are a 'fact of life' in the military. Although moving can be stressful, one aspect of moving you will never have to worry about is the cost. The government pays for all the costs associated with official moves. The amount of household goods you can move at government expense is determined by your rank.

Moves are performed by contracted companies who will not only move your possessions but will also pack, and on your arrival at your new home, unpack them and get rid of the packing material. If you prefer to move your own household goods, you may choose to do a Do-it-Yourself (or DITY) move. Military members are offered a cash incentive to perform their own moves. If you would like, you may also do a Partial DITY move, where professional movers move the bulk of your household goods, and you move a portion of the household goods.

In addition to moving household goods, military members are entitled to various other payments made to offset the cost of moving. These include payment for mileage, or air travel, lodging and meal expenses, as well as payments to cover temporary lodging costs while you are getting settled.

Military Retirement

One of the greatest benefits of military service is the retirement benefit after just twenty years of service. Although twenty years may seem like a long time, consider that if you enlisted in the military at age 18, you would be eligible for retirement pay at age 38. You would then be starting on a second career, while collecting retirement pay, at an age when many people are struggling with a first career and are likely almost thirty years from retirement.

The way military retirement pay is calculated has changed a great deal over the years. When I entered the military, it was calculated as 50 percent of base pay after twenty years of service, with increases in the percentage based on years served beyond twenty. The maximum amount of retirement pay allowable is 75 percent.

Presently, retirement pay is calculated as follows: The base pay of the highest thirty-six months (usually the last three years on Active Duty) is averaged. That average then is multiplied by 2.5 percent for each year of Active Duty.

For example, suppose that you retired with exactly twenty years of service and you earned $2000 a month your last year on Active Duty, $1800 the year before retirement, and $1700 the year before that. The three-year average would therefore be approximately $1833. You then multiply that number by 2.5 percent (.025) to give you $45.83, which is then multiplied by 20 to give you a monthly retirement pay of $916.60.

In addition to retirement pay, military retirees enjoy most of the same privileges they did on Active Duty, such as use of on-base facilities, healthcare benefits, and life insurance.

Presently, there is another retirement option for service members, called CSB/REDUX, or Career Status Bonus/REDUX. Under this plan, service members are given an option on their 15th anniversary of military service. They may keep the traditional high-three plan, or they may elect a $30,000 bonus payable at the 15-year point, and a reduction in retirement benefit to 40 percent after 20 years of service. While the appeal of a $30,000 bonus is tempting, there are some drawbacks, namely:

- Retirees are not eligible for Cost of Living Allowances, which may increase the monthly retirement pay significantly over the years.
- If, for any reason, a service member does not make it to the 20-year retirement mark, he or she will have to repay the entire $30,000.
- Just like most military pay, the bonus is subject to applicable state and federal taxes.

Because there are deployment locations around the world that exempt military pay from federal taxes, one way around paying federal taxes on the bonus is to ensure that you are deployed to one of those locations when your receive the bonus. Additionally, military members should only accept the CSB option if they are in heavy debt and the bonus would relieve them of that debt, or they are able to invest the money. Unfortunately, some service members spend their bonuses on purchases such as cars, boats, etc., and they are then faced with reduced pay at retirement.

Other Benefits

Some of the other benefits of military service include:

- Service Group Life Insurance (SGLI)—All military members can receive SGLI of up to $400,000 at a low rate. The cost of the premium comes directly out of the military member's pay.
- VA Home Loans—Military members are eligible to receive Veterans' Administration guaranteed home loans. By guaranteeing the loans, the VA makes it easier for military members to secure a mortgage.
- Military Discounts—Many establishments, especially in areas surrounding a military installation, offer small discounts to military members.
- Burial Expenses—Although not one of the benefits that drove me to join the military or one that I'm rushing to use, military members and veterans are entitled to a burial plot in a national cemetery, as well as a headstone.
- Family Life Insurance—Military members are also given the opportunity to insure their spouses and children at a low monthly rate.

Educational Benefits

Many people join the military for the educational benefits (there's nothing wrong with that) and end up staying in the military for the other benefits. The number of educational opportunities offered by the military is growing because it has become harder and harder to entice young people to join.

If you qualify for one of the special enlistment educational programs, such as the Army's Loan Repayment Program, make sure it's on your enlistment contract. Remember that if it's not listed in your contract, no matter who verbally promised it to you, it is not guaranteed.

Some educational programs, such as Tuition Assistance, are programs that a military member can use while on Active Duty. These types of programs are ongoing and are not on your enlistment contract. Your point of contact for these programs is your Base or Post Education Office.

Education Offices

These offices are your on-base guidance office to help you plan your education. They will assist you in determining your goals and help you decide on a course of action to achieve those goals.

How Educational Benefits Differ Among Branches

Basically, there are two types of educational benefits offered by the military. The first type represents programs that are common to all the branches, such as the Post-9/11 GI Bill, and the second type is branch-specific, such as the Army College Fund.

Although each branch has its own specific "programs," you'll find that overall they are similar. Some may have certain features that appeal to you over others, but the bottom line is that it becomes a matter of who can offer the best educational program for your particular needs.

Common Programs

The programs that are common to all military branches are the Post-9/11 GI Bill, the Tuition Assistance Program, the Defense Activity for Non-Traditional Education Support (DANTES) testing program, and credit for military school. Each of these programs has a specific and entirely different function.

POST-9/11 GI BILL

In this program, tuition payment is capped at the highest amount of established tuition and fees for the most expensive in-state public colleges; however, this does not mean that a service member must attend a public college. The service member makes no contribution to this program, but the member must use the benefit within fifteen years of his or her release from service. In addition, the Post-9/11 GI Bill will pay a housing allowance for students enrolled in a traditional "brick and mortar" college program and a reduced housing allowance for students enrolled in an online college program. Additionally, the GI bill program will also pay $1000 per year for books and equipment.

In addition, the amount of benefits that the service member receives is linked to the amount of time served in the military. In order to receive 100 percent of the Post-9/11 GI Bill benefits, a service member must serve at least 36 months. Another major benefit of the Post-9/11 GI Bill is that the benefits are transferable to the service member's spouse and children.

Although the Post-9/11 GI Bill is funded by the Department of Defense (DoD), it is administered by the Department of Veterans Affairs (VA). For the most up-to-date information about the Post-9/11 GI

Bill, visit the VA website at http://gibill.va.gov/benefits/post_911_gibill/index.html. The chart below outlines the percentage of benefits payable based on length of service.

Total Period of Active Duty	Percentage of Maximum Benefit Payable
At least 36 months	100%
At least 30 continuous days and discharged due to service-connected disability	100%
At least 30 months < 36 months	90%
At least 24 months < 30 months	80%
At least 18 months < 24 months	70%
At least 12 months < 18 months	60%
At least 6 months < 12 months	50%
At least 90 days < 6 months	40%

TUITION ASSISTANCE PROGRAM

One of the best educational benefits available to military members, the Tuition Assistance Program, is also one of the most underused. Presently, the Tuition Assistance Program typically pays $250 per semester hour towards the service member's college tuition, although most services do have an annual limit. Although the Post-9/11 GI Bill is designed for service members to use after their term of enlistment, Tuition Assistance (TA) is available to Active Duty members and Reserve members for use during their enlistment.

The only possible drawback to the Tuition Assistance Program is that the service member is limited to colleges in his or her local area or to online colleges. However, most military installations contract with several colleges to provide courses to their military members. This is how I earned my master's degree from Troy University in Alabama, while stationed at a base in the United Kingdom.

As good as the Tuition Assistance Program is, however, many (actually most) military members do not take advantage of it. For some, it may be a lack of initiative or the lack of desire to attend college; for others, however, it may be because the time demands of their jobs don't allow them to use TA. Therefore, it is important to consider your goals when selecting a job or even the branch of service you join. If you wish to pursue your degree in earnest while serving on Active Duty, you must consider whether you will have the time to do so.

I was fortunate. Although I enlisted in the Navy, I was stationed on a ship that rarely left port. I spent four years in Charleston, South Carolina, and, by coincidence, a local college, Baptist College at Charleston, now Charleston Southern University, had an excellent evening degree program. Because of this, I completed my undergraduate degree while stationed in Charleston using TA. Things would have been different, however, if I had been stationed on a submarine or a ship that went to sea more frequently.

Things have changed dramatically since I earned my undergraduate degree; in those days college students had no choice but to attend classes physically. Today, attending college has become much more convenient for military students. Many service members are able to attend college even when serving in deployed locations. Of course, if you are not motivated to attend college, you will find any excuse not to take advantage of TA, no matter how convenient it may be.

Servicemembers Opportunity Colleges (SOC)

SOC is made up of approximately 1900 member colleges that enroll hundreds of thousands of service members annually in associate, bachelor's, and graduate-level degree programs on school campuses, armories, and military installations within the United States and overseas and through a variety of distance learning methods. With the exception of the Air Force, all military branches have a version of SOC.

SOC allows service members to earn their degree as follows:

- The service member chooses a "home college" to begin the process.
- Members receive college credits for military schools and CLEP examinations.
- There is a guarantee for transfer of college credits as long as you attend any of the SOC-associated colleges.
- Degrees are awarded by the "home college."

For more information about Servicemembers Opportunity Colleges, visit www.soc.aasu.org or call (202) 667-0079.

DEFENSE ACTIVITY FOR NON-TRADITIONAL EDUCATION SUPPORT (DANTES)

DANTES testing, another fabulous educational benefit, is a great way to build college credits in a hurry and free of charge.

By using College-Level Examination Program (CLEP) tests, you may receive college credits for subject matter that you may have already mastered without taking a college course. These tests are similar to high school Advanced Placement (AP) tests, which allow you to demonstrate your knowledge in exchange for college credit. The main difference, however, is that CLEP examinations are offered free to military members.

CLEP examinations cover basic courses such as English, basic math, and science, but they are also available in other subjects such as calculus, marketing, and accounting.

Ultimately, it is up to the school you are attending to decide whether it will accept CLEP examinations for credit. Therefore, it is a good idea to check with the school first before wasting your time taking an examination that may not count. For more information about DANTES services, visit www.dantes. doded.mil and for specific information about CLEP, visit https://clep.collegeboard.org/military.

CREDIT FOR MILITARY SCHOOLS

Although not officially an "educational program," most military schools that you attend are eligible for college credit. Again, such as the case with CLEP examinations, it is up to the specific school whether it will award college credit and, if so, how much.

Depending on the military schools you have attended, the credits you receive may give your college journey a major "jump start." In my own case, I was trained in electronics and hydraulic theory (which, believe it or not, counted toward credits for physics). Counting Basic Training, I attended military schools for almost the first two years of my enlistment. The credits I received for my military education, coupled with the basic CLEP examinations I managed to pass, amounted to more than thirty credit hours toward my bachelor's degree! I was on my way to earning the required 126 hours necessary to graduate.

Branch-Specific Educational Programs

As stated, each branch has its own specific educational benefits in addition to the common programs that all of the services offer.

Although each branch offers its own unique programs, the bottom line is that, with few exceptions, the programs basically are all the same. You'll probably find the biggest difference in the programs for which you may qualify.

For example, maybe you'll be eligible, based on test scores or job selection, for more educational funding from the Army than from the Navy. Although they might have similar benefits, you may find yourself not qualifying for the benefits of one branch but qualifying for the benefits of another.

Remember, however, to consider all factors before making the decision to join a specific branch of the military for the educational benefits. For instance, I may not have received the same level of training that enabled me to earn all of those college credits if I had joined another branch of the military. In other words, how much money were those 30+ college credits worth?

In business management, we call those costs "opportunity costs"—the cost of doing one thing over another. You must look at all the opportunities and compare them to each other.

Branch-Specific Educational Benefits

This section covers the branch-specific educational benefits offered by each of the services. As stated earlier, things are changing so rapidly that the specifics of the benefits listed here probably changed before I even typed these words on my computer. Nevertheless, this will give you a good idea of the types of programs offered. I strongly encourage you to get the most current information from your recruiter.

AIR FORCE

Community College of the Air Force (CCAF)

The Community College of the Air Force (CCAF) is the only accredited institution belonging to any of the Armed Forces. The CCAF awards associate degrees in areas of study that relate to the service member's career field.

Air Force members earn college credits for military schools, CLEP examinations, and courses completed through civilian colleges. Enrollment in CCAF is free, and many Air Force members use their CCAF degrees as springboards to earning their bachelor's degrees. Enrollment in CCAF is also open to Reserve members.

Airman Education and Commissioning Program (AECP)

The Airman Education and Commissioning Program (AECP) is designed to allow outstanding enlisted personnel to complete the requirements for a bachelor's degree by attending college full-time and then applying for commissioning as an Air Force officer.

The AECP program requirements include the following:

- The airman must have completed at least one year of Active Duty.
- The airman must possess at least forty-five college credits.
- The airman must be able to be commissioned by his or her thirtieth birthday.

Other Programs Leading to a Commission

In addition to AECP, there are two programs that allow Air Force enlisted members to attend college full-time and then earn a commission:

- Leaders Encouraging Airmen Development—This allows deserving airmen, with fewer than six years of service, to attend the Air Force Academy.
- Scholarships for Outstanding Airmen to ROTC—This provides for two- and four-year Reserve Officer Corps scholarships for deserving enlisted members with fewer than six years of service.

Both of these programs offer an excellent opportunity for Air Force members to further their education.

ARMY

Loan Repayment

Certain types of federal student loans are eligible for this program. If you qualify, the Army will repay your loans at the rate of one third of the loan for each year of Active Duty served. A three-year enlistment could qualify you for up to $65,000 in loan repayments.

Concurrent Admissions Program (ConAP)

Administered by Army Recruiting Command, through a partnership with SOC, the Concurrent Admissions Program (ConAP) allows soldiers to enroll in one of 1900 participating schools. These schools guarantee on-campus enrollment after the soldier's initial term of enlistment. Also, all college credits earned while serving on Active Duty may be transferred. For more information, visit the SOC website or call (800) 368-5622.

SOCAD

SOCAD is the Army's partnership with SOC. For more information, visit the SOC website.

Green to Gold

The Green to Gold program allows deserving soldiers to apply for two-, three-, and four-year college scholarships that will ultimately lead to a commission as an Army officer. For more information, visit goarmy.com or call (502) 624-6937.

COAST GUARD

Coast Guard Institute

This program is similar to the Community College of the Air Force (CCAF) in that military schools, CLEP examinations, and civilian schools put together an official transcript. However, the Coast Guard Institute does not have the accreditation necessary to issue diplomas.

Pre-Commissioning Program for Enlisted Personnel

This program gives an opportunity to deserving enlisted members to complete their college education and then attend Officer Candidate School (OCS) to earn a commission as a Coast Guard Officer.

The program requirements and features include the following:

- be an active duty enlistee
- be a U.S. citizen
- have served on active duty for four years (two of which must be in the Coast Guard)
- have an SAT I combined score of 1100, an ACT score of 23, or an ASVAB GT score of 109
- meet physical requirements for commissioning
- be at least 21 years old but not older than 33 years
- be able to complete requirements for a four-year degree within twenty-four months and maintain a cumulative GPA of at least 2.5
- remain eligible for promotion while participating in the program
- continue to receive full pay and allowances while participating in the program

MARINE CORPS

Servicemembers Opportunity Colleges Degree Programs for the Marine Corps (SOCMAR)

SOCMAR is the Marine Corps partnership with SOC. For more information, visit the SOC website.

Marine Corps College Fund (GI Bill Kicker)

Combined with the GI Bill, the Marine Corps College Fund can help fund your college education. Besides meeting certain qualifications, you must enlist for at least four years to be eligible for the Marine Corps College Fund. Eligible Marines may begin using their benefits after completing four years of enlistment.

Other Programs Leading to a Four-Year Degree and Commission

There are several programs available to enlisted Marines that lead to earning a bachelor's degree and a commission as a Marine Corps officer. They include:

- Naval Reserve Officers Training Corps (NROTC)—NROTC scholarships are available for deserving enlisted Marines to attend one of seventy-one colleges nationwide that host NROTC units. Besides paying for tuition and books, NROTC scholarship recipients also receive a monthly stipend of $250 to $400.
- Naval Academy Preparatory School—Those selected for the Naval Academy Prep School will attend the school for one year to prepare them for admission to the Naval Academy.

NAVY

SOCNAV

SOCNAV is the Navy's partnership with SOC. For more information, visit the SOC website.

Program for Afloat College Education (PACE)

PACE is truly a mobile program, offering college courses on board Navy ships. PACE courses are free and are integrated fully into the SOC and SOCMAR programs.

The Navy College Fund (GI Bill Kicker)

Combined with the GI Bill, the Navy College Fund can help you fund your college education. Besides meeting certain qualifications, you must enlist for at least four years to be eligible for the Navy College Fund. Eligible Sailors may begin using their benefits after completing at least three years of enlistment.

Navy College Assistance/Student Headstart (Navy CASH) Program

The Navy CASH program allows applicants to enter Active Duty and receive pay and allowances for up to twelve months while attending college. To qualify, applicants must enlist either in the nuclear or submarine electronic/computer field or as a missile technician.

The Navy College Program

Similar to the Coast Guard Institute, the Navy College Program allows you to put all of your college credits, no matter where they were earned, into one transcript. For more information, visit www. navycollege.navy.mil.

Other Programs Leading to a Four-Year Degree and Commission

- Naval Reserve Officers Training Corps (NROTC)—NROTC scholarships are available for deserving enlisted Sailors to attend one of seventy-one colleges nationwide that host NROTC units. Besides paying for tuition and books, NROTC scholarship recipients also receive a monthly stipend of $250 to $400.
- Naval Academy Preparatory School—Those selected for the Naval Academy Prep School will attend the school for one year to get them prepared for admission to the Naval Academy.

NATIONAL GUARD AND RESERVE

Many of the programs listed in this chapter also are offered in one form or another by the National Guard and Reserve components. In addition, some states offer free tuition to state schools for members of their National Guard units.

Although many states offer "free" tuition, many restrictions do apply and are limited to budgetary constraints in some cases. Make sure you get all the facts before assuming that you will get a "free ride" to a state school.

SERVICE ACADEMIES AND RESERVE OFFICER TRAINING CORPS OPPORTUNITIES

Although I wrote this book for those interested in enlisting in the military, I thought it would be appropriate to mention the service academies and ROTC programs.

Many young people contact recruiters for information about the service academies and ROTC and enlist instead. Because the competition and requirements for entrance into the service academies and for ROTC scholarships are so stringent, many people enlist in the military hoping to earn a commission after earning a degree while serving on Active Duty.

As I've mentioned previously, if your sole goal is to attend college and you have the means to do so, then an enlistment in the military is probably not the right decision for you.

Service Academies

The Service Academies include:

- The Air Force Academy, Colorado Springs, Colorado
- The U.S. Military Academy (Army), West Point, New York
- The Coast Guard Academy, New London, Connecticut
- The Naval Academy, Annapolis, Maryland
- Merchant Marine Academy, Kings Point, New York

The purpose of the service academies is to provide an education and leadership training to future military officers. With the exception of the Merchant Marine Academy, all graduates of the four-year service academies serve as Active Duty officers on graduation. Merchant Marine Academy graduates enter the Naval Reserve on graduation, although many choose to enter Active Duty. Naval Academy graduates may choose to enter the Marine Corps after graduation because the Marines do not have a separate academy.

The cost of attending a service academy is minimal; in fact, students receive a stipend to attend. This, coupled with the quality of the education received, makes acceptance to a service academy difficult. Some of the basic requirements include:

- a minimum SAT score or the ACT equivalent (check websites for minimums; few people with minimum scores are chosen)

- a nomination from your state senator or local congressperson (this is not a requirement for the Coast Guard Academy)
- participation in high school team sports/clubs
- U.S. citizenship
- being single with no dependents
- meeting minimum physical requirements (see Chapter 1 for disqualifying factors)
- passing a physical fitness test
- having an outstanding high school academic record

Each academy has its own application process, which is long and tedious. Chapter 11 contains points of contact for more information about the service academies.

Reserve Officer Training Corps (ROTC)

Through Naval ROTC, the Air Force, Army, Navy, and Marine Corps offer programs that allow students to attend civilian colleges and, on graduation, receive a commission as an officer. Each year, ROTC graduates account for the highest percentage of officers entering Active Duty. ROTC units are in colleges and universities nationwide.

ROTC offers two-, three-, and four-year scholarships, although students do not have to be scholarship recipients to attend ROTC. Scholarships cover tuition, which usually has a cap, fees, and textbook costs. Scholarship recipients also receive a $250 to $400 (depending on year in college) per month stipend during the school year.

Requirements for an ROTC scholarship are similar to those of the service academies, with the exception of the congressional nominations and the dependency requirements. As with Service Academy applications, you should start the application process as early as possible. Ensure that you meet all deadlines and don't leave anything to chance. You will find points of contact for information about ROTC scholarships in Chapter 11.

> My oldest son, currently serving as an electrical engineer in the Air Force, attended college as the recipient of an ROTC scholarship. The college he attended also covered many of the costs not covered by his scholarship. The value of his scholarship, including the costs covered by the college, exceeded $250,000 by the time he graduated in 2005.

A Word About Taking the SAT/ACT

When applying for a service academy or ROTC scholarship, the more times you take the SAT or ACT the better. Because only your highest scores will count, you have nothing to lose and everything to gain by taking the examinations multiple times.

Summary

As you have seen, there are many benefits of military service in addition to the pay. When you consider the pay and other benefits, it all adds up to an attractive compensation package.

One important category of benefits that I covered in this chapter were the many educational benefits available to military members.

I think it is important to remind you one last time that the information contained in this chapter is only as current as the data that is available at the time of this writing. Military benefits, especially those related to education, change constantly. Therefore, it is important to check with your recruiter for new programs and changes to the ones listed here.

Above all, make sure that if you qualify for any special educational benefits you get your guarantee in writing. Do not accept a verbal promise; make sure you understand how much you will receive, how you will receive payment, and when you will receive payment or be able to start using the benefit.

10 OPPORTUNITIES IN THE GUARD AND THE RESERVE

Besides Active Duty, a great way to serve your country, get some excellent training, receive educational benefits, and get paid doing it is as a member of the Guard or Reserve. The purpose of this chapter is to familiarize you with the Reserve components and their many benefits.

Each branch of the service (Air Force, Army, Coast Guard, Marines, and Navy) has its own Reserve component. In addition, the Army National Guard and the Air National Guard play a unique role in our nation's defense. For the sake of simplicity, I'll refer to all Guard and Reserve members as "Reservists."

An entire book could be written describing the roles, capabilities, and history of the Reserve components; therefore, it is not the intent of this chapter to make you an expert. If you would like more detailed and up-to-date information, I suggest that you use the contact information provided in this book to obtain it.

The Purpose of the Reserve

Although each Reserve component has its own "mission statement," its basic purpose is no different from that of the Active Duty components: "to support and defend the Constitution of the United States against all enemies, foreign or domestic." The main difference is not how it does it but rather when it does it.

Where Most Reservists Come From

If you are reading this book, you probably have never served in any military branch. Therefore, you are an NPS (Non-Prior Service) applicant.

Although the number of NPS applicants joining the Reserve is increasing each year, the majority of Reserve members have had some military experience. Although some join the Reserve to protect their retirement pay and to continue receiving the many military benefits they enjoyed on Active Duty, others continue to serve because they like the camaraderie of the military and want to continue to serve their country.

Although Prior Service applicants can bring a wealth of knowledge to the Reserve, NPS applicants provide the "new blood" necessary to sustain the Reserve.

Why the Reserve?

If you have decided to join the military, why would you join the Reserve instead of Active Duty? There are many reasons people make that decision, including:

- searching for a good part-time job;
- the desire to stay in the local area;
- attending college and wanting to stay at that particular school;
- having a good job but wanting to learn new skills;
- family commitments that require them to remain in the local area; and
- the desire to serve their country without drastically changing their current lifestyle.

The reasons some people choose the Reserve over Active Duty are many, just as for others Active Duty is a better choice than the Reserve. The decision may be easier for you if you have used the "needs analysis" portion of this book.

What Makes the Reserve Components Different from Active Duty?

The basic difference between Active Duty military members and Reserve component members is that being on Active Duty is a full-time job, whereas Reserve members usually perform their duties one weekend a month and one two-week period a year.

However, there are usually opportunities for Reserve members to work additional time to support their Reserve unit. In addition, Reserve component members may be called on at any time to support worldwide operations. This is what happened during Operation Desert Storm when tens of thousands of Guard and Reserve members were "activated." An unfortunate phenomenon developed, however, when many Guard and Reserve members refused to go to the Middle East—they believed that they had joined for training and education, not to fight wars. For many of these Reservists, it was a case of not wanting to fulfill their obligation; for others, it resulted from a misrepresentation by the recruiter. These individuals more than likely did not belong in any branch of the military; they probably would not have joined if they knew that there was a chance they would have to "deploy." Unfortunately, they were more than likely told by their recruiters that there was little or no chance of them ever deploying, when, in reality, there is always a chance of being "called up."

Recent world events have tested the mettle of the nation's Reservists and Guardsmen. Once again, the majority of them answered the call and performed seamlessly with their Active Duty comrades. The one thing to remember is that if you become part of any Reserve component, including a Guard component, you are a member of the United States Armed Forces and, as such, may be called on at any time for activation to support the Active Duty military.

In addition, as a member of the Army National Guard or the Air National Guard, you may be activated by the Governor of your state to help during states of emergencies, such as floods, hurricanes, and tornadoes.

Military Benefits

As a Reservist, you are entitled to many of the same benefits available to Active Duty members. This section represents a sampling of some of the many benefits available. Because entitlements and regulations change, it is impossible to provide detailed information that is up-to-date. Therefore, I encourage you to get the details about benefits and entitlements from your recruiter. Ask specific questions about those benefits and entitlements in which you are interested, and, if your recruiter is unsure of the answers to your questions, ask him or her to research the answers for you.

BASE FACILITIES

As a Reservist, you can use most of the same on-base facilities as your Active Duty counterparts (see Chapter 9 for detailed information). However, there may be some exceptions and restrictions.

PAY AND ALLOWANCES

Because being a Reservist is a part-time job, you receive payment only for the time you are actually "on-duty," which is usually one weekend per month and one two-week period of Active Duty per year. Refer to the pay chart in Chapter 9 for details about Reserve Pay.

During Drill Weekends, Reservists receive payment for the equivalent of two days of Base Pay for every day served. During the two-week Annual Active Duty period, Reservists receive full pay, as well as allowances that include housing allowance, Basic Allowance for Subsistence (BAS), and any other special-duty pay authorized.

MEDICAL AND LIFE INSURANCE

As a Reservist, you are entitled to the same life insurance benefit as your Active Duty counterparts; however, the rules for medical and dental insurance differ. Reserve members are covered by military "medical benefits" only while engaged in Active Duty, and family members are not covered unless the member is on what is considered Extended Active Duty. Under certain circumstances, Reserve members and their families may have coverage under the military dental plan. For more information visit: http://www.tricare.mil/RESERVE.

ON-BASE HOUSING

Reserve members are not entitled to on-base housing and only receive housing allowance while serving on periods of Active Duty. However, the Reservist will get housing provisions when he or she is performing weekend drills and Active Duty. Facilities range from tents and dormitory rooms to off-base hotel accommodations, depending on the situation.

BASIC TRAINING

All NPS applicants are required to attend the same Basic Training (Boot Camp) as their Active Duty counterparts.

TECHNICAL TRAINING

Most Reservists attend the same technical schools as their Active Duty counterparts. Some of these schools are lengthy and, combined with Basic Training, require you to be on Active Duty status for some time. Therefore, you should consider how this would affect your civilian employment and/or college schedule.

You should use the "needs analysis" portion of this book to determine whether the technical training you have chosen fits your needs.

An added benefit of technical training, and perhaps the most important benefit to some, is that it may help to improve your skills in your civilian job or that it can open doors for new job opportunities in the civilian workforce.

ADVANCEMENT

Just as on Active Duty, you will have the opportunity for advancement as a Reservist. Although most NPS applicants enter the Reserve as E-1s, there are opportunities for enlistment at advanced pay grades based on college credits and participation in high school Junior ROTC programs, just like Active Duty.

It is imperative that you ask your recruiter if you qualify for advanced pay grade and then ensure that it is on your enlistment contract.

EDUCATIONAL BENEFITS

Reservists are entitled to many of the same educational benefits as their Active Duty counterparts. In some cases, the benefits for Reservists are even better!

Some of these benefits can include:

- post-9/11 G.I. Bill;
- tuition assistance;
- College Level Examination Program (CLEP) examinations; and
- participation in branch-specific programs, such as the Community College of the Air Force.

Also, some states offer members of the National Guard free tuition to state schools. However, be sure to find out all the facts, such as the amount of funding available, whether it is guaranteed funding, and what the restrictions are, if any.

RETIREMENT

As with Active Duty, Reservists may retire with as few as twenty years of service. There are two major differences, however, between an Active Duty retirement and a Reserve retirement:

- Instead of calculating retirement pay based on the number of years of service, pay is based on points that are awarded for each day of reserve duty—the higher the number of points, the higher the amount of retirement pay.
- Unlike Active Duty retirement pay, which starts immediately after retirement, the Reservist must wait until he or she turns sixty-years-old before collecting retirement pay. Retired Reservists, called "Gray Area Retirees," do not receive any healthcare until they are eligible for retirement pay.

Although not as lucrative as an Active Duty retirement, the Reservist with a retirement plan in his or her civilian job is, in fact, "contributing" to two retirement plans at once!

TRAVEL AND RECREATION

With few exceptions, Reservists have the same opportunity for travel and recreation as Active Duty members. Reservists and their families receive many of the same discounts offered to Active Duty members and their families. Most military recreation facilities and equipment are open to Reservists.

ENLISTMENT BONUSES

Depending on the branch of service you are entering and the specific job you choose, you may be entitled to an enlistment bonus. Usually a branch of service pays these bonuses to entice people into hard-to-fill "critical" jobs. Besides cash bonuses, some services are offering increased educational benefits for people who are enlisting in certain jobs. You should consider all of this before enlisting. As stated earlier, however, don't give a high priority to enlistment bonuses unless you are enlisting only for the money.

Before you enlist, make sure that you understand all the terms of the enlistment bonus. For example, ensure that you find out when you will receive the bonus and whether you will receive it in one lump sum or is paid out in increments during a certain amount of time. As with everything that is "promised" to you, ensure that the enlistment bonus is part of your enlistment contract. If it is not listed, plain and simple, you haven't been promised it, no matter what has been promised verbally.

Chapter Summary

Now more than ever, the lines that distinguish the Active Duty Military from their Reserve counterparts have become blurred, the major difference lying in not what they do but rather when they do it. Gone are the days of the "weekend warriors" who were considered by many on Active Duty as second-class citizens. Today, Reservists fill a vital role in the defense of our nation.

Chapter 11 contains contacts for more information about joining the Reserve or Guard.

CONTACTS AND OTHER USEFUL INFORMATION

To aid you in your research for more information on joining the military, this chapter provides you with contact points for information about each military branch, for Department of Defense websites, and commercial websites that deal with military careers. This chapter also contains other useful information that will help you get a head start on Basic Training.

As with any military service literature, "Recruiting" websites are vehicles for advertising. Just as you would expect an automobile manufacturer's website to "push" its product, military recruiting websites do the same thing. Take in the information you find, digest it, and apply the skills you have learned from reading this book.

E-Recruiting

E-business is big in today's society. Many, if not most, large companies engage in it, and the military is no exception. Many of the services have, or plan to have in the near future, e-recruiting sites as part of their recruiting websites, Usually, these sites are chat rooms, where you can "speak" with recruiters and get immediate answers to your questions. Of course, the recruiters in these chat rooms are not your local recruiters; they solely are dedicated to e-recruiting and may be located anywhere in the country.

Official Recruiting Websites and Telephone Numbers

ACTIVE DUTY

Air Force
www.airforce.com
800-423-8723

Marine Corps
www.marines.com
800-627-4637

Army
www.goarmy.com
800-872-2769

Navy
www.navy.com
800-872-6289

Coast Guard
www.gocoastguard.com
There is no national phone number;
see website for recruiter locator

RESERVE COMPONENTS

Air Force Reserve
www.afreserve.com
800-257-1212

Coast Guard Reserve
www.gocoastguard.com
See website

Air National Guard
www.goang.com
800-864-6264

Marine Corps Reserve
www.marines.com
800-627-4637

Army National Guard
www.1800goguard.com
800-464-8273

Navy
wwwnavyreserve.com
800-872-8767

Army Reserve
www.goarmyreserve.com
800-872-2769

EDUCATIONAL OPPORTUNITIES

Coast Guard Institute
www.uscg.mil

Coast Guard Pre-commissioning Program for Enlisted Personnel
www.uscg.mil/hq/capemay/education/e-oprograms3.asp

Community College of the Air Force
www.au.af.mil/au/ccaf

Defense Activity for Non-Traditional Education Support (DANTES)
http://www.dantes.doded.mil/DANTES_Homepage.html

Department of Defense Education Activity
www.dodea.edu

Green to Gold
www.goarmy.com/rotc/enlisted-soldiers

Navy College
https://www.navycollege.navy.mil

Navy Enlisted Commissioning Program (now called the Seaman to Admiral-21 Program)
www.sta-21.navy.mil

Post-911 GI Bill
www.gibill.va.gov

Scholarship for Outstanding Airmen to ROTC
www.afoats.af.mil

Servicemembers Opportunity Colleges
www.soc.aascu.org

United Services Military Apprenticeship Program
https://usmap.cnet.navy.mil

SERVICE ACADEMIES

Air Force Academy
www.academyadmissions.com
800-443-9266

Merchant Marine Academy
www.usmma.edu
516-773-5391

U.S. Military Academy
www.usma.edu
845-938-4041

Naval Academy
www.usna.edu
410-293-4361

Coast Guard Academy
www.cga.edu
800-883-8724

ROTC

Air Force
www.afrotc.com
800-522-0033

Navy/Marines
www.nrotc.navy.mil
800-628-7682

Army
www.goarmy.com/rotc
800-872-7682

Department of Defense/Government Sponsored Websites

The websites listed below are either Department of Defense (DoD) or other U.S. government-owned and -operated sites. Some of the sites specifically focus on recruiting, whereas others, such as www. dfas.mil, provide information to those already serving in the military.

Remember that when visiting any recruiting website, regardless if it is for a specific branch of the military or a DoD site, the information on the site is designed to "sell" the military. Again, get the information from the website and use it to make an informed decision.

- **Air Force Historical Research Agency**—official repository for Air Force historical documents. **www.afhra.af.mil**
- **AFCrossroads.com**—operated by the Air Force, this website, designed with the service member in mind, contains information and news about all of the military branches, including information about military bases and military benefits. There are also many helpful links to other websites. **www.afcrossroads.com**

- **Coast Guard History**—history, images, and information pertaining to the Coast Guard **www.uscg.mil/history/h_index.asp**
- **Defense Finance and Accounting Service**—information for all money matters. Contains up-to-date and proposed pay charts. **www.dfas.mil**
- **DefenseLink**—Official website of the Department of Defense (DoD). Includes information about DoD and the military branches, as well as up-to-date news and articles pertaining to military matters. **www.defenselink.mil**
- **House Committee on Armed Forces**—news, information, press releases, hearing schedules, transcripts, etc. **www.house.gov/hasc**
- **Joint Chiefs of Staff**—official website of the JCS, includes up-to-date information pertaining to the military. **www.dtic.mil/jcs**
- **Myfuture.Com**—joint-service recruiting website that is somewhat disguised as a "career/college planner" but is a site for military recruiting. **www.myfuture.com**
- **National Security Council**—website of the president's "forum" for deciding national security and foreign policy. **www.whitehouse.gov/nsc**
- **Naval Historical Center**—website of the navy's official history program. **www.history.navy.mil**
- **TodaysMilitary.com**—specifically designed for individuals who may be able to influence young men and women of enlistment age. This includes parents, guidance counselors, and youth-group leaders. Includes a tremendous amount of information about "today's military" opportunities. **www.todaysmilitary.com**
- **U.S. Army Center of Military History**—website of the Army's official history program. **www.army.mil/cmh-pg**
- **U.S. Senate Committee on Armed Services**—News, information, press releases, hearing schedules, transcripts, etc. **www.senate.gov/~armed_services**
- **The White House**—everything you've ever wanted to know about the White House, the president, the vice president, and history. Also has a virtual library. **www.whitehouse.gov**

Commercial Websites

If you have browsed the Internet for information about the military, you have undoubtedly come across at least a few commercial, non-government-sponsored websites. The unfortunate thing about alot of these sites is that their sole purpose is to give a negative view of the military.

Frequently, groups or individuals who have some kind of grudge against the military established these websites. Oftentimes, people who have had a bad experience with the military establish these sites.. Please keep this in mind if you come across any of these negative websites to not allow them to cloud your judgment when deciding whether the military is right for you.

Another word of caution: some websites offer unbiased advice about joining the military; they promise to give the "real" answers to your questions about joining the military. However, many are private websites that sell your information to the military and their answers, therefore, are biased.

The websites included in this section, although from commercial sources, provide a positive view about the military.

- **Army and Air Force Exchange Service**—the official website of the army and air force "department store." This site will not give you any information about the military, although you will get a look into some of the shopping privileges available to military members. **www.aafes.com** (A related site is the **Navy Exchange System: www.mynavyexchange.com**)
- **The U.S. Constitution**—Okay, maybe this isn't a military website, but I thought we could all refresh our minds on the reasons why we serve in the military. **www.law.cornell.edu/constitution**
- **MilitaryCity.com**—the official website of Army Times Publishing. There is some military news as well as some excellent image and audio downloads. **www.militarycity.com**
- **USmilitary.com**—A powerful website containing information about the military along with articles on current military topics written by military experts. **www.usmilitary.com**

Military Time

Have you ever watched a war movie and wondered what the heck they were talking about when they said, "We'll rendezvous at zero six thirty"? Well, I'm about to unravel the mystery for you, and it really isn't that difficult to learn!

Civilian time is based on a 12-hour clock, with the two halves of the day divided into a.m. and p.m. Military time is based on a 24-hour clock, which starts counting at midnight. The following table shows how to translate military time into civilian time, hour by hour. It also indicates how to pronounce military time. Civilian a.m. times are pronounced "oh" followed by the time in hundreds. For example, 1 a.m. is pronounced "oh one hundred." Civilian p.m. times are pronounced as hundreds, such as "sixteen hundred" for 4 p.m.

TIME CONVERSION AND PRONUNCIATION

Civilian	Military	Pronunciation
12 a.m.	0000	zero-zero-zero-zero
1 a.m.	0100	oh one hundred
2 a.m.	0200	oh two hundred
3 a.m.	0300	oh three hundred
4 a.m.	0400	oh four hundred
5 a.m.	0500	oh five hundred
6 a.m.	0600	oh six hundred
7 a.m.	0700	oh seven hundred
8 a.m.	0800	oh eight hundred
9 a.m.	0900	oh nine hundred
10 a.m.	1000	ten hundred

Civilian	Military	Pronunciation
11 a.m.	1100	eleven hundred
12 p.m.	1200	twelve hundred
1 p.m.	1300	thirteen hundred
2 p.m.	1400	fourteen hundred
3 p.m.	1500	fifteen hundred
4 p.m.	1600	sixteen hundred
5 p.m.	1700	seventeen hundred
6 p.m.	1800	eighteen hundred
7 p.m.	1900	nineteen hundred
8 p.m.	2000	twenty hundred
9 p.m.	2100	twenty-one hundred
10 p.m.	2200	twenty-two hundred
11 p.m.	2300	twenty-three hundred

For exact times, it's as simple as adding the number of minutes to the hour. For example, if it's 2:15 p.m. civilian time, you start with the 1400 and add 15, which makes it 1415, or "fourteen fifteen," military time. Notice that it isn't "fourteen hundred fifteen," as you might think it would be. That's because when expressing a more exact p.m. time, the hundred is dropped from the pronunciation.

Here are a few more pronunciation tips:

- For any time between 1 and 9 minutes past the hour, you add "zero" to the minutes: 0905 is "oh nine zero five," and 1607 is "sixteen zero seven."
- You can also say "zero" instead of "oh" at the beginning of a time, as in "zero nine hundred" for 0900.
- The time 0005 is pronounced "zero zero zero five" and 0030 is pronounced "zero zero thirty."

An easy way to convert from civilian to military time (for p.m.) is to add 12 to the civilian time (hour). For example, 2:15 plus 12 equals 1415. To convert from military to civilian (for p.m.), subtract 12 from the first two digits (1415 minus 12 equals 2:15).

Phonetic Alphabet

Just as there is a specific way to express the time, there is a specific way to express each letter of the alphabet. Have you ever had to spell your name for someone who has responded, "Is that 'B' as in 'boy'?" Someone else may ask, "Is that 'B' as in 'ball'?"

The military has an established a set of words that express each letter. Study the following chart, and you'll memorize them in no time.

MILITARY ALPHABET

Letter	Name	Letter	Name	Letter	Name	Letter	Name
A	ALFA (Alpha)	H	HOTEL	O	OSCAR	U	UNIFORM
B	BRAVO	I	INDIA	P	PAPA	V	VICTOR
C	CHARLIE	J	JULIETT	Q	QUEBEC	W	WHISKEY
D	DELTA	K	KILO	R	ROMEO	X	X-RAY
E	ECHO	L	LIMA	S	SIERRA	Y	YANKEE
F	FOXTROT	M	MIKE	T	TANGO	Z	ZULU
G	GOLF	N	NOVEMBER				

Military Terminology and Acronyms

A complete dictionary of military terminology and acronyms would take up this entire book and, for the most part, would be overkill. Fortunately, there is a complete dictionary available online for your use. The official *Department of Defense Dictionary of Military and Associated Terms* are at http://www.dtic.mil/doctrine/.

The list below contains some essential (and a few nonessential) terms that you may find helpful.

A

AD—Active Duty.

AFSC—Air Force Specialty Code. A number designation for all Air Force jobs.

ASVAB—Armed Services Vocational Aptitude Battery (see Chapter 4).

AWOL—Absent Without Leave. Term used by the Army and Air Force for a person who has failed to show up for work even though he or she has not been granted leave.

B

Billeting—on-base quarters. Usually a temporary arrangement.

Brig—The Navy and Marine Corps versions of jail.

Bulkhead—a wall to us landlubbers (but not to those in the Navy, Coast Guard, or Marines).

C

Call Sign—any combination of characters or pronounceable words, which identifies a communication facility, a command, an authority, an activity, or a unit; used primarily for establishing and maintaining communications.

Chaplain—any military member of the clergy (chaplains hold commissioned-officer rank).

Chain-of-Command—an organizational chart of a military organization; as a recruit, you are at the bottom of the chain-of-command.

Check Your Six—be careful of what might be behind you (look behind you).

Chow—a meal (most times served in the "Chow Hall").

Company—the group to which Coast Guard recruits are assigned to for Basic Training.

Company Commander—the primary person responsible for a recruit's Basic Training in the Coast Guard.

CONUS—Continental United States (if you were stationed in Texas, you would be CONUS; if you were stationed in England, you'd be OCONUS—outside CONUS.

Cover—a uniform hat.

D

DI—Drill Instructor. For the Army and Marine Corps, this is the primary person responsible for a recruit's Basic Training.

Division—the group to which Navy recruits are assigned for Basic Training.

DoD—Department of Defense.

Dog Tags—metal ID tags worn on a metal necklace.

Double Time—run in formation or do something quickly.

E

Echelon—separate level of command. As compared to a regiment, a division is a higher echelon; a battalion is a lower echelon.

F

Field Day—a thorough cleaning of a workspace or living quarters.

First Shirt—another name for First Sergeant (usually the top enlisted person in a military organization whose job it is to care for the welfare of the unit members).

Flight—the group to which Air Force recruits are assigned during Basic Training; also refers to the smallest part of an Air Force Squadron.

G

GEDUNK—a Navy term meaning junk food, or snacks, or the place on board ship where they are purchased. Navy folklore says the name comes from the sound a soda can makes when it falls to the bottom of the machine.

GI—any U.S. military member (comes from the words "Government Issue").

Grunt—refers to members of the infantry, also describes hard manual labor—"grunt work."

H

Head—a bathroom to Marine Corps, Navy, and Coast Guard members.

Hollywood Shower—a long shower taken aboard ship where water is scarce and usually conserved; the proper showering method is to turn on the water, get wet, turn off the water, soap-up, turn on the water, rinse off, and turn off the water.

I

I.G.—Inspector General; answers service members' complaints and conducts inspections.

Intel—short for intelligence, meaning any type of information.

J

JAG—Judge Advocate General (military lawyers).

K

KP—Kitchen Police in charge of cleaning the kitchen.

L

Ladder—stairs on board ships.
Latrine—what soldiers and airmen call a bathroom.
Leave—vacation.
LES—Leave and Earnings Statement; a monthly report of your pay, allowances, and leave balance.
Liberty—time off (away from work) for sailors and marines.

M

Mess Deck—the place where sailors and marines eat aboard a ship.
MOS—Military Occupational Specialty.
MP—Military Police.
MRE—Meals Ready to Eat; food packaged in foil pouches usually eaten when regular meals are not available.

N

NATO—North Atlantic Treaty Organization; a group of countries (of which the United States is one) that was formed for mutual protection of member countries originally in response to the Communist threat.
NCO—Non-Commissioned Officer in the Army, Marine Corps, and Air Force. Enlisted members in the pay grades of E-4 or E-5 (depending on service) through E-9.
NCO Club—(also known as Enlisted Club); a place where enlisted personnel can go to unwind and enjoy a meal or drink.

O

O'Dark Thirty—slang for very early in the morning.
Officer—refers to commissioned officers.
O Club—Officers' Club; a place that commissioned officers can go to dine and drink.

P

Passageway—a hallway aboard ships.
PCS—Permanent Change of Station; a move to a new base, post, ship, etc.
Platoon—Part of a company composed of three squads. Also, the group to which Army and Marine recruits are assigned for Basic Training.
Police—to cleanup an area.
PX—Post Exchange; on-post stores where soldiers can shop for items.

Q

Quarters—where you live.

R

Rate—job specialty in the Navy and Coast Guard.

Rations—another word for food (or meals).

RDC—Recruit Division Commander; the primary person responsible for a Navy recruit's Basic Training.

Recycled—During Basic Training, to be put back in training (sort of like being left back in school).

S

Scuttlebutt—rumors (may also refer to a water fountain).

SEAL—Sea Air Land. The name of the Navy's Special Forces.

SECDEF—the Secretary of Defense; the top position in the Department of Defense (held by a civilian).

Skivvies—underwear.

T

TAD—Temporary Assigned Duty; duty away from home station.

TDY—Temporary Duty Assignment; same as TAD for Army and Air Force members.

U

Underway—refers to a ship at sea.

V

Voice Call Sign—a call sign provided primarily for voice communication.

W

Wash out—to fail (as in washing out of Basic Training or technical school).

X

XO—Executive Officer; usually the number two position in a military unit, directly under the commanding officer.

Y

YTD—year-to-date (for example: "you have earned $10,000 YTD").

Z

ZULU Time—a universal worldwide time used to coordinate military operations; (for example, 1600Z is the same in the United States as it is in Europe, Asia, etc.).

Military Rank Insignia Charts

You may want to familiarize yourself with military rank insignia before you leave for Basic Training. The following links illustrate rank insignia for all branches of the U.S. military:

- Enlisted Insignia: www.defense.gov/about/insignias/enlisted.aspx
- Officer Insignia: www.defense.gov/about/insignias/officers.aspx

One Last Link

I invite you to visit the Guide to Joining the Military Facebook page (www.facebook.com/guidetojoiningthemilitary). I want to know what you think of this book and any suggestions you may have to improve its contents. Also, I'd like to hear from those of you with any "recruiter or Basic Training story" (good or bad). However, please do not ask me specific questions about enlistment opportunities (your recruiter can answer these better than I can).

Summary

The links provided in this chapter are up-to-date as of this writing; however, they may have changed by the time you read this book. In addition, I cannot control the contents of any of the websites listed here. I have visited all of these sites and found them to be acceptable. Of course, your view of the contents may be different from mine; therefore, you should use your own judgment when viewing each site.

Although the links provided in this chapter could keep you occupied for a while, I suggest that you do some Internet surfing on your own to find others. If, by chance, you stumble across one you find helpful that is not in this book, please visit my Facebook page and leave the address for me.

The information about military time, the phonetic alphabet, military terminology and acronyms, and military rank insignias in this chapter will give you an edge over other recruits. The more you know before arriving at Basic Training, the less you'll have to learn when you get there. While others are struggling to memorize information, you'll already be ahead of the game.

APPENDIX

Forms

This appendix contains examples of three important forms that are filled out during the enlistment process:

- DD Form 1966, which is the Record of Military Processing–Armed Forces of the United States (your application for enlistment)
- DD Form 2807-2, which is the Medical Prescreen of Medical History Report
- DD Form 2808, which is the Report of Medical Examination

Note that although the actual forms may have been revised by the time you read this book, they are not likely to be substantially different.

RECORD OF MILITARY PROCESSING - ARMED FORCES OF THE UNITED STATES

(Read Privacy Act Statement and Instructions on back before completing this form.)

OMB No. 0704-0173
OMB approval expires
Jul 31, 2014

The public reporting burden for this collection of information is estimated to average 20 minutes per response, including the time for reviewing instructions, searching existing data sources, gathering and maintaining the data needed, and completing and reviewing the collection of information. Send comments regarding this burden estimate or any other aspect of this collection of information, including suggestions for reducing the burden, to the Department of Defense, Washington Headquarters Services, Executive Services Directorate, Information Management Division, 1155 Defense Pentagon, Washington, DC 20301-1155 (0704-0173). Respondents should be aware that notwithstanding any other provision of law, no person shall be subject to any penalty for failing to comply with a collection of information if it does not display a currently valid OMB control number.

PLEASE DO NOT RETURN YOUR FORM TO THE ABOVE ORGANIZATION.

A. SERVICE PROCESSING FOR	B. PRIOR SERVICE: YES ☐ NO ☐ NUMBER OF DAYS:	C. SELECTIVE SERVICE CLASSIFICATION	D. SELECTIVE SERVICE REGISTRATION NO.

SECTION I - PERSONAL DATA

1. SOCIAL SECURITY NUMBER — —

2. NAME *(Last, First, Middle Name (and Maiden, if any), Jr., Sr., etc.)*

3. CURRENT ADDRESS *(Street, City, County, State, Country, ZIP Code)*

4. HOME OF RECORD ADDRESS *(Street, City, County, State, Country, ZIP Code)*

5. CITIZENSHIP *(X one)*
- a. U.S. AT BIRTH *(If this box is marked, also X (1) or (2))*
  - (1) NATIVE BORN
  - (2) BORN ABROAD OF U.S. PARENT(S)
- b. U.S. NATURALIZED   ALIEN REGISTRATION NUMBER *(If issued)*
- c. U.S. NON-CITIZEN NATIONAL
- d. IMMIGRANT ALIEN *(Specify)*
- e. NON-IMMIGRANT FOREIGN NATIONAL *(Specify)*

6. SEX *(X one)*
- a. MALE
- b. FEMALE

7.a. RACIAL CATEGORY *(X one or more)*
- (1) AMERICAN INDIAN/ ALASKA NATIVE
- (2) ASIAN
- (3) BLACK OR AFRICAN AMERICAN
- (4) NATIVE HAWAIIAN OR OTHER PACIFIC ISLANDER
- (5) WHITE

7.b. ETHNIC CATEGORY
- (1) HISPANIC OR LATINO
- (2) NOT HISPANIC OR LATINO

8. MARITAL STATUS *(Specify)*

9. NUMBER OF DEPENDENTS

10. DATE OF BIRTH *(YYYYMMDD)*

11. RELIGIOUS PREFERENCE *(Optional)*

12. EDUCATION *(Yrs/Highest Ed Gr Completed)*

13. PROFICIENT IN FOREIGN LANGUAGE *(If Yes, specify. If No, enter NONE.)*   1st   2nd

14. VALID DRIVER'S LICENSE *(X one)* YES ☐ NO ☐ *(If Yes, list State, number, and expiration date)*

15. PLACE OF BIRTH *(City, State and Country)*

SECTION II - EXAMINATION AND ENTRANCE DATA PROCESSING CODES
(FOR OFFICE USE ONLY - DO NOT WRITE IN THIS SECTION - Go on to Page 2, Question 20.)

16. APTITUDE TEST RESULTS

a. TEST ID	b. TEST SCORES	AFQT PERCENTILE	GS	AR	WK	PC	MK	EI	AS	MC	AO	VE

17. DEP ENLISTMENT DATA

a. DATE OF ENLISTMENT - DEP *(YYYYMMDD)*	b. PROJ ACTIVE DUTY DATE *(YYYYMMDD)*	c. ES	d. RECRUITER IDENTIFICATION	e. STN ID	f. PEF

g. T-E MOS/AFS	h. WAIVER (1) (2)	(3)	(4)	(5)	(6)	i. PAY GRADE	j. SVC ANNEX CODES	k. MSO *(YYWW)*	l. AD OBLIGATION *(YYWW)*

18. ACCESSION DATA

a. DATE OF ENLISTMENT *(YYYYMMDD)*	b. ACTIVE DUTY SERVICE DATE *(YYYYMMDD)*	c. PAY ENTRY DATE *(YYYYMMDD)*	d. MSO *(YYWW)*	e. AD/RC OBLIGATION *(YYMMWWDD)*

f. WAIVER (1) (2)	(3)	(4)	(5)	(6)	g. PAY GRADE	h. DATE OF GRADE *(YYYYMMDD)*	i. ES	j. YRS./HIGHEST ED GR COMPL

k. RECRUITER IDENTIFICATION	l. STN ID	m. PEF	n. T-E MOS/AFS	o. PMOS/AFS	p. YOUTH	q. OA	r. STATE GUARD

s. SVC ANNEX CODES	t. REPLACES ANNEXES	u. TRANSFER TO (UIC)

19. SERVICE REQUIRED CODES

1	2	3	4	5	6	7	8	9	10	11	12	13	14	15	16	17	18	19	20	21	22	23	24	25
26	27	28	29	30	31	32	33	34	35	36	37	38	39	40	41	42	43	44	45	46	47	48	49	50
51	52	53	54	55	56	57	58	59	60	61	62	63	64	65	66	67	68	69	70	71	72	73	74	75	76	77	78	79	80
81	82	83	84	85	86	87	88	89	90	91	92	93	94	95	96	97	98	99	100	101	102	103	104	105	106	107	108	109	110
111	112	113	114	115	116	117	118	119	120	121	122	123	124	125	126	127	128	129	130	131	132	133	134	135	136	137	138	139	140

DD FORM 1966/1, AUG 2011   PREVIOUS EDITION IS OBSOLETE.   Adobe Professional 8.0

PRIVACY ACT STATEMENT

AUTHORITY: 10 U.S.C. Sections 136, 504, 505, 12102; 14 U.S.C. Sections 351 and 632; DoDI 1304.2; DoDI 1304.26; AR 601-270; OPNAVINST 1100.4C Ch-1; AFI 36-2003_IP; MCO 1100.75E; COMDTINST M 1100.2E; AR 601-210; AFPD 36-20; and E.O. 9397, as amended (SSN).

PRINCIPAL PURPOSE(S): The information collected on this form is used to obtain data for use in determining the eligibility of applicants for accession into the Armed Forces and establishing official records for those who are accepted and enlist. Completed forms are covered by recruiting and official military personnel file SORNs maintained by each of the Services.

ROUTINE USE(S): The DoD Blanket Routine Uses found at http://privacy.defense.gov/blanket_uses.shtml apply to this collection.

DISCLOSURE: Voluntary. However, failure by an applicant to provide the information not annotated as "optional" may result in a denial of your enlistment application. An applicant's SSN is used during the recruitment process to keep all records together during the enlistment process, ensure testing and results are properly recorded and perform background screening.

WARNING

Information provided by you on this form is FOR OFFICIAL USE ONLY and will be maintained and used in strict compliance with Federal laws and regulations. The information provided by you becomes the property of the United States Government, and it may be consulted throughout your military service career, particularly whenever either favorable or adverse administrative or disciplinary actions related to you are involved.

YOU CAN BE PUNISHED BY FINE, IMPRISONMENT OR BOTH IF YOU ARE FOUND GUILTY OF MAKING KNOWING AND WILLFUL FALSE STATEMENT ON THIS DOCUMENT.

INSTRUCTIONS

(Read carefully BEFORE filling out this form.)

1. Read Privacy Act Statement above before completing form.

2. Type or print LEGIBLY all answers. If the answer is "None" or "Not Applicable", so state. "Optional" questions may be left blank.

3. Unless otherwise specified, write all dates as 6 digits (with no spaces or marks) in YYYYMMDD fashion. June 1, 2010 is written 20100601.

DD FORM 1966/1, AUG 2011   Back of Page 1

20. NAME *(Last, First, Middle Initial)*				21. SOCIAL SECURITY NUMBER	

SECTION III - OTHER PERSONAL DATA

22. EDUCATION

a. List all high schools and colleges attended. *(List dates in YYYYMM format.)*

				(5) GRADUATE	
(1) FROM	(2) TO	(3) NAME OF SCHOOL	(4) LOCATION	YES	NO

	YES	NO
b. Have you ever been enrolled in ROTC, Junior ROTC, Sea Cadet Program or Civil Air Patrol?		

23. MARITAL/DEPENDENCY STATUS AND FAMILY DATA *(If "Yes," explain in Section VI, "Remarks.")*

	YES	NO
a. Is anyone dependent upon you for support?		
b. Is there any court order or judgment in effect that directs you to provide alimony or support for children?		
c. Do you have an <u>immediate relative</u> (father, mother, brother, or sister) who: (1) is now a prisoner of war or is missing in action (MIA); or (2) died or became 100% permanently disabled while serving in the Armed Services?		
d. Are you the only living child in your immediate family?		

24. PREVIOUS MILITARY SERVICE OR EMPLOYMENT WITH THE U.S. GOVERNMENT *(If "Yes," explain in Section VI, "Remarks.")*

a. Are you now or have you ever been in any regular or reserve branch of the Armed Forces or in the Army National Guard or Air National Guard?		
b. Have you ever been rejected for enlistment, reenlistment, or induction by any branch of the Armed Forces of the United States?		
c. Are you now or have you ever been a deserter from any branch of the Armed Forces of the United States?		
d. Have you ever been employed by the United States Government?		
e. Are you now drawing, or do you have an application pending, or approval for: retired pay, disability allowance, severance pay, or a pension from any agency of the government of the United States?		

25. ABILITY TO PERFORM MILITARY DUTIES *(If "Yes," explain in Section VI, "Remarks.")*

a. Are you now or have you ever been a conscientious objector? (That is, do you have, or have you ever had, a firm, fixed, and sincere objection to participation in war in any form or to the bearing of arms because of religious belief or training?)		
b. Have you ever been discharged by any branch of the Armed Forces of the United States for reasons pertaining to being a conscientious objector?		
c. Is there anything which would preclude you from performing military duties or participating in military activities whenever necessary (i.e., do you have any personal restrictions or religious practices which would restrict your availability)?		

26. DRUG USE AND ABUSE *(If "Yes," explain in Section VI, "Remarks.")*
Have you ever tried, used, sold, supplied, or possessed any narcotic (to include heroin or cocaine), depressant (to include quaaludes), stimulant, hallucinogen (to include LSD or PCP), or cannabis (to include marijuana or hashish), or any mind-altering substance (to include glue or paint), or anabolic steroid, except as prescribed by a licenced physician?

DD FORM 1966/2, AUG 2011   Page 2

27. NAME *(Last, First, Middle Initial)*	28. SOCIAL SECURITY NUMBER

SECTION IV - CERTIFICATION

29. CERTIFICATION OF APPLICANT *(Your signature in this block must be witnessed by your recruiter.)*

a. I certify that the information given by me in this document is true, complete, and correct to the best of my knowledge and belief. I understand that I am being accepted for enlistment based on the information provided by me in this document; that if any of the information is knowingly false or incorrect, I could be tried in a civilian or military court and could receive a less than honorable discharge which could affect my future employment opportunities.

b. TYPED OR PRINTED NAME *(Last, First, Middle Initial)*	c. SIGNATURE	d. DATE SIGNED *(YYYYMMDD)*

30. DATA VERIFICATION BY RECRUITER *(Enter description of the actual documents used to verify the following items.)*

a. NAME *(X one)*	b. AGE *(X one)*	c. CITIZENSHIP *(X one)*
(1) BIRTH CERTIFICATE	(1) BIRTH CERTIFICATE	(1) BIRTH CERTIFICATE
(2) OTHER *(Explain)*	(2) OTHER *(Explain)*	(2) OTHER *(Explain)*
d. SOCIAL SECURITY NUMBER (SSN) *(X one)*	e. EDUCATION *(X one)*	f. OTHER DOCUMENTS USED
(1) SSN CARD	(1) DIPLOMA	
(2) OTHER *(Explain)*	(2) OTHER *(Explain)*	

31. CERTIFICATION OF WITNESS

a. I certify that I have witnessed the applicant's signature above and that I have verified the data in the documents required as prescribed by my directives. I further certify that I have not made any promises or guarantees other than those listed and signed by me. I understand my liability to trial by courts-martial under the Uniform Code of Military Justice should I effect or cause to be effected the enlistment of anyone known by me to be ineligible for enlistment.

b. TYPED OR PRINTED NAME *(Last, First, Middle Initial)*	c. PAY GRADE	d. RECRUITER I.D.	e. SIGNATURE	f. DATE SIGNED *(YYYYMMDD)*

32. SPECIFIC OPTION/PROGRAM ENLISTED FOR, MILITARY SKILL, OR ASSIGNMENT TO A GEOGRAPHICAL AREA GUARANTEES

a. SPECIFIC OPTION/PROGRAM ENLISTED FOR *(Completed by Guidance Counselor, MEPS Liaison NCO, etc., as specified by sponsoring service.) (Use clear text English.)*

b. I fully understand that I will not be guaranteed any specific military skill or assignment to a geographic area except as shown in Item 32.a. above and annexes attached to my Enlistment/Reenlistment Document (DD Form 4).	c. APPLICANT'S INITIALS

33. CERTIFICATION OF RECRUITER OR ACCEPTOR

a. I certify that I have reviewed all information contained in this document and, to the best of my judgment and belief, the applicant fulfills all legal policy requirements for enlistment. I accept him/her for enlistment on behalf of the United States *(Enter Branch of Service)*

_____ and certify that I have not made any promises or guarantees other than those listed in Item 32.a. above. I further certify that service regulations governing such enlistments have been strictly complied with and any waivers required to effect applicant's enlistment have been secured and are attached to this document.

b. TYPED OR PRINTED NAME *(Last, First, Middle Initial)*	c. PAY GRADE	d. RECRUITER I.D. OR ORGANIZATION	e. SIGNATURE	f. DATE SIGNED *(YYYYMMDD)*

SECTION V - RECERTIFICATION

34. RECERTIFICATION BY APPLICANT AND CORRECTION OF DATA AT THE TIME OF ACTIVE DUTY ENTRY

a. I have reviewed all information contained in this document this date. That information is still correct and true to the best of my knowledge and belief. If changes were required, the original entry has been marked "See Item 34" and the correct information is provided below.

b. ITEM NUMBER	c. CHANGE REQUIRED		

d. APPLICANT		e. WITNESS		
(1) SIGNATURE	(2) DATE SIGNED *(YYYYMMDD)*	(1) TYPED OR PRINTED NAME *(Last, First, Middle Initial)*	(2) RANK/ GRADE	(3) SIGNATURE

DD FORM 1966/3, AUG 2011

Page 3

35. NAME *(Last, First, Middle Initial)*	36. SOCIAL SECURITY NUMBER

SECTION VI - REMARKS
(Specify item(s) being continued by item number. Continue on separate pages if necessary.)

DD FORM 1966/5 ATTACHED? *(X one)*	YES	
	NO	

SECTION VII - STATEMENT OF NAME FOR OFFICIAL MILITARY RECORDS

37. NAME CHANGE.
If the preferred enlistment name (name given in Item 2) is not the same as on your birth certificate, and it has not been changed by legal procedure prescribed by state law, and it is the same as on your social security number card, complete the following:

a. NAME AS SHOWN ON BIRTH CERTIFICATE	b. NAME AS SHOWN ON SOCIAL SECURITY NUMBER CARD

c. I hereby state that I have not changed my name through any court or other legal procedure; that I prefer to use the name of _____ by which I am known in the community as a matter of convenience and with no criminal intent. I further state that I am the same person as the person whose name is shown in Item 2.

d. APPLICANT

(1) SIGNATURE	(2) DATE SIGNED *(YYYYMMDD)*

e. WITNESS

(1) TYPED OR PRINTED NAME *(Last, First, Middle Initial)*	(2) PAY GRADE	(3) SIGNATURE

DD FORM 1966/4, AUG 2011

38. NAME *(Last, First, Middle Initial)*	39. SOCIAL SECURITY NUMBER

USE THIS DD FORM 1966 PAGE ONLY IF EITHER SECTION APPLIES TO THE APPLICANT'S RECORD OF MILITARY PROCESSING.

SECTION VIII - PARENTAL/GUARDIAN CONSENT FOR ENLISTMENT

40. PARENT/GUARDIAN STATEMENT(S) *(Line out portions not applicable)*

a. I/we certify that *(Enter name of applicant)* _____

has no other legal guardian other than me/us and I/we consent to his/her enlistment in the United States
(Enter Branch of Service)

_____

I/we acknowledge/understand that he/she may be required upon order to serve in combat or other hazardous situations. I/we certify that <u>no promises of any kind</u> have been made to me/us concerning assignment to duty, training, or promotion during his/her enlistment <u>as an inducement</u> to me/us to sign this consent. I/we hereby authorize the Armed Forces representatives concerned to perform medical examinations, other examinations required, and to conduct records checks to determine his/her eligibility. I/we relinquish all claim to his/her service and to any wage or compensation for such service. I/we authorize him/her to be transported unsupervised to/from the Military Entrance Processing Station via public conveyance and to stay unsupervised at a government contracted hotel facility.

b. FOR ENLISTMENT IN A RESERVE COMPONENT.

I/we understand that, as a member of a reserve component, he/she must serve minimum periods of active duty for training unless excused by competent authority. In the event he/she fails to fulfill the obligations of his/her reserve enlistment, he/she may be recalled to active duty as prescribed by law. I/we further understand that while he/she is in the ready reserve, he/she may be ordered to extended active duty in time of war or national emergency declared by the Congress or the President or when otherwise authorized by law, and may be required upon order to serve in combat or other hazardous situations.

c. PARENT

(1) TYPED OR PRINTED NAME *(Last, First, Middle Initial)*	(2) SIGNATURE	(3) DATE SIGNED *(YYYYMMDD)*

d. WITNESS

(1) TYPED OR PRINTED NAME *(Last, First, Middle Initial)*	(2) SIGNATURE	(3) DATE SIGNED *(YYYYMMDD)*

e. PARENT

(1) TYPED OR PRINTED NAME *(Last, First, Middle Initial)*	(2) SIGNATURE	(3) DATE SIGNED *(YYYYMMDD)*

f. WITNESS

(1) TYPED OR PRINTED NAME *(Last, First, Middle Initial)*	(2) SIGNATURE	(3) DATE SIGNED *(YYYYMMDD)*

41. VERIFICATION OF SINGLE SIGNATURE CONSENT

DD FORM 1966/5, AUG 2011   Page 5

INSTRUCTIONS FOR DD FORM 2807-2,
MEDICAL PRESCREEN OF MEDICAL HISTORY REPORT

1. This form is to be completed by each individual who requires medical processing in accordance with Army Regulation 40-501 Chapter 2 standards, or Department of Defense Directive 6130.3, "Physical Standards for Appointment, enlistment, or Induction." The form should be completed by the applicant with the assistance of the recruiter, parent(s), or guardian, as needed (see page 2).

2. Use of this form will also facilitate efficient, timely, and accurate medical processing of individuals applying for service in the United States Armed Forces or Coast Guard. The form is designed to assist recruiters in the medical pre-screening of applicants.

3. The individual completing the DD Form 2807-2 will submit the form, at a minimum, 1 processing day in advance to the MEPS projected to process the individual. A minimum of 2 processing days in advance is required if support documentation (e.g., private physicians paperwork, treatment records, etc.) is required to augment the MEPS CMO review.

EXPLANATION OF CODES.

Items are followed by numbers that refer to the following:

(1) If the applicant has been seen by a physician and/or has been hospitalized for the condition, obtain medical documentation with a medical release form and submit records to the MEPS Medical Section. After the MEPS Medical Officer reviews the provided information, the appropriate recruiting service member will be informed of the examinee's processing status, or if additional record review or specialty consultation may be required for further processing or qualification determination.

    a. If the applicant was evaluated and/or treated on an out-patient basis, obtain a copy of actual treatment records of the private medical doctor (PMD) or health care provider (HCP), to include (if any):
- office or clinic assessment and progress notes, including the initial assessment and subsequent evaluation and treatment documents, and record and date when released from doctor's care to full, unrestricted activity;
- emergency room (ER) report;
- study reports (e.g., x-ray report(s), magnetic resonance imaging (MRI) report(s), or Computerized Tomography (CT) scan report(s), etc.);
- procedure reports (e.g., arthroscopy, electroencephalogram (EEG; brain wave test), echocardiogram (ultrasound of the heart), etc.);
- pathology reports (e.g., if tissue specimens taken from the body and sent to lab for microscopic diagnosis, etc.);
- specialty consultation records (e.g., neurologist, cardiologist, OB/Gynecologist, gastroenterologist, orthopedic surgeon, pulmonologist, allergist, etc.).

    b. If the applicant was hospitalized, then obtain a copy of the hospital record, to include (if any): ER report, admission history and physical, study reports, procedure reports, operative report (especially necessary for surgery to bone or joint), pathology report, specialty consultation reports, and discharge summary.

(2) If an applicant has been diagnosed or treated since age 12 for any attention disorder (Attention Deficit Disorder (ADD) or Attention Deficit Hyperactivity Disorder (ADHD), etc.), academic skills or perceptual defect, or has had an Individual Education Plan (IEP), call the MEPS for additional instructions.

(3) Condition to be discussed with the examining Medical Officer at time of the medical examination.

(4) Call MEPS Medical Section to discuss examinee's medical history BEFORE sending the individual in for physical examination.

(5) Send medical reports to MEPS for review before sending applicant for physical ("papers only" medical review), and MEPS Medical Section will advise regarding further medical processing. Records pertaining to non-psychiatric diagnoses may be sent to the Medical Section of the processing MEPS, with the envelope stating: "CONFIDENTIAL: MEPS MEDICAL SECTION."

(6) Send all documentation relating to ANY past or present evaluation, treatment or consultation with a psychiatrist, psychologist, counselor or therapist, on an inpatient or out-patient basis for any reason, including but not limited to counseling or treatment for adjustment or mood disorder, family or marriage problem, depression, treatment or rehabilitation for alcohol, drug or other substance abuse, directly from the treating clinician and/or hospital to the MEPS Chief Medical Officer. The envelope must bear the following statement: "CONFIDENTIAL: FOR EYES OF THE MEDICAL OFFICER ONLY."

(7) May require an orthopedic consult, scheduling to be coordinated by the MEPS CMO and Medical Section.

DD FORM 2807-2, AUG 2011

MEDICAL PRESCREEN OF MEDICAL HISTORY REPORT

(Chapter #2 Physicals Only)

OMB No. 0704-0413
OMB approval expires
Aug 31, 2014

The public reporting burden for this collection of information is estimated to average 10 minutes per response, including the time for reviewing instructions, searching existing data sources, gathering and maintaining the data needed, and completing and reviewing the collection of information. Send comments regarding this burden estimate or any other aspect of this collection of information, including suggestions for reducing the burden, to the Department of Defense, Washington Headquarters Services, Executive Services Directorate, Information Management Division, 1155 Defense Pentagon, Washington, DC 20301-1155 (0704-0413). Respondents should be aware that notwithstanding any other provision of law, no person shall be subject to any penalty for failing to comply with a collection of information if it does not display a currently valid OMB number.

PLEASE DO NOT RETURN YOUR FORM TO THE ABOVE ORGANIZATION. RETURN COMPLETED FORM AS INDICATED ON PAGE 2.

PRIVACY ACT STATEMENT

AUTHORITY: 10 U.S.C. 136, DoD Instruction 6130.03, and E.O. 9397 (SSN).

PRINCIPAL PURPOSE(S): The primary collection of this information is from individuals seeking to join the Armed Services. The information collected on this form is used to obtain medical data for a determination of medical fitness for enlistment, induction and appintment of individuals in the Armed Forces.

ROUTINE USE(S): The DoD Blanket Routine Uses found at http://privacy.defense.gov/blanket_uses.shtml apply to this collection.

DISCLOSURE: Voluntary. However, failure by an applicant to provide the information may result in delay or possible rejection of the individual's application to enter the Armed Forces. An applicant's SSN is used during the recruitment process to keep all records together and when requesting civilian medical records.

WARNING: The information you have given constitutes an official statement. Federal law provides severe penalties (up to 5 years confinement or a $10,000 fine or both), to anyone making a false statement. If you are selected for enlistment, commission, or entrance into a commissioning program based on a false statement, you can be tried by military courts-martial or meet an administrative board for discharge and could receive a less than honorable discharge that would affect your future.

1. APPLICANT

a. LAST NAME - FIRST NAME - MIDDLE INITIAL (SUFFIX)	b. DATE OF BIRTH *(YYYYMMDD)*	c. SOCIAL SECURITY NUMBER

d. HEIGHT	e. WEIGHT	f. MAXIMUM WEIGHT	g. SERVICE/COMPONENT			Regular	h. DATE SCREENED *(YYYYMMDD)*
		lbs.	Army	Marine Corps	Coast Guard	Reserve	
			Navy	Air Force		National Guard	

2. Mark each item "YES" or "NO". Every item marked "YES" must be fully explained in Item 2b.

a. HAVE YOU EVER HAD OR DO YOU NOW HAVE:	YES	NO		YES	NO
(1) Asthma, wheezing, or inhaler use (4)			(24) Any other heart problems (4)		
(2) Dislocated joint, including knee, hip, shoulder, elbow, ankle or other joint (1)(7)			(25) High blood pressure (4)		
			(26) Discharged from military service for medical reasons (4)		
(3) Epilepsy, fits, seizures, or convulsions (4)			(27) Ulcer *(stomach, duodenum or other part of intestine)* (4)		
(4) Sleepwalking (4)			(28) Received disability compensation for an injury or other medical condition (4)		
(5) Recurrent neck or back pain (4)(1)(7)					
(6) Rheumatic fever (4)			(29) Hepatitis *(liver infection or inflammation)* (4)		
(7) Foot pain (3)			(30) Intestinal obstruction *(locked bowels)*, or any other chronic or recurrent intestinal problem, including small intestine or colon problems, such as Crohn's disease or colitis (4)		
(8) A swollen, painful, or dislocated joint or fluid in a joint *(knee, shoulder, wrist, elbow, etc.)* (1)(7)			(31) Detached retina or surgery for a detached retina (4)		
(9) Double vision (4)			(32) Surgery to remove a portion of the intestine *(other than the appendix)* (4)		
(10) Periods of unconsciousness (4)					
(11) Frequent or severe headaches causing loss of time from work or school or taking medication to prevent frequent or severe headaches (4)			(33) Any other eye condition, injury or surgery (4)		
			(34) Are you over 40? *(If so, call the MEPS for information on special requirements for over-40 physicals)* (4)		
(12) Wear contact lenses *(If so, bring your contact lens kit and solution so you can remove your contact when we test your vision at the MEPS; also, if you have a pair of eyeglasses, bring them with you no matter how old they are.)*			(35) Gall bladder trouble or gall stones (4)		
			(36) Jaundice (4)		
(13) Fainting spells or passing out (4)			(37) Missing a kidney (4)		
(14) Head injury, including skull fracture, resulting in concussion, loss of consciousness, headaches, etc. (4)			(38) Allergy to common food *(milk, bread, eggs, meat, fish or other common food)* (4)		
(15) Back surgery (4)			(39) *(Females only)* Abnormal PAP smear or gynecological problem (4)		
(16) Seen a psychiatrist, psychologist, social worker, counselor or other professional for any reason *(inpatient or outpatient)* including counseling or treatment for school, adjustment, family, marriage or any other problem, to include depression, or treatment for alcohol, drug or substance abuse (6)(2)			(40) *(Males only)* Missing a testicle, testicular implant, or undescended testicle (4)		
(17) Any of the following skin diseases:			(41) Broken bone requiring surgery to repair *(with or without pins, plates, screws or other metal fixation devices used in repair)* (1)(7)		
(a) Eczema (5)			(42) Ruptured or bulging disk in your back or surgery for a ruptured or bulging disk (4)		
(b) Psoriasis (5)					
(c) Atopic dermatitis (5)			(43) Thyroid condition or take medication for your thyroid (4)		
(18) Irregular heartbeat, including abnormally rapid or slow heart rates (4)			(44) Limitation of motion of any joint, including knee, shoulder, wrist, elbow, hip or other joint (4)(1)(7)		
(19) Allergic to bee, wasp, or other insect stings *(itching/swelling all over and/or get short of breath)* (4)			(45) Drug or alcohol rehab (4)		
(20) Heart murmur, valve problem or mitral valve prolapse (4)			(46) Kidney, urinary tract or bladder problems, surgery, stones or other urinary tract problems (4)		
(21) Allergic to wool (4)			(47) Sugar, protein or blood in urine (4)		
(22) Heart surgery (4)			(48) Surgery on a bone or joint *(knee, shoulder, elbow, wrist, etc.)* including Arthroscopy with normal findings (1)(7)		
(23) Been rejected for military service *(temporary or permanent)* for medical or other reasons (4)			(49) Taking any medications *(If so, list reason in Item 2b.)*		

DD FORM 2807-2, AUG 2011   PREVIOUS EDITION IS OBSOLETE.   Page 2 of 6 Pages

MEDICAL PRESCREEN

LAST NAME - FIRST NAME - MIDDLE INITIAL (SUFFIX)			SOCIAL SECURITY NUMBER	

2a. (Continued) HAVE YOU EVER HAD OR DO YOU NOW HAVE:	YES	NO		YES	NO
(50) Pain or swelling at the site of an old fracture (4)(1)(7)			(64) Shoulder, knee, or elbow problem *(out of place)* (4)(1)(7)		
(51) Perforated ear drum or tubes in ear drum(s) (4)			(65) Locking of the knee or other joint (4)(1)(7)		
(52) Anemia (4)			(66) Giving way of knee or other joint (4)(1)(7)		
(53) Ear surgery, to include mastoidectomy or repair of perforated ear drum, hearing loss or need/use a hearing aid (4)			(67) Cataracts or surgery for cataracts (4)		
(54) Night blindness (4)			(68) Eye surgery, including radial keratotomy, lens implant or other eye surgery to improve your vision (4)		
(55) Arthritis (4)			(69) Collapsed lung or other lung condition (4)		
(56) Absence or disturbance of the sense of smell (4)			(70) Bed wetting since age 12 (4)		
(57) Absence or removal of the spleen, or rupture or tear of the spleen without removal (4)			(71) Evaluation, treatment, or hospitalization for alcohol abuse, dependence, or addiction (4)(6)		
(58) Anorexia or other eating disorder (4)			(72) Taken medication, drugs, or any substance to improve attention, behavior, or physical performance (2)(1)(6)		
(59) Cracked bone or fracture(s) (4)					
(60) Bursitis (4)			(73) Do you smoke? *(If yes:)*		
(61) Braces *(If you wear or are planning on obtaining braces for your teeth, have the orthodontist submit a letter stating that braces will be removed before active duty date; release form and sample format can be found in the Recruiter's Medical Guide.)*			(a) Type ☐ Cigarettes ☐ Cigars ☐ Smokeless tobacco		
			(b) How many per day? (c) Date last used		
(62) Loss of finger, toe or part thereof (4)			(74) Evaluation, treatment, or hospitalization for substance use, abuse, addiction or dependence *(including illegal drugs, prescription medications, or other substances)*		
(63) Loss of the ability to fully flex *(bend)* or fully extend a finger, toe or other joint (4)(1)(7)			(75) Any illnesses, surgery, or hospitalization not listed above		

b. **EXPLAIN ALL "YES" ANSWERS TO QUESTIONS (1) - (75) ABOVE.** *(Describe answer(s), give date(s) of problems, name doctor(s), clinic(s), hospital(s), treatment given and current medical status. Attach additional sheet(s) if necessary.)*

DD FORM 2807-2, AUG 2011

MEDICAL PRESCREEN

LAST NAME - FIRST NAME - MIDDLE INITIAL (SUFFIX)	SOCIAL SECURITY NUMBER

b. EXPLAIN ALL "YES" ANSWERS TO QUESTIONS (1) - (74) ABOVE. *(Continued)*

3. CURRENT PRIMARY CARE PHYSICIAN(S)/PRACTITIONER(S) AND/OR CLINIC(S) *(Attach additional sheets if necessary)*

a. NAME(S)	b. ADDRESS *(Include ZIP Code)*	c. TELEPHONE *(Include Area Code)*

4. PREVIOUS PRIMARY CARE PHYSICIAN(S)

a. NAME(S)	b. ADDRESS *(Include ZIP Code)*	c. TELEPHONE *(Include Area Code)*

5. CURRENT INSURANCE PROVIDER

a. NAME	b. ADDRESS *(Include ZIP Code)*	c. INSURANCE ID NUMBER

6. PREVIOUS INSURANCE PROVIDER(S)

a. NAME(S)	b. ADDRESS *(Include ZIP Code)*	c. INSURANCE ID NUMBER

STOP AND READ: THE FOLLOWING STATEMENTS APPLY TO SIGNATURES AT ITEMS 7 AND 8

- I certify the information on this form is true and complete to the best of my knowledge and belief, and no person has advised me to conceal or falsify any information about my physical and mental history.

- I further understand that I may be requested to provide medical documentation regarding issues within my medical history.

- I authorize any of the doctors, hospitals, clinics or insurance company(ies) to furnish the Department of Defense medical authority a complete transcript of my medical record for purposes of processing my application for military service.

7. APPLICANT

a. SIGNATURE	b. DATE SIGNED *(YYYYMMDD)*

8. PARENT OR GUARDIAN SIGNATURE FOR MINOR *(Mandatory)* **OR PARENT ASSISTING TO COMPLETE FORM** *(Voluntary)*

a. NAME *(Last, First, Middle Initial)*	b. SIGNATURE	c. DATE SIGNED *(YYYYMMDD)*

9. RECRUITING REPRESENTATIVE: I certify all information is complete and true to the best of my knowledge. I have conducted the medical prescreening requirements as directed by service regulations.

a. NAME *(If representative was used)* *(Last, First, Middle Initial)*	b. PAY GRADE	c. SIGNATURE	d. DATE SIGNED *(YYYYMMDD)*

DD FORM 2807-2, AUG 2011

Page 4 of 6 Pages

MEDICAL PRESCREEN

LAST NAME - FIRST NAME - MIDDLE INITIAL (SUFFIX)	SOCIAL SECURITY NUMBER

10. PHYSICIAN'S SUMMARY AND ELABORATION OF ALL PERTINENT DATA *(Physician shall comment on all positive answers in questions (1) - (74). Physician may develop by interview any additional medical history deemed important, and record any significant findings here.)*

a. COMMENTS

11. MEDICAL OFFICER'S PRESCREENING COMMENTS: Based on information provided, further processing is:

a. ON PRESCREEN:

☐ (1) AUTHORIZED ☐ (2) NOT JUSTIFIED *(Permanent Disqualification (PDQ))*: ☐ (3) DEFERRED *(See Comments above)*:

    ☐ (a) Profile Serial _____ ICD _____   ☐ (a) Pending review of additional documentation

    ☐ (b) Process for Waiver *(CMO initials)* _____   ☐ (b) RJ Date *(If applicable)* _____ *(CMO initials)* _____

b. ON EXAM:

☐ (1) APPROVED ☐ (2) DEFERRED:/   ☐ (a) Additional information needed *(See DD Form 2808)*

    ☐ (3) NOT JUSTIFIED: ☐ (b) Information different than on prescreen

        ☐ (c) Form not prescreened by MEPS

(4) MEPS USE:

☐ (a) AE ☐ (c) PRI

☐ (b) RE ☐ (d) N/A

c. TYPED OR PRINTED NAME OF EXAMINER	d. SIGNATURE	e. DATE SIGNED *(YYYYMMDD)*	12. NUMBER OF ATTACHED SHEETS

DD FORM 2807-2, AUG 2011

MEDICAL PRESCREEN

LAST NAME - FIRST NAME - MIDDLE INITIAL (SUFFIX)	SOCIAL SECURITY NUMBER

13. COMMENTS *(Continued)*

REPORT OF MEDICAL EXAMINATION	1. DATE OF EXAMINATION (YYYYMMDD)	2. SOCIAL SECURITY NUMBER

PRIVACY ACT STATEMENT

AUTHORITY: 10 USC 504, 505, 507, 532, 978, 1201, 1202, and 4346; and E.O. 9397.

PRINCIPAL PURPOSE(S): To obtain medical data for determination of medical fitness for enlistment, induction, appointment and retention for applicants and members of the Armed Forces. The information will also be used for medical boards and separation of Service members from the Armed Forces.

ROUTINE USE(S): None.

DISCLOSURE: Voluntary; however, failure by an applicant to provide the information may result in delay or possible rejection of the individual's application to enter the Armed Forces. For an Armed Forces member, failure to provide the information may result in the individual being placed in a non-deployable status.

3. LAST NAME - FIRST NAME - MIDDLE NAME (SUFFIX)	4. HOME ADDRESS (Street, Apartment Number, City, State and ZIP Code)	5. HOME TELEPHONE NUMBER (Include Area Code)

6. GRADE	7. DATE OF BIRTH (YYYYMMDD)	8. AGE	9. SEX	10.a. RACIAL CATEGORY (X one or more)	b. ETHNIC CATEGORY
			☐ Female ☐ Male	☐ American Indian or Alaska Native ☐ Asian ☐ Black or African American ☐ White ☐ Native Hawaiian or Other Pacific Islander	☐ Hispanic/Latino ☐ Not Hispanic/Latino

11. TOTAL YEARS GOVERNMENT SERVICE a. MILITARY b. CIVILIAN	12. AGENCY (Non-Service Members Only)	13. ORGANIZATION UNIT AND UIC/CODE

14.a. RATING OR SPECIALTY (Aviators Only)	b. TOTAL FLYING TIME	c. LAST SIX MONTHS

15.a. SERVICE	b. COMPONENT	c. PURPOSE OF EXAMINATION	16. NAME OF EXAMINING LOCATION, AND ADDRESS (Include ZIP Code)
☐ Army ☐ Coast Guard ☐ Navy ☐ Marine Corps ☐ Air Force	☐ Active Duty ☐ Reserve ☐ National Guard	☐ Enlistment ☐ Medical Board ☐ Other ☐ Commission ☐ Retirement ☐ Retention ☐ U.S. Service Academy ☐ Separation ☐ ROTC Scholarship Program	

CLINICAL EVALUATION (Check each item in appropriate column. Enter "NE" if not evaluated.)

	Normal	Abnorm	NE
17. Head, face, neck, and scalp			
18. Nose			
19. Sinuses			
20. Mouth and throat			
21. Ears - General (Int. and ext. canals/Auditory acuity under item 71)			
22. Drums (Perforation)			
23. Eyes - General (Visual acuity and refraction under items 61 - 63)			
24. Ophthalmoscopic			
25. Pupils (Equality and reaction)			
26. Ocular motility (Associated parallel movements, nystagmus)			
27. Heart (Thrust, size, rhythm, sounds)			
28. Lungs and chest (Include breasts)			
29. Vascular system (Varicosities, etc.)			
30. Anus and rectum (Hemorrhoids, Fistulae) (Prostate if indicated)			
31. Abdomen and viscera (Include hernia)			
32. External genitalia (Genitourinary)			
33. Upper extremities			
34. Lower extremities (Except feet)			
35. Feet (See Item 35 Continued)			
36. Spine, other musculoskeletal			
37. Identifying body marks, scars, tattoos			
38. Skin, lymphatics			
39. Neurologic			
40. Psychiatric (Specify any personality deviation)			
41. Pelvic (Females only)			
42. Endocrine			

44. NOTES: (Describe every abnormality in detail. Enter pertinent item number before each comment. Continue in item 73 and use additional sheets if necessary.)

35. FEET (Continued) (Circle category)

Normal Arch	Mild	Asymptomatic
Pes Cavus	Moderate	
Pes Planus	Severe	Symptomatic

43. DENTAL DEFECTS AND DISEASE (Please explain. Use dental form if completed by dentist. If dental examination not done by dental officer, explain in Item 44.)

☐ Acceptable

☐ Not Acceptable   Class

DD FORM 2808, OCT 2005   DoD exception to SF 88 approved by ICMR, August 3, 2000. PREVIOUS EDITION IS OBSOLETE.

Page 1 of 3 Pages
Adobe Professional 7.0

LAST NAME - FIRST NAME - MIDDLE NAME (SUFFIX)		SOCIAL SECURITY NUMBER

LABORATORY FINDINGS

45. URINALYSIS	a. Albumin	46. URINE HCG	47. H/H	48. BLOOD TYPE
	b. Sugar			

TESTS	RESULTS	HIV SPECIMEN ID LABEL	DRUG TEST SPECIMEN ID LABEL
49. HIV			
50. DRUGS			
51. ALCOHOL			
52. OTHER			
a. PAP SMEAR			
b.			
c.			

MEASUREMENTS AND OTHER FINDINGS

53. HEIGHT	54. WEIGHT	55. MIN WGT - MAX WGT	MAX BF %	56. TEMPERATURE	57. PULSE
	lbs.				

58. BLOOD PRESSURE			59. RED/GREEN *(Army Only)*	60. OTHER VISION TEST
a. 1ST	b. 2ND	c. 3RD		
SYS.	SYS.	SYS.		
DIAS.	DIAS.	DIAS.		

61. DISTANT VISION		62. REFRACTION BY AUTOREFRACTION OR MANIFEST			63. NEAR VISION		
Right 20/	Corr. to 20/	By	S.	CX	Right 20/	Corr. to 20/	by
Left 20/	Corr. to 20/	By	S.	CX	Left 20/	Corr. to 20/	by

64. HETEROPHORIA *(Specify distance)*

ES°	EX°	R.H.	L.H.	Prism div.	Prism Conv CT	NPR	PD

65. ACCOMMODATION		66. COLOR VISION *(Test used and result)*	67. DEPTH PERCEPTION *(Test used and score)* AFVT	
Right	Left	PIP /14	Uncorrected	Corrected

68. FIELD OF VISION	69. NIGHT VISION *(Test used and score)*	70. INTRAOCULAR TENSION	
		O.D.	O.S.

71a. AUDIOMETER	Unit Serial Number						71b. Unit Serial Number						72a. READING ALOUD TEST	
Date Calibrated *(YYYYMMDD)*							Date Calibrated *(YYYYMMDD)*							
HZ	500	1000	2000	3000	4000	6000	HZ	500	1000	2000	3000	4000	6000	SAT UNSAT
Right							Right							72b. VALSALVA
Left							Left							SAT UNSAT

73. NOTES *(Continued)* **AND SIGNIFICANT OR INTERVAL HISTORY** *(Use additional sheets if necessary.)*

DD FORM 2808, OCT 2005   Page 2 of 3 Pages

LAST NAME - FIRST NAME - MIDDLE NAME (SUFFIX)		SOCIAL SECURITY NUMBER

74.a. EXAMINEE/APPLICANT *(check one)*

☐ IS QUALIFIED FOR SERVICE
☐ IS NOT QUALIFIED FOR SERVICE

75. I have been advised of my disqualifying condition.

a. SIGNATURE OF EXAMINEE	b. DATE *(YYYYMMDD)*

b. PHYSICAL PROFILE

P	U	L	H	E	S	X	PROFILER INITIALS	DATE *(YYYYMMDD)*

76. SIGNIFICANT OR DISQUALIFYING DEFECTS

ITEM NO.	MEDICAL CONDITION/DIAGNOSIS	ICD CODE	PROFILE SERIAL	RBJ DATE *(YYYYMMDD)*	QUALI-FIED	DIS-QUALI-FIED	EXAMINER INITIALS	WAIVER RECEIVED	
								SERVICE	DATE *(YYYYMMDD)*

77. SUMMARY OF DEFECTS AND DIAGNOSES *(List diagnoses with item numbers) (Use additional sheets if necessary.)*

78. RECOMMENDATIONS - FURTHER SPECIALIST EXAMINATIONS INDICATED *(Specify) (Use additional sheets if necessary.)*

79. MEPS WORKLOAD *(For MEPS use only)*

WKID	ST	DATE *(YYYYMMDD)*	INITIAL	WKID	ST	DATE *(YYYYMMDD)*	INITIAL

80. MEDICAL INSPECTION DATE

	HT	WT	%BF	MAX WT	HCG	QUAL	DISQ	PHYSICIAN'S SIGNATURE

81.a. TYPED OR PRINTED NAME OF PHYSICIAN OR EXAMINER	b. SIGNATURE

82.a. TYPED OR PRINTED NAME OF PHYSICIAN OR EXAMINER	b. SIGNATURE

83.a. TYPED OR PRINTED NAME OF DENTIST OR PHYSICIAN *(Indicate which)*	b. SIGNATURE

84.a. TYPED OR PRINTED NAME OF REVIEWING OFFICER/APPROVING AUTHORITY	b. SIGNATURE

85. This examination has been administratively reviewed for completeness and accuracy.

a. SIGNATURE	b. GRADE	c. DATE *(YYYYMMDD)*

86. WAIVER GRANTED *(If yes, date and by whom)*

☐ YES
☐ NO

87. NUMBER OF ATTACHED SHEETS

DD FORM 2808, OCT 2005

Page 3 of 3 Pages

ABOUT THE AUTHOR

Dr. Scott A. Ostrow is a high school Air Force JROTC teacher and retired military officer who started his military career as an enlisted Navy member shortly after graduating from Copiague High School (New York) in 1978. After serving in the Navy for more than seven years, Scott attended Air Force Officer Training School and was commissioned as a second lieutenant in July 1986.

Scott has served as a Poseidon Missile Technician, Navy Recruiter, Air Force Missile Officer, Fighter Squadron Executive Officer, Recruiting Squadron Operations Officer, and Medical Service Corps Officer (as a Reservist), and he was also Chief of Recruiter Training, Chief of Health Professions Recruiting, and, Chief, Recruiting Operations and Training Division with Air Force Reserve Recruiting. He holds a Bachelor of Science degree in business administration (management) from Baptist College at Charleston (now Charleston Southern University), a Master of Public Administration degree from Troy University, and a Doctor of Education degree in Organizational Leadership from Argosy University.

Scott retired from the Air Force in 2005 and has been teaching high school since then. He is married and has six children, two of whom are currently serving in the Air Force.

NOTES

NOTES

NOTES

NOTES

NOTES

NOTES

NOTES

NOTES

NOTES

NOTES

NOTES

NOTES

NOTES

NOTES

NOTES